D1475359

EUROPE'S NEUTRAL AND NONALIGNED STATES

EUROPE'S NEUTRAL AND NONALIGNED STATES

Between NATO and the Warsaw Pact

Edited by
S. Victor Papacosma
Mark R. Rubin

A Scholarly Resources Imprint
WILMINGTON, DELAWARE

The paper used in this publication meets the minimum requirements of the American National Standard for permanence of paper for printed library materials, Z39.48, 1984.

Scholarly Resources Inc.
104 Greenhill Avenue
Wilmington, Delaware 19805-1897

Library of Congress Cataloging-in-Publication Data

Europe's neutral and nonaligned states.

    Includes bibliographies and index.
    1. Europe--Neutrality. 2. Europe--Nonalignment.
I. Papacosma, S. Victor, 1942-   . II. Rubin,
Mark R., 1944-   .
JX4031.E87 1988   341.6'4'094   87-33545
ISBN 0-8420-2269-4

Contents

Preface

This volume is the fifth in a series of publications sponsored by the Lyman L. Lemnitzer Center for NATO Studies. Its predecessors are: *NATO after Thirty Years* (1981), *The Warsaw Pact: Political Purpose and Military Means* (1982), *NATO and the Mediterranean* (1985), and *East-West Rivalry in the Third World: Security Issues and Regional Perspectives* (1986).

The Lemnitzer Center coordinated the efforts of specialists in producing this volume on the neutral and nonaligned states of Europe. The project benefited from the participation of scholars and officials in discussions on the individual papers and the overall project theme: Lt. Col. Ernst Bartolmé, assistant armed forces attaché, Embassy of Switzerland, Washington, DC; Morris Honick, chief historian, SHAPE; Prof. John T. Hubbell, Kent State University; Prof. Joseph Kruzel, The Mershon Center, Ohio State University; Dr. Nils Ørvik Queen's University; Michael Sternberg, U.S. Embassy, Vienna, Austria.

Prof. Lawrence S. Kaplan, director of the Lemnitzer Center, and Prof. Robert W. Clawson, associate director (Research) of the center and director of Kent State's Center for International and Comparative Programs, provided important advice and support in the organization of the project. Ruth Young, the center's administrative assistant, once again displayed her indispensable organizational and secretarial abilities; her services and enthusiasm are greatly appreciated. Students associated with the center--Nancy Brendlinger, James Carlton, Andrew Herrmann, Jason Reichel--provided assistance in various support activities.

S. Victor Papacosma and
Mark R. Rubin
Kent State University

About the Contributors

BOLESLAW A. BOCZEK is professor of political science at Kent State University and an associate of the Lyman L. Lemnitzer Center for NATO Studies. He holds a doctorate in international law from Jagiellonian University and a Ph.D. in political science from Harvard University. Author of *Flags of Convenience* (1962) and *Taxation in Switzerland* (1976), he also has written numerous articles, monographs, and reviews dealing with international law and organization. He has a special interest in NATO, the Warsaw Pact, and international security in Europe.

JOAN JOHNSON-FREESE is associate professor of political science at the University of Central Florida. Her Ph.D. is from Kent State University. She has pursued research and published on international space policy and disarmament issues.

JOHN LOGUE is professor of political science at Kent State University and an associate of the Lyman L. Lemnitzer Center for NATO Studies. He received his Ph.D. from Princeton University and is the author of numerous articles and monographs on Scandinavian politics and policy. He has held visiting teaching and research appointments at Roskilde University in Denmark and the Universities of Gothenburg and Linköping (Sweden).

JOSEPH P. O'GRADY is professor of history at La Salle University, having also served as chairman of the department. He holds a Ph.D. from the University of Pennsylvania. His research interests have centered on Irish-American issues, and he has published *How the Irish Became Americans* (1973) and *Irish-Americans and Anglo-American Relations, 1880-1888* (1976).

S. VICTOR PAPACOSMA is professor of history at Kent State University and associate director of the Lyman L. Lemnitzer Center for NATO Studies. He received his Ph.D. from Indiana University with a concentration in Balkan history. He has written extensively on twentieth-century Greek issues, including *The Military in Greek Politics: The 1909 Coup d'Etat* (1977).

MARK R. RUBIN is assistant professor of French, associate director of the Center for International and Comparative Programs, and administrative coordinator of the Lyman L. Lemnitzer Center for NATO Studies at Kent State University; his doctorate is from Princeton University. He has written a number of articles on French and Swiss military affairs.

JOHN P. VLOYANTES is professor of political science at Colorado State University. He received his Ph.D. from the University of Utah, and has published on Finnish foreign relations. He is the author of *Silk Glove Hegemony: Finnish-Soviet Relations, 1944-1974* (1975).

LAURENT WEHRLI is an apprentice journalist with the 24 Heures group in Switzerland. He is currently working for the newspaper *Le Matin* in Lausanne. He received his *Licence ès Lettres* from the Université de Lausanne in 1987 and is an artillery lieutenant in the Swiss Army.

Introduction: The Conceptual and Legal Framework of Neutrality and Nonalignment in Europe

Boleslaw A. Boczek

Broadly conceived, foreign policy can be analyzed as a country's general orientation toward its external environment-- that is, the fundamental attitudes and principles that guide its behavior in relations with other states.[1]   It is this conception of foreign policy that is implicit in frequently made references to "neutral," "permanently neutral," "neutralist," or "nonaligned" nations of Europe.

Apart from their imprecise and vague use, these terms presuppose the existence of a triangular relationship in which a party adopts an attitude of not taking sides with either of the two other parties in conflict with each other.   In the European context these terms are associated with those states which, despite (in some cases) fundamental differences between them, have one thing in common: nonmembership in either of the Cold War alliances, NATO and the Warsaw Pact.   More generally, these states refuse to commit their respective military capabilities for the pursuance of other states' objectives and in their security policy are determined to rely upon their own resources.   Beyond this common denominator there are variations in the scope of each country's engagement in the international system, the nature of the commitment implementing its respective orientation, and the historical circumstances under which each of them adopted its fundamental posture.   It also must be borne in mind that they are ideologically a heterogeneous group. Although most of them are Western capitalist democracies, two profess the Marxist ideology: Yugoslavia follows a more "liberal" form of this ideology, whereas Albania represents the most extreme and doctrinaire Stalinist edition of Marxism-Leninism (apart from the fact that its foreign policy behavior in many respects approaches an isolationist model).

In analyzing the varieties of what, in a preliminary and colloquial way, can be referred to as "alliance-free policy" in the European context,[2] it is imperative to clarify the semantic confusion that exists in regard to such terms as neutrality, neutralization, neutralism, and nonalignment, which are frequently used interchangeably and without precision as popular terms rather than as clearly defined analytical concepts. Since the foreign policy of the European permanently neutral countries has historical linkages to classical neutrality in the legal sense of the term, the latter institution will have to be examined first. The central sections of the study will analyze the concept of permanent neutrality, legal as well as factual, which guides the policies of the principal European neutrals. The term neutralization also will be clarified in this context. Since two or--if one includes the geographically Middle Eastern (that is, Asian) but politically European Greek Cyprus--three European states belong to the nonaligned group, the concept of nonalignment will be dealt with, but only insofar as it is relevant within the European context. Having established terminological and conceptual parameters, the study will present a concise but comprehensive typology of the states concerned, which also will include such unique cases as the semi-isolationist Albania, the qualified neutrality case of Ireland, and the permanently neutral ministates of Europe. Some brief generalizations on the determinants of neutral policy and conclusions will complement this definitional and thematic introduction to a more detailed analysis of the individual neutral and nonaligned countries of Europe.

NEUTRALITY

Colloquially, the term neutrality means impartiality, that is, not taking sides in a dispute between third parties. In this sense any state can be viewed as neutral in relation to a specific controversial issue between other states. Thus, a member of an alliance may follow a neutral line on an issue that does not involve its commitment as an alliance member. In view of the multiplicity of foreign policy issues and crisscrossing interests in international politics, one theoretically could envisage a continuum ranging from an orientation of absolute neutrality (which then would equal isolation in practice) to a strategy of absolute alliance.[3] For example, on a number of issues the recent behavior of Greece reminds one of a neutral, rather than an aligned, foreign policy orientation. This kind of phenomenon has prompted some international relations theorists to view present international politics as evolving into some kind of a "nonaligned international system."[4] However, neutrality, a word derived from the Latin *neuter,* meaning neither, is a term of art and institution of traditional international law. It refers to the status of a state during an ongoing war between other states, whereby that state adopts an attitude of impartiality toward the belligerents, which they recognize and which creates rights and duties under international law between the neutral state and the belligerents.[5] This institution of neutrality (sometimes referred to as "ordinary" or "occasional" neutrality, to distinguish it from "permanent" neutrality) became a part of the law of nations (today known more often as international law) in the seventeenth century. In the classical multipolar balance-of-power era it developed into a system of, primarily, customary law of neutrality, subsequently codified in 1907 at the Second Hague Peace Conference in Hague Conventions V (neutrality in case of war on land) and XIII (neutrality in naval war).[6]

Under the traditional law of neutrality, a neutral state is obliged to treat the belligerents with strict impartiality. It must abstain from providing them with military support and prevent them from engaging in military activities on its territory--for example, by establishing bases or recruitment offices. However, since neutral rights and obligations are vested in the state and not in its nationals, under the traditional law a neutral state has no obligation to prevent its citizens from going abroad and offering their services to a belligerent.[7] Similarly under the same law, reflecting nineteenth-century laissez-faire philosophy, although a neutral state as such was prohibited from furnishing war materiel and services to a belligerent, its nationals were allowed to engage in such activities. This distinction is clearly obsolete in today's world where armed conflicts have acquired a total character and where arms trade and, in many states, foreign trade as a whole are a state monopoly, or at least under strict governmental control.

A neutral state has the right[8] to defend its neutrality by force of arms against a belligerent state; if it fails to do so, the other belligerent may attack the enemy on the neutral territory. A neutral state, however, must acquiesce in legitimate acts of belligerents with respect to the commerce of its nationals, such as search and seizure of vessels carrying contraband.

The twentieth century has witnessed the decline of the institution of traditional neutrality, which frequently was violated by belligerents on land and at sea.[9]   Violations of neutral duties by neutral states also took place. In fact, during World War II some such states--for example, the United States prior to joining the war and Spain--adopted the position of what became known as "nonbelligerency" or "quasi neutrality." This refers to the status of a nonbelligerent state which, while not participating in an ongoing war, does not observe impartiality but favors one side in the conflict.

The League of Nations collective security system seemed to render the institution of neutrality largely obsolete, but upon its obvious failure a number of small states, including Ireland and Finland, declared that they would remain neutral in a future war. The prohibition of the use of force in the UN Charter[10] again raised the question of the relevance of neutrality in the UN collective security system in which, strictly speaking, an attitude of impartiality toward the belligerents, some of which were aggressors while others acted in self-defense, would be impermissible. However, in practice, the collective security system did not prove feasible, as a result of which traditional neutrality of individual states in case of an armed conflict remained a possibility.

Yet in the numerous post-World War II conflicts the nonparticipating states have been reluctant to proclaim neutrality according to the traditional rules for a number of reasons. First, a formal proclamation of neutrality somehow would imply recognition of the legitimacy of war in international relations. Second, virtually all the armed conflicts that have erupted following World War II have been waged without any declarations of war; hence, no neutral status was legally possible with regard to such "nonwar" armed conflicts. What exactly in legal terms is the status of states not participating in such conflicts still remains to be clarified in international law.[11]   Third, proclaiming neutrality in an armed conflict might be detrimental to the economic interests of nonbelligerents and would otherwise hamper their international and domestic legal relations and political standing.

Despite all its uncertainties and ambiguities, the institution of neutrality has not become altogether obsolete. A number of international instruments, such as, for example, the Geneva Conventions of 1949,[12] refer to neutral states and, in general, accept neutrality as a fact of international life. Permanent neutrality, which also imposes certain legal duties in peacetime, remains a significant institution of international law in the European context where Switzerland and Austria are legally obligated to observe it. In addition to this legal permanent neutrality, there is factual permanent neutrality, followed as a foreign policy orientation and without legal obligation by Sweden and Finland. Permanent neutrality in its two general editions will be examined in the following sections of this study.

PERMANENT NEUTRALITY: LEGAL AND FACTUAL

In General

Whereas neutrality denotes the legal status of a state not participating in an ongoing war between other states, permanent[13] neutrality legally obligates a state to remain neutral not only during a war but also in peacetime. In the classical formulation of the duties of a permanently neutral state, such state is bound never to take up arms against any other state except in self-defense, to defend its neutrality, and to "do everything not to get involved in a war and abstain from anything that might involve it in a war; that is, it must . . . avoid taking sides in conflicts between third states. It is obliged to follow the policy of neutrality."[14] Switzerland, the classical model of this status, and Austria are such permanently neutral states under international law. Malta is a special case, and among the ministates Vatican City also enjoys the status of legal permanent neutrality. A permanent neutrality type of foreign policy orientation may be practiced in reality without any international legal obligation to do so, as was the case of the Swiss Confederation prior to 1815 (apart from the Napoleonic interlude). Today, it is the case of Sweden, which prefers to call itself "not aligned," Finland, and, subject to certain reservations and doubts, Ireland. Liechtenstein and San Marino are also de facto permanently neutral.

The similarities between the foreign policies of the legally and factually permanently neutral countries demonstrate that actual political behavior, rather than formal international legal commitment, can be taken as the criterion for classifying their foreign policy orientations. Legal permanent neutrality imposes definite restrictions upon a neutral state's exercise of sovereignty, but at the same time it offers the advantages of predictability and greater credibility in the perception of other states. As a matter of fact, the foreign policy of a legally permanently neutral country represents the most straightforward and clear-cut type of policy in which there exists the highest degree of consistency between such a country's fundamental guiding principle and its translation into concrete foreign policy behavior. For this reason, unlike other general foreign policy orientations, the nonalignment of Third World states--for example, the policies of de jure permanently neutral states--can be classified as a quite rigorous category of foreign policy. The same is, to a large extent, true of the de facto permanently neutral states except that, in the absence of legal restraints, a country like Sweden, which has deliberately avoided any legal commitments to permanent neutrality either in its constitution or under international law, has more flexibility in its foreign policy actions.[15] This was demonstrated by the Swedish offer to Norway and Denmark in 1948 to set up a Scandinavian defense alliance of neutral countries, something that Switzerland would not be allowed to consider.[16]

The status of legal permanent neutrality can be created by two methods: 1) a unilateral policy or declaration of such neutrality, followed by recognition by other states (as was the case of Switzerland and Austria), formalized in a treaty or according to some other method valid under international law (such as a diplomatic note or simply acquiescence, which normally produces a customary rule of law);[17] or 2) the imposition of such status upon a state at the initiative of and by a collective agreement of other powers, joined by the state concerned. The latter method, historically applied to Belgium (1839), Luxembourg (1867), and the rather unusual case of the "Republic of Cracow" (1815), constitutes in the strict sense of the term what is known as neutralization, although the term is frequently used with regard to states acquiring a status of permanent neutrality according to the first procedure, especially where the independence and neutrality of a state are guaranteed or at least expressly recognized by the great powers. For this reason, Austria and Switzerland are sometimes referred to as neutralized states. Neutralization may be resented by the neutralized state as an unjustified limitation of its sovereignty in return for recognition of independence. (Such was the case of Belgium, whose neutralization was terminated by Article 31 of the Treaty of Versailles in 1919.[18]) The Austrian government, however, has always emphasized that it adopted the status of permanent neutrality out of its own free will, but it is clear that political circumstances had indirectly imposed it upon Austria. On the other hand, this status turned out to be the right option to choose and has become part and parcel of

Austria's political culture, shared by an overwhelming majority of the population.[19]

The term neutralization is used sometimes instead of the more appropriate term demilitarization, in situations involving not states but only parts of them, or such areas as rivers, canals, or outer space, all of which cannot have any rights and duties under international law.[20] A unilateral declaration alone (self-neutralization) cannot create a status of permanent neutrality. In the absence of recognition by other states, it has merely the force of municipal (domestic) law.[21] The international political impact of such declarations varies depending upon the circumstances of the case.

Legal permanent neutrality entails obligations also for third powers. A distinction must be made between powers merely recognizing the permanent neutrality of a state and those that guarantee it. Thus, the permanent neutrality and territorial integrity of Switzerland were guaranteed by Austria, France, Great Britain, Prussia, and Russia in 1815,[22] but its permanent neutrality has been recognized by all states and reaffirmed in the treaties ending World War I in 1919.[23] The status of Switzerland as a permanently neutral country, originally recognized in treaty form only by the great powers, has become such a firmly established institution of public international law that it is binding upon all states as a customary rule of law.[24] The permanent neutrality of Austria has been recognized explicitly or by acquiescence by all states and also can be considered as a rule of customary international law.[25] The permanent neutrality proclaimed by Malta in 1980 has been recognized by a limited number of states including, in addition to Italy, the Soviet Union, China,[26] France, and Algeria, and under a five-year treaty of friendship and cooperation (1984) by Libya.[27]

As far as the legal effects of the guarantee of its permanent neutrality are concerned, Switzerland reserves to itself the right to decide when such a guarantee becomes operative, emphasizing that it does not entail the right of the guaranteeing powers to intervene without Switzerland's consent. This principle must be considered as applying to all cases where a neutralization agreement would include provisions on guarantees.[28] In general, Switzerland and Austria are very sensitive on the point of their exclusive right to interpret the obligations of their status, an issue which, fortunately for them, has not been pressed by the great powers. Austria has never sought an international guarantee of its neutrality, principally because of its desire to exclude any outside interference with the interpretation of its neutrality.[29]

Switzerland and Austria also stress that, beyond certain relatively clear neutral obligations, they have the right to pursue a policy which, while compatible with their status, depends entirely upon their discretionary power.   The duties of the de jure permanently neutral states will be analyzed in the following paragraphs, but it must not be forgotten that the de facto neutrals, Sweden and Finland, in general follow the same behavior pattern without any legal obligation under international law.   Therefore, unless expressly stated otherwise, the discussion applies to both legal and factual permanent neutrality.

Obligations of Permanently Neutral States

A legally permanently neutral state has the obligation to observe neutrality during an ongoing war.   In armed conflicts that are not formally "wars" (and, as noted, virtually all the armed conflicts of the post-World War II era belong to this category), a permanently neutral state must do everything not to get involved in hostilities and to remain impartial.   Neutrality also must be observed in the case of a civil war, especially since such wars tend to be internationalized.   In peacetime, the whole policy of a permanently neutral state must be geared to the fundamental principle of abstaining from any act or omission that might jeopardize its neutral status in any future war.

The content of permanent neutrality obligations, developed historically in the customary practice of permanently neutral countries, is presented in its classical form in the official Swiss conception of neutrality of 1954.   This model is recognized as valid also for Austria.[30]   Under its conception there are two categories of obligation of a permanently neutral state: primary and secondary, as discussed below.

Primary Obligations

The primary obligations include: 1) the now otherwise peremptory rule of international law (*jus cogens*) not to start a war, and 2) the obligation to defend independence, territorial integrity, and neutrality of the state.[31]   That second primary obligation implies that the neutrality of a permanently neutral state must be "armed" neutrality; that is, such a state has not just the right but the duty to provide in advance for its armed defense, thereby deterring any potential aggressor and strengthening its credibility as a neutral in the eyes of other nations.[32] If attacked, a permanently neutral state has the right to call for help of other states, especially of the guarantors of its neutrality, and to appeal to a collective security organization, such as the United Nations. Having successfully repulsed an aggression, a permanently neutral country continues its legal status as before.

In their defense strategy, the permanently neutral countries, realizing that they would not be able to repulse an all-out attack, have opted for what in the Swiss defense conception is known as the "high entrance and occupation price" strategy. This approach conveys to the would-be aggressor the message that any benefit that might accrue to him from attacking and occupying the neutral country would be far outweighed by the costs incurred in terms of casualties, loss of war materiel, time, and political damage.[33] The extent of the defense preparations required of a permanently neutral state depends on the circumstances, but in general it must be determined by the international standard, that is, by the military effort of comparable neighboring countries. The share of gross national product (GNP) spent on defense per year, possibly combined with per capita defense expenditures, could be used as such a standard.[34] A glance at the statistics reveals that Switzerland meets this standard of armed permanent neutrality, but Austria lags behind it. The factually neutral Sweden can, in its defense effort, be compared to Switzerland, whereas Finland and Austria spend less for defense than those two countries. It is significant that the new neutrals, Austria and Finland, eager to develop an appropriate image and credibility in their status, emphasize the political tools of an "active" foreign policy in the interests of international peace rather than military instruments, even though their geostrategic situation makes them more vulnerable than Sweden and Switzerland. The latter two countries have been spending consistently more on defense than Austria and Finland.[35]

The primary obligation of a permanently neutral country to defend itself is closely related to the military aspect of its secondary obligations, which will be examined below. It can be noted here that the obligation to preserve independence and territorial integrity entails the prohibition, without the recognizing powers' consent, of merger with or joining another state and, except for minor border rectifications, cession or acquisition of territory.[36]

Secondary Obligations

It is a fundamental duty of a permanently neutral country to practice a credible policy of neutrality. This involves adherence to the general principle of refraining from any acts or situations which would make it impossible or difficult to comply with the obligations of ordinary neutrality during a future war and thus jeopardize its permanent neutrality status. The resulting obligations, which bind a permanently neutral state (sometimes referred to as anticipatory effects, or *Vorwirkungen*), are of a political, military, and economic nature.[37]

Political Obligations. The general principle underlying the secondary obligations offers a rather vague standard of behavior, yet it does impose at least one clear legal obligation--namely, prohibition of entering into treaties that would oblige a permanently neutral country to enter a war, specifically treaties of alliance or guarantee. Such a country cannot even enter into an alliance with another permanently neutral state or guarantee that state's neutrality.[38] However, as already noted, the status of permanent neutrality does not bar a state from having other states' guarantees or requesting assistance if attacked.[39] The experience of Austria demonstrates that participation in a universal collective security organization, such as the United Nations, can be made compatible with the obligations of neutrality, as discussed below.

The secondary obligations must be interpreted restrictively. If a neutral state does more than is clearly required by its status, its actions should not be considered as meeting a legal obligation but as prompted by political motives and designed to strengthen the confidence of other states in the determination of the neutral state to uphold its status.[40] Moreover, the secondary obligations apply only to the foreign policy acts of the authoritative organs of government and not to all governmental activities, let alone opinions and actions of a neutral state's nationals. As stated in the official Swiss conception, international law obligations of neutrality are not vested in an individual.[41] This means that legal and political neutrality cannot interfere with the ideological posture of a permanently neutral state: "There exists no obligation to so-called moral neutrality."[42] The permanently neutral countries are ideologically Western democracies and have often criticized other states' actions which they found objectionable on moral or legal grounds. For example, the Soviet intervention in Afghanistan was condemned by the Swiss and Austrian governments,[43] and Sweden's censure of the U.S. involvement in Vietnam is a matter of public record. On the other hand, neither Switzerland nor Austria joined the boycott of the Moscow Olympic Games, nor did they participate in the economic sanctions against Iran, resulting from the hostage crisis in 1979-80.[44] One consequence of the rule that permanent neutrality binds only the state in its official foreign policy relations is that neutrality does not require restricting the neutral state's freedom of the press.[45]

Apart from creating zones of stability in a divided Europe and to a certain extent separating NATO from the Warsaw Pact (like Switzerland and Austria),[46] the neutral states, within their modest possibilities, have played an active role in promoting peace and security. Examples of these efforts are representation of diplomatic and consular interests (for sixteen countries by Switzerland alone), good offices and mediation, contribution to UN peace-keeping operations, hosting international conferences and organizations, and humanitarian services. However limited in its effects, the mediatory role of the European neutral and nonaligned states (the n+n group) at the Conference on Security and Cooperation in Europe (CSCE) and its follow-up meetings must not be underestimated.[47] This kind of international behavior, although not required by law, strengthens the image of neutral states and also demonstrates the usefulness of the institution of permanent neutrality to the states forming part of the two alliances which divide the European continent.

The discretionary power of a permanently neutral state to implement its foreign policy orientation is illustrated by the fact that whereas Switzerland has not become a member of the United Nations, Austria has done so without finding such membership incompatible with its status.[48] In principle, membership in the United Nations seems to conflict with the status of permanent neutrality. Regarding Austria, the only de jure permanently neutral state and UN member, the prevalent opinion is that should the Security Council decide upon coercive measures under the UN Charter's Chapter VII, it would have to exempt Austria from participating in sanctions that conflicted with its status, a procedure possible under Article 48(3) of the Charter.[49] It is also Austria's position, stated on the occasion of the UN sanctions against Southern Rhodesia in 1967, that the question of whether Austria is to be bound by the decision of the Security Council must be decided in each case with due regard to its UN membership obligations and its status of permanent neutrality.[50] In any case, Austria is not likely to be confronted with the UN-permanent neutrality dilemma because the collective security system of the United Nations has turned out to be virtually a dead letter.   Still, Austria, in a desire to take advantage of a world arena to build up the image of its newly acquired neutral status, has been contributing much to the work of the organization, including hosting UN agencies and providing troops for UN peace-keeping operations.[51]

Switzerland, haunted by the failure of its membership in the League of Nations with the status of "differential" neutrality,[52] has not joined the United Nations, but it is party to the Statute of the International Court of Justice[53] and a number of specialized agencies.[54]   It hosts a major UN headquarters and several UN agencies and is universally known as contributing financially and materially, but not in the form of troops, to UN peace-keeping operations and humanitarian activities.   The membership issue has been on the agenda of the Swiss government and a subject of national debate for decades.   The matter received extensive analysis by the Federal Council, which submitted reports to that effect to the Federal Assembly in 1969, 1971, 1977, and 1981.   The last report, backed by the Federal Assembly, recommended membership.   The required popular referendum took place in March 1986, and an overwhelming majority of the voters and cantons decided against joining the United Nations.[55]

The official Swiss conception of neutrality established guidelines on the participation of Switzerland in international diplomatic conferences and organizations which can be applied to permanently neutral states in general.   It distinguished between conferences and organizations that are predominantly political and those that are primarily economic, technical, cultural, and similarly nonpolitical in nature.   Participation in the former, with observance of strict impartiality, may be considered only if they are of a universal nature and include the principal representatives of political blocs, in particular both parties to a possible conflict.[56]   The rationale of this position is that permanent neutrality would be less exposed to risks of involvement in conflicts and charges of partiality if membership were as universal as possible.   Thus, Switzerland and the other neutral and nonaligned countries of Europe (the n+n group) took part in the Helsinki Conference on Security and Cooperation and its follow-up meetings because the Helsinki framework includes all the European countries, except Albania.[57]

Since membership in the United Nations can be made compatible with permanent neutrality, it is a matter of the discretionary policy of a neutral state whether or not to join this otherwise abortive collective security system.   The paths followed by Switzerland and Austria illustrate this proposition.   Switzerland, a well-established model of permanent neutrality, believes that it can do without UN membership, whereas Austria, a newcomer to the post-World War II political scene, seized the opportunity to become a member and has found the United Nations a useful forum in which to strengthen its credibility as a permanently neutral state.   The de facto neutrals, nonaligned Yugoslavia and even isolationist Albania, also appreciate UN membership for their respective foreign policy goals.

Military Obligations.   The defense policy of a permanently neutral state must be consistent with its fundamental political obligation to defend its neutrality, independence, and territorial integrity and not to enter into any alliances.   Defense consultations with other countries appear to be allowed in case of incontrovertible evidence of an impending attack upon the neutral state.[58]   The obligations of military neutrality further include the prohibition of allowing foreign military bases in the neutral state's territory and supplying troops to other countries.[59]   A neutral state is not liable, however, for its nationals enrolling in foreign armed services as mercenaries.[60]

If a permanently neutral state were to implement ideally its obligation of maintaining a minimum international standard of defense efforts while avoiding obligations during peacetime that might compromise its neutrality in a future war, it would have to rely exclusively on native arms production in its weapons acquisition policy.   The borderline between the legal obligation of self-defense and the national security policy of implementing this obligation cannot be clearly determined.   However, excessive dependence on arms imports from one country would cast doubt upon the neutral importer's credibility as a permanently neutral state.   No permanently neutral country is entirely self-sufficient in weaponry and equipment.[61]   Sweden, which learned its lesson during the early years of World War II,[62] relies, with certain exceptions, on its own munitions industry.[63]   Switzerland does possess an armaments industry of its own but must still rely heavily upon NATO technology for both its own production and imports.[64]   Austria and Finland import much of their military hardware and, more than Switzerland or Sweden, adjust their acquisition policy to the sensitive requirements of the policy of permanent neutrality.[65]

While emancipating a neutral country from excessive dependence upon foreign imports, self-reliance often leads to the need to export materiel for which the relatively small domestic market does not have sufficient demand.   Hence, arms sales by a neutral country, especially those to a member of a Cold War alliance, may place it in a position that might be construed as economic dependence upon an aligned power, or even outright partiality.[66]   Therefore, it is a policy of the European neutrals not to export weapons to areas involved in an armed conflict or tension.[67]

Although a permanently neutral state is required to maintain a reasonably strong military establishment, it may be subjected to restrictions under a treaty, as witnessed by the Austrian State Treaty of 1955.[68]   Such restrictions are not thought to be incompatible with the status of permanent neutrality.[69]   Unless a permanently neutral country is barred by treaty from acquiring nuclear weapons, it is allowed to possess them.[70]   At this time the issue is of little significance since, even though until 1965 Sweden kept the nuclear option open,[71] both that country and Switzerland eventually rejected it as inappropriate and lacking credibility in the strategic and military conditions of the contemporary international system. Both these countries and the other permanently neutral states are parties to the partial test-ban treaty of 1963 and the nonproliferation treaty of 1978.[72]   They have supported international measures for nuclear and other arms control, but since the balance of power between the two blocs is the very basis and prerequisite of a permanently neutral country's status, such a country may logically join a multilateral arms control arrangement only if it does not jeopardize such a balance.   In fact, it is an axiom of the security policy of the European neutral, as well as of nonaligned countries, that a military balance between NATO and the Warsaw Pact is an essential element of global and, therefore, their own security.[73]

Economic Obligations.   The status of permanent neutrality indirectly affects the foreign economic policy of the neutral state, in particular with regard to its participation in international or supranational integration schemes.   European integration confronted the European neutrals with a dilemma.   On the one hand, joining the European Community would offer them economic and other advantages, but on the other, they realized that legal and political considerations excluded membership in an organization that, albeit primarily economic in nature, was ultimately designed as a vehicle for an eventual political integration of the member countries.   Only membership in the European Free Trade Association (EFTA), a rather loose arrangement without any aspirations toward economic, let alone political, integration and with basically majority rule in its major organs, was open to the European neutrals.   Consequently,

Austria, Switzerland, and Sweden joined that organization. Because of its special relationship to the Soviet Union, Finland had to make a special arrangement with EFTA (FINEFTA), but not without balancing this turn toward the West by granting equal trade and tariff concessions to the Soviet Union.[74]

The Swiss conception of neutrality states clearly that "a permanently neutral state cannot conclude any customs and economic alliances."[75] There is one historical precedent confirming the customary-law nature of this principle, namely, the great powers' protests at France's negotiations with the then permanently neutral Belgium on the conclusion of a customs union in 1841-42.[76] Also legally relevant is the Advisory Opinion of the Permanent Court of International Justice (1931), which stated that Austria's customs union with Germany would compromise the former's independence.[77]

There is almost universal consensus that membership of Austria and Switzerland in the European Economic Community (EEC) would conflict with their international legal status or, at best, jeopardize their credibility as permanently neutral states, particularly in the eyes of the Soviet Union.[78] Such membership also would create difficult problems for the neutrals if economic sanctions were to be imposed by the European Community against a country in armed conflict with a community member. The position of a permanently neutral state would be even more awkward following the 1986 reform of the EEC decision-making system allowing more scope for majority rule in the Council of Ministers, the Community's crucial organ. In addition, because of the ultimately supranational objectives of the EEC, membership of a neutral state in the EEC would potentially entail the end of the neutral state's independent existence, which clearly would be incompatible with its primary obligations. For all these reasons Switzerland and Austria, as well as Sweden, opted, after mutual consultations, only for free-trade agreements with the EEC in 1972. These agreements include provisions safeguarding the permanent neutrality of each of these states.[79] Finland's 1973 agreement is even more cautious, since, unlike the other three, it lacks the so-called evolution clause providing for the possibility of expanding cooperation with the EEC in case of its further evolution on the road to closer integration.[80] It is characteristic of Finland's delicate position that, in order to demonstrate its balanced neutral posture, it simultaneously concluded an association agreement with the Soviet-sponsored Council of Mutual Economic Assistance (CMEA).[81]

It is primarily within the context of the economic obligations of permanently neutral states that the position of Ireland as a neutral must be considered.   Ireland had no political qualms in joining the European Community as a full-fledged member in 1973, thereby disregarding one of the major prohibitions restricting a permanently neutral country's foreign policy.   For this reason, Ireland cannot be counted among the permanently neutral states like Sweden.   It is significant that, while proclaiming its bloc-free position, Ireland was not a member of the neutral and nonaligned nations (the n+n group) at the CSCE and the follow-up meetings but coordinated its policy with the Western group in the context of the European political cooperation of the EEC member countries.[82] Therefore, among the European neutrals, Ireland occupies a special position which departs from the model of permanent neutrality.[83]

NEUTRALISM: A DEPRECIATED TERMINOLOGY

Unlike the terms neutrality, legal permanent neutrality, and even the relatively precise factual permanent neutrality, the rather colloquial and very political term neutralism lacks conceptual precision.   It frequently is used interchangeably with those terms and even more often with the term nonalignment, in the meaning of the policy of noninvolvement by the Third World countries in the alliances generated by the Cold War.

Historically, the term neutralism, as opposed to interventionism, first appeared in the context of the debate in Italy prior to that country's decision to join the allies in World War I.[84]   The term reappeared after World War II as a result of the rise of bipolarity, institutionalized in the Cold War alliances, and of the emergence of many new states in the decolonized areas of the world.   Whereas neutrality meant legally nonparticipation in a war, the term neutralism acquired the meaning of a policy of noncommitment in the Cold War.   It is interesting to follow the vicissitudes and nuances in its meaning in the post-World War II era.   Whereas today, especially in the European context, it does not have any pejorative connotations and in some eyes it has even acquired respectability, during the early postwar years and then in the climate of the beginning Cold War it was considered by many in the West as an "immoral and short-sighted conception."[85]   For their part, the leaders of the neutralist Third World countries, rejecting the negative and passive associations of the term with its implication of indifference and isolation from world politics, decided to use the term nonalignment rather than neutralism. Already in 1954, Marshal Tito and Jawaharlal Nehru jointly proclaimed that theirs was not a policy of neutrality or neutralism but a constructive and positive action leading to collective peace.[86] Since the first Belgrade summit meeting in 1961, the term nonalignment has been used officially by the movement of the nonaligned nations.[87] The term neutralism has become a colloquial expression referring indiscriminately to all kinds of international noncommitment; therefore, it has lost its usefulness for purposes of this analysis.

NONALIGNMENT

In General

As a term of art, nonalignment is relevant for purposes of this study because Yugoslavia and Malta (and, if one wants to add it to the European region, Cyprus) are members of the nonaligned movement.[88] Nonalignment must be distinguished from the term *not alignment*, sometimes used in Sweden's political vocabulary to denote the Swedish policy of permanent neutrality.

It is far beyond the scope of this discussion to examine in detail the otherwise "amorphous and vague concept" of alignment.[89] The following analysis will be limited to the essentials, with particular reference to those aspects which pertain to the European members of the nonaligned movement. As crystallized by declarations and conferences of the nonaligned countries, beginning with the 1961 Belgrade Conference, nonalignment can be defined as a foreign policy orientation toward the East-West conflict. It has been embraced primarily by newly emerged African and Asian states but also by Latin America and, in Europe, by Yugoslavia, Malta, and Cyprus. These states do not participate in the military alliances functioning in the context of great-power conflicts but are committed to play an active role as intermediaries in the Cold War and as supporters of the peace-keeping efforts of the United Nations. On the other hand, according to the criteria laid down for membership in the nonaligned movement, a bilateral military alliance with a great power, participation in a regional defense pact outside of great-power conflicts, or the granting of military bases to a foreign power outside of such conflict are not incompatible with the prin-

ciple of nonalignment.[90]   These are all rather contradictory and
not entirely precise guidelines which, if liberally interpreted, would
allow acceptance in the movement of any country claiming to be
nonaligned.   In this context, attendance in the capacity of guests,
not only of the European neutrals--Austria, Switzerland, Sweden,
Finland, San Marino, and the Vatican--but also especially of such
countries as Romania, Spain, and even Portugal is significant.[91]   It
must be added, however, that China and Albania are not members
of the nonaligned movement; for the latter country, that movement
is another form of imperialist conspiracy.   Additional conditions for
belonging are support of selected national liberation movements and
the struggle against all forms of racism.

Although the nonaligned countries profess themselves uncom-
mitted in the East-West conflict, they are much more critical of
the West than of the Soviet Union.   Moreover, some of them, led
by Cuba, have been pressing for closer ties with the Soviets and
the Warsaw Pact as protagonists of the "struggle against imperialism," putting forward the concept of a "natural alliance between
nonaligned and socialist countries" and urging exclusion from the
movement of "reactionary," that is, pro-Western members.   A show-
down between the radical and moderate groups occurred at the 1979
Havana meeting, which is of interest for purposes of this study
because of the role played by Yugoslavia at the nonaligned conference.   As a spokesman of the moderate group, that European country successfully upheld the element of impartiality in the concept
of nonalignment, arguing that any commitment to either side in the
East-West conflict would negate the concept.[92]

The nonaligned countries do not consider themselves as a bloc
with a common strategy on all issues of global and regional policies.
On the contrary, it is common knowledge that regional conflicts
and changing alliances abound among the nonaligned countries.   The
movement is not based on any charter, and it does not enter into
international agreements.   Hence, its members are not bound by any
rules of international law emanating from it.   Institutionalization of
the nonaligned movement is still rather limited.[93]   A confrontation
of the concept of nonalignment against that of permanent neutrality,
both legal and factual, will make it easier to understand in what
way the two concepts differ from each other and in what way they
are similar.

Nonalignment and Permanent Neutrality

At first sight the two concepts appear to have much in common. A closer look, however, discloses not only parallel traits but also considerable differences, especially insofar as the objective situation of states following the two concepts of foreign policy is concerned.[94] Furthermore, unlike the case of the European neutrals, the analysis of the nonaligned countries' policy is impeded by the gap that sometime exists between the concept of nonalignment and the actual foreign policy behavior of the states professing to follow it. However, it must be added that the latter observation applies least of all to Yugoslavia, whose policy approximates that of the European neutrals rather than that of the Afro-Asian nonaligned countries.

Nonparticipation in Cold War military alliances is the most obvious common denominator of the concepts of nonalignment and permanent neutrality, but the analogy ends there. Outside of the great-power conflict, nonalignment allows bilateral military alliances with a great power or the leasing of a military base to such a power as well as participation in regional military pacts, all of which are illegal for a de jure permanently neutral country and unthinkable from the point of view of factual neutrals. Yugoslavia's behavior in this respect is more like that of such neutrals than that of the nonaligned states.[95] Still, even that country has a limited naval repair agreement with the Soviet Union and purchases most of its major military equipment from it.[96] Under Malta's Declaration of Permanent Neutrality, warships of the superpowers cannot use Maltese shipyards,[97] but under a 1981 agreement Malta granted the Soviet Union the right to refuel its ships using Maltese oil storage facilities.[98] The declaration allows the use of Malta's military facilities by foreign forces in the exercise of Malta's right of self-defense or in pursuance of the enforcement measures ordered by the UN Security Council, or "whenever there is a threat to [Malta's] sovereignty, independence, neutrality, unity, or territorial integrity." It also allows admission in "reasonable numbers" of foreign personnel assisting in the defense of the country or in civil works and activities.[99] All those provisions clearly are incompatible with the status of permanent neutrality as it is understood by the European neutrals. In addition, the duty of the nonaligned to support national liberation movements would be difficult to reconcile with such status.

There are some similarities in the foreign policy attitude of the neutrals and nonaligned countries. The former are, in general, more sympathetic than the other Western European nations to the anticolonial stand and to the demands for a New International Economic Order (NIEO), the current focus of the nonaligned states' policy.[100] Both groups of countries are for an active foreign policy under the auspices of the United Nations. Within the European context, the neutral and nonaligned (n+n) group of states coordinated their position at the Helsinki CSCE and the follow-up meetings.

Still, permanent neutrality and nonalignment differ both in concept and in the nature of the states embracing the respective orientations. Permanent neutrality is an exceptional institution in international politics. It is essentially a West European phenomenon which evolved historically in the conditions of the European balance-of-power system, whereas nonalignment emerged in the post-World War II era as a result of decolonization and in reaction to the bipolar alignment of the two blocs in the North. The origin of Yugoslavia's nonalignment is different in that it was embraced in reaction to Soviet hegemony in Eastern Europe as a security policy to deter any possible Soviet intervention. Yugoslavia also developed ties with the nonaligned nations of the Third World and sought assistance from the West without military alignment with NATO, and eventually also from the Soviet bloc itself.

The basic difference between legal permanent neutrality and nonalignment is that the former is a legal status with rights and duties under international law (which are also followed by the de facto neutrals, but without any legal obligation), whereas nonalignment is a rather ill-defined political doctrine that can be used flexibly and according to expediency by the countries concerned.

A TYPOLOGY OF THE EUROPEAN STATES
OUTSIDE OF NATO AND THE WARSAW PACT

Having established the conceptual and legal parameters of neutrality and nonalignment in the European context, it will now be possible to categorize the European states remaining outside of the alliance systems. The core group is constituted by two legally permanently neutral states: the classical model, Switzerland, "neutralized" in 1815; and Austria, which followed it much later in 1955. The sovereign ministate of Vatican City also must be included in this category. The 1929 Lateran Treaty with Italy and the 1984 treaty between the Holy See and Italy established Vatican City as a perpetually neutral and inviolable territory, a principle which must be regarded as part of general international law.[101] Sweden and Finland are de facto permanently neutral states, for which permanent neutrality is not a legal obligation but a principle of foreign policy. Sweden, in fact, often refers to itself as a not-aligned neutral country. Finland's Treaty of Friendship, Cooperation, and Mutual Assistance with the Soviet Union (1948) merely states what a de facto permanently neutral country like Sweden would do in any case: namely, defend its territorial integrity and independence. Any Soviet assistance would have to be mutually agreed to in prior consultations. This is the interpretation of the crucial Article 2 of the treaty to which the Soviet Union consented in 1961.[102] Still, as is well known, the foreign policy behavior of Finland is very much determined by the need not to provoke any adverse Soviet reaction. Ultimately, however, Sweden must not antagonize the Soviet Union either.

Two ministates, Liechtenstein and San Marino, also can be classified as de facto permanently neutral (Monaco and Andorra may be overlooked as not fully sovereign states). Ireland represents a special case since, although it remains outside of any military alliance, its membership in the European Community is incompatible with the conduct of a permanently neutral country. Malta's status of "neutrality strictly founded on the principles of nonalignment" entails a contradiction since, as already noted, despite certain similarities, the concepts of permanent neutrality and nonalignment are incompatible. Some provisions of Malta's Declaration of 1980 also conflict with the military obligations of a permanently neutral state. Hence, Malta's status is a hybrid between neutrality and nonalignment. Yugoslavia, a cofounder of the nonaligned movement, is a full-fledged member of the group and provides a linkage between the European neutrals and the nonaligned countries of the Third World. Cyprus is also nonaligned (there are two British air bases on Cypriot territory, but they are under the sovereignty of the United Kingdom). Finally, Albania stands out as a unique case in the European context and even the international system as a whole. Despite some diplomatic and economic contacts with selected countries, its ideologically intransigent attitude and self-reliant foreign policy warrant the label of semi-isolation to be applied to this anachronistic remnant of Stalinism and former Warsaw Pact member in the Balkans.

DETERMINANTS OF NEUTRALITY
AND NONALIGNMENT

The inquiry into the nature of the concepts of permanent neutrality and nonalignment in Europe can now be complemented by an
examination of the circumstances under which the states concerned
have adopted and successfully maintained their respective foreign
policy orientations.   It is difficult to generalize on these determinants of neutrality and nonalignment in the European context,
which vary from case to case in diverse combinations.   In general,
it is possible to distinguish two broad clusters of variables, systemic
and internal, accounting for the choice and success of these orientations in each particular case.

Systemic Variables

The systemic, or external, variables include primarily the
geostrategic factor and certain aspects of the structure of the
international system.   While it is true that such geographical variables as location, size, and topography of a country fall into the
internal, or domestic, category if taken in their absolute magnitude
and representing a national attribute as such, they can also be
perceived as elements of an international system if viewed in their
relation to other elements of the system.[103]   Taking size as an
example, it cannot be denied that the European neutrals and nonaligned belong to the category of rather small states.   This absolute
fact must both determine their domestic requirements and limit the
scope of their foreign involvement.   At the same time, this fact
forms part of the perception of other states and must be approached
relative to elements and interactions in the international system as
such.
Without necessarily endorsing the position of geographic deter-
minism, it can be said that the geostrategic location of Switzerland
and its topography, as perceived by others, has helped that model
of neutrality to sustain its policy and status throughout the centuries.   Similarly, Sweden's relative distance from the focus of
international conflict must have played a role in the great powers'
perception to the benefit of Sweden's policy of permanent neutrality.
There is likewise no doubt that the geographical location of Yugoslavia and Albania has been a major factor contributing to the

successful assertion by these countries of their respective independent foreign policy lines.

A favorable structure of the international system in the meaning of the distribution of power is a major condition for the success of permanent neutrality. Tight bipolarity by definition negates any idea of neutrality. On the other hand, a diffuse balance-of-power system of the nineteenth century was an ideal structure for this institution, but, as it turned out, permanent neutrality can flourish in the European continent divided by a bipolar conflict. It was in the interest of the European balance of power that the great powers decided to legalize the de facto permanent neutrality of Switzerland, decoupling that strategic area of Alpine passes from their rivalry. The neutralization of Switzerland was a classic balance-of-power deal, whereby each of the great powers agreed to renounce its influence over the Swiss cantons on the condition that its rivals do likewise.

Similarly, after World War II when neither bloc was willing to leave Austria to the other side, the neutralization of that country, located on the borderline of the two antagonistic alliances, offered both a reasonable guarantee that Austria would stay out of the East-West confrontation. At the same time, in exchange for giving up any thought of alignment with the West, Austria achieved the withdrawal of Soviet troops from its territory. Moreover, Sweden's policy of permanent neutrality also meets the interests of the two blocs, constituting as it does a central factor in the Nordic balance of power in which the neutral Finland plays a sensitive role. Since the superpowers perceive the continued existence of permanent neutrality in Europe as an essential element of the balance of power between the two alliances, stability of that balance is of vital significance for the neutrals. As put by Austria's foreign minister, "stability of balance of power--a rough or approximate military balance between NATO and the Warsaw Pact--is an essential element in global, European, and therefore Austrian security."[104]

To what extent the intensity of the bipolar conflict affects the security of the neutrals is a matter of speculation.[105] There seems to exist a certain optimum in the spectrum of tension-détente, when the neutrals' position in the system is at its best. High-intensity conflict tends to rigidify bipolarity and reduce the acceptance of a neutral foreign policy by the conflicting blocs. Moreover, whatever its behavior, a neutral state may be confronted by the dilemma of antagonizing either one or the other bloc. The experience of such neutrals as Belgium and Luxembourg (and more recently the neutralization of Laos) demonstrates that extreme conflict situations, let alone a large-scale war, are likely to bring about the loss or abandonment of neutrality. On the other hand, too much détente might tempt the bloc leaders to make a deal at the expense of the neutrals. Hence, the position of such states may be most advantageous at a level of conflict that is neither too high nor too low.[106] "We have a vested interest in a low intensity of conflict between the two blocks," once said the Austrian foreign minister.[107] Not only do the neutral countries then have maximum freedom of action, but they can also prove their usefulness to the antagonistic blocs by assuming the functions of intermediaries. With rising intensity of conflict, such functions become increasingly difficult.[108]

Finally, in the conditions of the loose bipolar system the growth of the nonaligned movement has conferred a certain respectability upon the policy of noninvolvement in the East-West conflict. This development has contributed positively to the success of neutrality and nonalignment also in Europe.

Internal Variables

The historical experience of Switzerland and Sweden and the current situation of all the European neutrals demonstrate the importance of domestic determinants in the emergence and continued success of the policy of neutrality. It is significant that both Switzerland and Sweden embarked upon such a policy following the collapse of their expansionist policies in the sixteenth and seventeenth centuries, respectively. Today in these countries and in the new post-World War II neutrals, Austria and Finland, the policy of neutrality enjoys the general consensus of the population and support of the major political groupings, which in turn strengthens the international position and credibility of these countries. Related to this is the need for internal stability as an essential condition for a viable policy of neutrality in an ideologically heterogeneous international system, preventing or at least making more difficult any foreign attempt to interfere in the domestic affairs of a neutral state.[109] An adequate military establishment also adds to the credibility of neutral policy. A neutral state will contribute to the success of its foreign policy by building up an image of an honest broker and, in general, by trying to convince the superpowers that its neutral orientation is actually beneficial to their interests.

One significant sociopolitical variable that cannot be overlooked as a determinant of a permanently neutral or nonaligned policy is the feeling of special identity of the country concerned, such as the Swiss historical awareness of their being a confederation of republican cantons surrounded by European monarchies. In more recent times, the adoption of an independent foreign policy orientation has been largely influenced by feelings of nationalism. Ireland refused to join NATO because it could not psychologically bear association with Great Britain. Yugoslavia's nonalignment originated in nationalist resistance against Soviet hegemony, and even Albania's break with Moscow was in essence a manifestation of nationalism, despite appearances of an ideological conflict.

CONCLUSIONS

Although in a general sense all the European neutral and nonaligned countries follow the foreign policy orientation of remaining outside the Cold War alliances, there are significant variations in the way they conceptualize and apply in practice their respective policies. The traditional international law institution of temporary neutrality during an ongoing war has, for all practical purposes, become obsolete. On the other hand, permanent neutrality, a unique European institution, has provided the conceptual basis for the foreign policy orientation of the core of European neutrals, all of them linked by ideological ties to Western Europe. The analysis of the concept of permanent neutrality has disclosed two general models: the classic Swiss one of permanent neutrality subject to the rules of international law, more recently adopted by Austria; and the model of factual permanent neutrality, followed as a political doctrine and without any obligation by Sweden and, subject to the special position vis-à-vis the Soviet Union, Finland. Yet the element of formal, legal commitment does not play a decisive role in the conduct of foreign policy by these four principal neutrals. Despite some variations, their respective foreign policies are guided by the need to behave in a way that would sustain and strengthen the credibility of their commitment to neutrality in any future war or other armed conflict between third states. It is true, however, that, while generating greater predictability and trust, legal permanent neutrality has the drawback of rigidity stemming from the neutral state's formal obligations under international law.

Apart from the ministates, two other West European nations have chosen a policy of staying outside of military alliances. Ireland's status must be considered as that of qualified permanent neutrality in view of that country's membership in the European Community. Malta has initiated a new foreign policy conception that combines the elements of permanent neutrality with those of nonalignment. The two East European states which follow independent foreign policies display contrasting approaches in their independence. Yugoslavia is a member of the nonaligned movement and, as such, constitutes a link between its Afro-Asian members and the West European neutrals with whom, like Cyprus, it actively cooperates within the framework of European security conferences. On the other hand, Albania, ideologically at odds with the rest of the world, has chosen the path of self-reliant semi-isolation colored by certain traits of ethnocentric nationalism.

Yet, even Albania's anachronistic isolationism is playing a positive systemic role in the politico-strategic context of European politics. All the nonbloc countries, including that bizarre outpost of Stalinism in the Balkans, have prevented the European continent from being totally partitioned into opposing bloc structures, thus effectively interrupting the line of military confrontation between NATO and the Warsaw Pact and contributing to the loosening of bipolarity in Europe.

In the final analysis, the foreign policy conceptions of all European nonbloc nations can be explained as their own individual ways of coping with the perceived threats to their security. In this sense, permanent neutrality, nonalignment, and similar strategies in the European context are not only foreign policy orientations but also national security policies of the countries concerned.

NOTES

[1]For some theoretical thoughts on this approach see K. Holsti, *International Politics: A Framework for Analysis* (Englewood Cliffs, NJ: Prentice Hall, 1983), pp. 93-98; James N. Rosenau, "The Study of Foreign Policy," in James N. Rosenau, Kenneth W. Thompson, and Gavin Boyd, eds., *World Politics* (New York: Free Press, 1976), p. 16.

[2]Although a good deal has been written, mostly in German, on the individual neutral countries of Europe, there has not been much theoretical comparative analysis of their status in law and international politics, even in conference papers on this subject, such as those organized by the Austrian Institute for International Affairs. See Karl E. Birnbaum and Hanspeter Neuhold, eds., *Neutrality and Non-Alignment in Europe* (Vienna: Braumüller, 1981), Laxenburg Papers; Hanspeter Neuhold and Hans Thalberg, eds., *The European Neutrals in International Affairs* (Vienna: Braumüller, December 1984), Laxenburg Papers. See, however, Annemarie Grosse Jütte and Rüdiger Jütte, "Neutralität und Blockfreiheit in Europa: Sicherheits-und Verteidigungspolitik im Vergleich," *Aus Politik und Zeitgeschichte* (weekly supplement to *Das Parlament* Bonn) 18 (1983): 39-53. Most of the relevant literature originates in the neutral countries themselves. Among theoretical analyses one can mention studies by Harto Hakovirta. See Harto Hakovirta, "Neutral States and Bloc-Based Integration," *Cooperation and Conflict* 13 (1978): 109-32; Harto Hakovirta, "The International System and Neutrality in Europe 1946-1980-1990," *Yearbook of Finnish Foreign Policy* (Helsinki: Finnish Institute of International Affairs, 1980), pp. 39-48; Harto Hakovirta, "The Soviet Union and the Varieties of Neutrality in Western Europe," *World Politics* 34 (1983): 536-85. A panel at the 25th Annual Convention of the International Studies Association, Atlanta, 1984, dealt with "The Neutral Democracies and the New Cold War" (Chair: Bengt Sundelius). And in November 1986 a major conference on the European neutrals was held in Washington, DC, under the auspices of the Wilson International Center for Scholars. See also Bengt Sundelius, ed., *The Neutral Bureaucracies and the New Cold War* (Boulder, CO: Westview, 1986).

[3]It is this flexible perspective that is adopted in a major theoretical study of neutrality by Daniel Frei. See Daniel Frei, *Dimensionen neutraler Politik: Ein Beitrag zur Theorie der internationalen Beziehungen* (Geneva: Institut Universitaire de Hautes Etudes, 1969). For an attempt to measure alignment along the alliance-nonalignment continuum using a set of indicators, see Henry Teune and Sig Synnestvedt, "Measuring International Alignment," *Orbis* 9 (Spring 1965): 171-89.

[4]See John W. Burton, *International Relations: A General Theory* (Cambridge: Cambridge University Press, 1965); John W. Burton, *System, States, Diplomacy and Rules* (Cambridge: Cambridge University Press, 1968).

[5]See Marjorie M. Whiteman, *Digest of International Law* (Washington, DC: Government Printing Office, 1968), 11:141-42, containing definitions of neutrality according to the U.S. Department of the Army, *Field Manual* (1956), and the Department of the Navy, *Law of Naval Warfare* (1955, as amended July 1959). See also Robert Bledsoe and Boleslaw A. Boczek, *Dictionary of International Law* (Santa Barbara, CA: ABC-Clio, 1987), chap. 12.

[6]The law of neutrality became a standard part of major treatises of international law.   See, for example, Oppenheim's classical textbook, H. Lauterpacht, *Oppenheim's International Law* 2 (New York: McKay, 1952). For a more recent textbook see Gerhard von Glahn, *The Law among Nations*, 5th ed. (New York: Macmillan, 1986).   For a detailed examination, with excerpts from international practice and publicists, see   Whiteman, *Digest of International Law* 11:139-475.   See also Erik J. Castrén, *The Present Law of War and Neutrality* (Helsinki: Suomalainen Tiedeakemial, 1954).

[7]For example, neutral Sweden was in no breach of international law when it allowed several thousand volunteers to join Finland in its Winter War against the Soviet Union in 1939-40.   On the other hand, Sweden violated its neutral duties in World War II when, for a brief period, it allowed recruitment by Finland of such volunteers on its territory.   A breach of neutrality occurred also at the end of the war in 1945, when Sweden allowed 12,000 Norwegian troops to prepare for action against Germany on its territory.   Daniel Woker, *Die skandinawischen Neutralen: Prinzip und Praxis der schwedischen und der finnischen Neutralität* (Bern: Paul Haupt, 1978), pp. 70-71.

[8]A permanently neutral state has not just the right but the duty to behave in this way.

[9]Of interest here may be the violation of Sweden's neutrality by Germany in World War II.   Germany pressured that neutral country into allowing transit privileges to unarmed German troops and supplies to Norway in 1940-1943 and, in 1941, into allowing an armed German SS division transit through Sweden from Norway to Finland. Woker, *Die skandinawischen Neutralen*, p. 7.

[10]Article 2(4).

[11]One vexing question is, for example, whether a party to a "nonwar" armed conflict can exercise belligerents' rights of search and visit vis-à-vis vessels of states staying outside the conflict, an issue that arose in connection with the stopping of U.S. and other flag vessels in the Persian Gulf by warships of Iran engaged in a "nonwar" armed conflict with Iraq.

[12]These are four conventions, revising, codifying, and developing the international humanitarian law on the protection of the victims of war.

[13]The adjectives "perpetual" or "permanent," modifying the term neutrality, are used to distinguish this status from temporary neutrality--that is, neutrality only during a war--and in no way imply that the status of permanent neutrality cannot be altered or terminated by agreement of all parties concerned.   The term *neutralité permanente* was used for the first time in the Treaty of Amiens (1802) with regard to the island of Malta. The German term is *dauernde Neutralität*.   Sometimes the term perpetual

neutrality (*neutralité perpetuelle*, or *immerwährende Neutralität*) is also used. It appeared first in the Declaration of 20 March 1815 of the eight Congress powers calling for the recognition and guarantee of the "perpetual neutrality" of Switzerland. See the text in *Martens Nouveau Recueil* 2:157; *British and Foreign State Papers* 2:142; Gordon E. Sherman, "The Permanent Neutrality Treaties," *Yale Law Journal* 24 (1915): 223-25.

[14]The official Swiss conception of neutrality, 26 November 1954, in *Verwaltungsentscheide der Bundesbehörden aus dem Jahr 1954*, no. 24 (1954), reprinted in *Schweizerisches Jahrbuch für internationales Recht* 14 (1957): 195 (hereafter referred to as "Swiss Conception"). Also in Stephen Verosta, *Die dauernde Neutralität--Ein Grundriss* (Vienna: Manz, 1967), pp. 113-17. Permanent neutrality has been a subject of extensive analysis, primarily by Swiss and then Austrian authors. Among comprehensive studies see Verosta (this note) and, more recently, Manfred Rotter, *Die dauernde Neutralität* (Berlin: Duncker and Humblot, 1981). Political aspects of neutralization are examined in Cyril E. Black, Richard A. Falk, Klaus Knorr, and Oran R. Young, *Neutralization and World Politics* (Princeton: Princeton University Press, 1968). For the international legal aspects see materials in Whiteman, *Digest of International Law* 1:342-63. For the literature on the neutrality of Switzerland see items listed in Claudio Caratsch and Luzius Wildhaber, "The Permanent Neutrality of Switzerland," in Birnbaum and Neuhold, eds., *Neutrality and Non-Alignment in Europe*, pp. 42-43.

For Austria see items listed in Hanspeter Neuhold, Wolfgang Loibl, and Hans-Georg Rudofsky, "The Permanent Neutrality of Austria," in Birnbaum and Neuhold, eds., *Neutrality and Non-Alignment in Europe*, pp. 107-9; and Paul Luif, "Neutrality and External Relations: The Case of Austria," *Cooperation and Conflict* 21, no. 1 (1986): 25-41. For Sweden see items in Nils Andrén and Frank Belfrage, "The Neutrality of Sweden," in Birnbaum and Neuhold, eds., *Neutrality and Non-Alignment in Europe*, pp. 130-31. For Finland see items in Raimo Väyrynen and Aimo Pajunen, "The Neutrality of Finland," in Birnbaum and Neuhold, eds., *Neutrality and Non-Alignment in Europe*, pp. 165-67. For Sweden and Finland, the bibliography in Woker, *Die skandinawischen Neutralen*, pp. 103-7 is also useful. For a comprehensive comparative analysis of the permanent neutrality of Switzerland, Austria, Sweden, and Finland see Hanspeter Neuhold, "Permanent Neutrality in Contemporary International Relations: A Comparative Perspective," in *Irish Studies in International Affairs* 1, no. 3 (1982): 13-21.

For the Soviet view of the permanently neutral democracies see Harto Hakovirta, "The Soviet Union and the Varieties of Neutrality in Western Europe," with rich bibliographical references. See also A. Alexandrov, "Soviet-Swiss Relations: Past and Prospects," *International Affairs* (Moscow), no. 4 (1986): 90-94. The institution of permanent neutrality also has been studied in other Eastern European countries. For Hungary see Janos I. Szirtes, "Az állandó semlegesség" [Permanent neutrality], *Jogtudomanyi Közlöny* 35 (1980): 583-91 (1980); László Valki, "Neutrality: A Hungarian View," in Neuhold and Thalberg, eds., *European Neutrals in International Affairs*, pp. 105-17. For the Polish view see Rudolf Buchala, "Neutralnosc w Europie" [Neutrality in Europe], *Sprawy Miedzynarodowe* 36, no. 12 (1982): 21-34; Rudolf Buchala, "Modele trwalej neutralnosci: Szwajcaria-Austria" [Models of permanent neutrality: Switzerland-Austria], *Sprawy Miedzynarodowe* 36, no. 3 (1983): 109-20. See also J. Sutor, *Panstwa neutralne i niezaangazowane* [The neutral and nonaligned states] (Warsaw: PWN, 1972). For a Yugoslav analysis see R. Petkovic, *Teorijski pojmovi neutralnosti* [The theoretical conception of neutrality] (Belgrade, 1982).

[15]See Andrén and Belfrage, "The Neutrality of Sweden," pp. 114-15.

[16]This Swedish idea has been extensively analyzed. See, for example, Ch. Lange and Kjeil Coldmann, "A Nordic Defense Alliance 1949-1965-197?," *Cooperation and Conflict* 1, no. 1 (1966): 46; Johan J. Holst, ed., *Five Roads to Nordic Security* (Oslo: Universitetsvorlaget, 1972); Barbara G. Haskel, *The Scandinavian Option: Opportunities and Opportunity Costs in Postwar Scandinavian Foreign Policies* (Oslo: Universitetsforlaget, 1976); Bengt Sundelius, ed., *Foreign Policies of Northern Europe* (Boulder, CO: Westview Press, 1982).

[17]An interesting legal question is whether factual permanent neutrality could, by customary law, evolve into legal permanent neutrality. It is clear that, in the absence of the de facto permanently neutral country's consent internationally to legalize its status, factual neutrality could never crystallize into an international law rule even if acquiesced to by all other states. Sweden is a case in point.

[18]See André Roussel Le Roy, *L'abrogation de la neutralité de la Belgique, ses causes et ses effets* (Paris, 1923), referred to in Black et al., *Neutralization and World Politics*, pp. 25-26. The Republic of Cracow, a creation of the Congress of Vienna, lasted from 1815 until 1846.

[19]Hanspeter Neuhold, "The Permanent Neutrality of Austria: Background Factors," in Birnbaum and Neuhold, eds., *Neutrality and Non-Alignment in Europe*, pp. 57-59. Such consensus also exists in the other permanently neutral countries.

[20]By an agreement, states may prohibit the use of an area for military purposes, as was the case of the Åland Islands in the Baltic, demilitarized in 1856; or they may undertake not to subject it to their sovereignty, an obligation frequently combined with the demilitarization of the area. A historical example is offered by Malta, "neutralized" in 1802. See H. P. Schmitt, "Ursprung und Untergang der ersten immerwährenden Neutralität: Malta," *Österreichische Zeitschrift für öffentliches Recht* 22, no. 1 (1971):

57-72. Other major examples of such "neutralization" include Chablais and Faucigny (1815-1919), the Ionian Islands (1863-1891), the International Zone of Tangier (1923-1940, 1945-1956), and the Free Territory of Trieste (1945-1954). See Black et al., *Neutralization and World Politics*, pp. 15-16. The demilitarization of Antarctica under the Antarctic Treaty of 1959, *United Nations Treaty Series* 402:71, is a current example of demilitarization.

[21]Among historical, short-lived examples of self-neutralization are Iceland (1918) and Cambodia (1957). Black et al., *Neutralization and World Politics*, p. 32. Estonia also proclaimed itself permanently neutral in 1918. Whiteman, *Digest of International Law* 1:347.

[22]Act of Paris, 20 November 1815; *Martens Nouveau Recueil* 2:379, 419; *American Journal of International Law (Supp.)* 3 (1909): 106. Today this guarantee appears to bind only France, Great Britain, Italy, Sweden, and Spain. The permanent neutrality of Belgium and Luxembourg was also guaranteed by the great powers. Verosta, *Die dauernde Neutralität*, p. 105. On the methods of guaranteeing permanent neutrality, see Whiteman, *Digest of International Law* 1:344-45.

[23]Treaty of Versailles, art. 435, *American Journal of International Law (Supp.)* 13 (1919): 151; Treaty of St. Germain, art. 375, ibid. *(Supp.)* 14 (1920): 176-77; Treaty of Trianon, art. 358, William M. Malloy, *Treaties* 3:3539, 3691; Treaty of Neuilly, art. 291, *American Journal of International Law* 14 (1920): 185, 302.

[24]See Report of the International Law Commission on the Work of the Second Part of Its Session, 3-28 January 1966. *Supp.* 9; UN Doc. A/6309/Rev. 1 (1966) in *American Journal of International Law* 61 (January 1967): 255, 375.

[25]Verosta, *Die dauernde Neutralität*. The U.S. Department of State interprets American recognition of Austria's permanent neutrality as meaning only the U.S. obligation to respect this neutrality and Austria's territorial integrity, that is, "to refrain from taking those actions with regard to [Austria] which might violate the accepted concepts of a neutral state in the international community," but not implying any guarantee. See Office of the Legal Advisor, Memorandum of the United States in response to the declaration of Austria's neutrality, 16 November 1955, in Whiteman, *Digest of International Law* 1:344, 349-50. For U.S. political relations with the four European neutrals in general see Robert A. Bauer, "The United States and the European Neutrals," in Neuhold and Thalberg, eds., *European Neutrals in International Affairs*, pp. 81-91.

[26]Natalino Ronzitti, "Malta's Permanent Neutrality," *Italian Yearbook of International Law* 5 (1981): 171. See also Jean-François Flauss, "La neutralité de Malte," *Annuaire français de droit international* 29 (1983): 175-93.

[27]*The Military Balance, 1986-1987* (London: International Institute for Strategic Studies, 1986), p. 80.

[28]Dietrich Schindler, "Europäische Neutralitätserfahrung und- theorie aus schweizerischer Sicht," in Gerd Kaminski, ed., *Neutralität in Europa und Südostasien* (Bonn: Wehling Verlag, 1979), pp. 67, 71.

[29]"Austria between the Block Systems," Lecture of the Austrian Foreign Minister Willibald Pahr at the Royal Institute of International Relations, Brussels, 17 February 1983, in *Österreichische Zeitschrift für Aussenpolitik* 23, no. 1 (1983): 50. For this reason the speech of Ambassador H. Eugene Douglas, coordinator of refugee affairs for the U.S. government, before the Political Academy of the Austrian People's Party in 1982, caused a furor in Austria because this U.S. representative undiplomatically criticized that country for its handling of Qaddafi's visit in Vienna, Austria's relations with the PLO, attitudes of Austrian socialists toward U.S. policy in Central America, and Austria's dealings with the CMEA countries. The U.S. government made it clear that Douglas's views were strictly personal. Bauer, "The United States and the European Neutrals," pp. 83-84.

[30]The Soviet Union expressly recognized this in its Memorandum of 15 April 1955 concerning the conversations between the governments of Austria and the Soviet Union, in *American Journal of International Law (Supp.)* 49 (1955): 162, 191-92.

[31]Under Article I(1) of the Federal Constitutional Act on Austria's Neutrality "[f]or the purpose of the permanent maintenance of its external independence and . . . the inviolability of its territory Austria of its own free will declares . . . its permanent neutrality which it is resolved to maintain and defend with all the means at its disposal." Under Article 102(9) of the Swiss constitution (1874), the Federal Council (the Swiss executive authority) is obliged to act as guardian of the external security, independence, and neutrality of Switzerland. The principle of permanent neutrality itself is not, however, expressly anchored in the constitution.

[32]See, generally, Hans Rudolf Kurz, *Bewaffnete Neutralität--Die militärische Bedeutung der dauernden schweizerischen Neutralität* (Frauenfeld: Huber, 1967). For the obligation of self-defense see Verosta, *Die dauernde Neutralität*, pp. 69-77; Josef Pokstefl, "Die Verteidigungs-und Rüstungspflicht der dauernd neutralen Staaten," *Österreichische Zeitschrift für Politikwissenschaft* 7, no. 3 (1978): 357-68; D. Späni and P. Spinnler, "Die militärischen Vorbereitungspflichten des dauernd Neutralen nach völkerrechtlichem Neutralitätsrecht," *Revue de droit international, de sciences diplomatiques et politiques* 52 (1974): 169-84. One historical exception to the rule of armed permanent neutrality was the neutralization of Luxembourg, 1867-1919 (or 1940, in the Grand Duchy's view), which was also demilitarized. See Black et al., *Neutralization and World Politics*, pp. 26-27, referring to

Marcel Junod, *Die Neutralität des Grossherzogtums Luxemburg von 1867 bis 1948* (Luxembourg, 1951).

[33]See Report of the Federal Council to the Federal Assembly on the security policy of Switzerland (Conception of "total defense," *Gesamtverteidigung*), 27 June 1973; the Guidelines for national military defense in the '80s, 29 September 1975; and the Intermediate Report on security policy, 3 December 1979. For Switzerland see also Peter Gaupp, *Gesamtverteidigung: Operationalisierung der sicherheitspolitischen Ziele und strategischen Hauptaufgaben der Schweiz* (Bern: Studien zur Sicherheitspolitik, no. 11, 1974); Curt Gasteyger, *La sécurité de la Suisse: Les défis de l'avenir* (Geneva: Institut Universitaire de Hautes Etudes, 1983); Erich A. Kägi, *Wie hoch ist der Eintrittspreis? Schweizer Landesverteidigung heute und morgen* (Zurich: Neue Zürcher Zeitung, 1985); Rudolf Bindschedler, "Neutralitätspolitik und Sicherheitspolitik," *Österreichische Zeitschrift für Aussenpolitik* 16 (1976): 339-54.

For the Austrian doctrine of total territorial defense (*Gesamtraumverteidigung*) see Emil Spannocchi, "Verteidigung ohne Zerstörung," in Emil Spannocchi and Guy Brosselet, eds., *Verteidigung ohne Schlacht* (Munich: Hauser Verlag, 1976), p. 175. See also Walter Fürnholzer, *Grundzüge der militärischen Landesverteidigung* (Vienna: Österreichische Gesellschaft zur Förderung der Landesverteidigung, 1980).

For Finland see, for example, Woker, *Die skandinavischen Neutralen*, pp. 39-43; Aimo Pajunen, "Some Aspects of Finnish Security Policy," in Birnbaum and Neuhold, eds., *Neutrality and Non-Alignment in Europe*, pp. 156-64; and Kari Möttölä, "The Politics of Neutrality and Defence: Finnish Security Policy since the Early 1970s," *Cooperation and Conflict* 17, no. 4 (1982): 287-313. For Swedish defense policy see generally Woker, *Die skandinavischen Neutralen*, pp. 73-83. See also Nils Andrén, "Swedish Defence Doctrines and Changing Threat Perspectives," *Cooperation and Conflict* 17, no. 1 (1982): 29; and *Elva åsikter om svensk säkerhetspolitik* [Eleven views on Swedish security policy] (Stockholm: Folk och Försvar, 1979).

[34]Neuhold, "Permanent Neutrality in Contemporary International Relations," p. 20.

[35]In the years 1981 and 1984 the percentage of the GNP spent on defense by Austria amounted to 1.2 and 1.2, respectively, and that of Finland to 1.4 and 1.6. The corresponding figures for the other permanent neutrals are 3.5 and 3.0 percent (Sweden) and 2.0 and 2.1 percent (Switzerland). In 1984 per capita defense expenditures in Austria and Finland were $106 and $168, respectively, whereas the figures for Sweden and Switzerland were $341 and $301.

Switzerland spends by far a greater percentage of its government expenditures on defense than the other neutrals: 21.3 percent in 1984.

The figures for the other neutrals are: 3.6 percent (Austria), 5.7 percent (Finland), and 7.2 percent (Sweden). In 1984, Ireland spent 1.6 percent of its GNP on defense ($80 per capita), which represented 2.9 percent of government expenditures. In the same year nonaligned Yugoslavia spent 3.8 percent of its GNP on defense. The figure for Malta was 1.5 percent and for Cyprus, 0.9 percent. Albania's share of defense expenditures in total government spending was 11 percent, but per capita defense expenditure in that semi-isolationist country was estimated to be $43, quite low compared to the neutrals. *Military Balance, 1986-1987*, p. 212.

[36]Of interest here is the story of the incorporation of Neuchâtel into the newly established federal Switzerland in 1848, against the protest of Prussia (claiming old rights to this new Swiss canton), but recognized by the guarantee powers in the Treaty of Paris in 1857; and the cession by Belgian King Leopold II of the permanently neutral "independent state of the Congo" to the permanently neutral Belgium in 1907-08. In still another case, after World War I, Switzerland refused to admit Austrian Vorarlberg into the Swiss federation, one reason being the lack of consent of the guarantee powers. Verosta, *Die dauernde Neutralität*, p. 72.

[37]For "Swiss Conception," see note 14. See, also, for example, Dietrich Schindler, "Die Lehre von den Vorwirkungen der Neutralität," in*Festschrift für Rudolf Bindschedler* (Bern: Haupt, 1980), pp. 563-82.

[38]Historically it was for this reason that the once permanently neutral Belgium was exempt under the London Treaty (1867) from the obligation to guarantee the permanent neutrality of Luxembourg. Verosta, *Die dauernde Neutralität*, p. 81.

[39]The Swiss general staff made arrangements with the armies of neighboring countries (Austria and Germany in World War I and France on the eve of World War II) concerning common military measures in case of an attack on Switzerland. These activities were and still are incompatible with the traditional interpretation of Swiss neutrality. Claudio Caratsch, "The Permanent Neutrality of Switzerland," in Birnbaum and Neuhold, eds., *Neutrality and Non-Alignment in Europe*, p. 16.

[40]Swiss conception in *Verwaltungsentscheide der Bundesbehörden aus dem Jahr 1954*, p. 199.

[41]Ibid., p. 196.

[42]Ibid. Ideological aspects of permanent neutrality are examined in Daniel Frei, "Ideologische Dimensionen neutraler Politik," *Österreichische Zeitschrift für Aussenpolitik* 8 (1968): 207-14; Frei, *Dimensionen neutraler Politik*, pp. 166-84.

[43]For Switzerland see Caratsch, "The Permanent Neutrality of Switzerland," p. 23. For Austria see the statement of the Austrian foreign minister in his speech before the UN General Assembly, 2 October 1980, in

Österreichische Zeitschrift für Aussenpolitik 20 (1980): 329. Austria joined the majority of the UN General Assembly in calling for the withdrawal of foreign troops from Afghanistan. Willibald Pahr, "Austria between the Block Systems," p. 52.

[44]Caratsch, "The Permanent Neutrality of Switzerland," pp. 31, 36; Hanspeter Neuhold, "The Permanent Neutrality of Austria," in Birnbaum and Neuhold, eds., *Neutrality and Non-Alignment in Europe*, pp. 70-71, 89-90.

[45]However, during World War II the Swiss government, yielding to German pressures, did restrict the freedom of the Swiss press. Verosta, *Die dauernde Neutralität*, pp. 96-100.

[46]This contribution is emphasized in Hans Thalberg, "The European Neutrals and Regional Stability," in Neuhold and Thalberg, eds., *European Neutrals in International Affairs*, pp. 125-31.

[47]The Swiss role in this respect is reviewed in Pierre du Bois, "Neutrality and Political Good Offices: The Case of Switzerland," in Neuhold and Thalberg, eds., *European Neutrals in International Affairs*, pp. 7-16. See also Raymond Probst, "La politique étrangère de la Suisse et ses missions de 'bons offices,'" *Revue roumaine d'études internationales* 15, no. 5 (1981): 485-94. For Finland see Harto Hakovirta, "An Interpretation of Finland's Contributions to European Peace and Security," in Neuhold and Thalberg, eds., *European Neutrals in International Affairs*, pp. 25-37. See also more generally A. Aebi, *Der Beitrag neutraler Staaten zur Friedenssicherung untersucht am Beispiel Österreichs und der Schweiz* (Zurich: Schweizerischer Aufklärungsdienst, 1976) (Thèse No. 286, Genève); H. F. Köck, "The Contribution of Permanent Neutrality to World Peace," *Peace and the Sciences* 2 (1980): 1-12; Ljubivoje Acimovic, "In Search of Peace and Security: The Role of European Neutrals--A Yugoslav Point of View," in Neuhold and Thalberg, eds., *European Neutrals in International Affairs*, pp. 119-24.

[48]For a detailed analysis of the relationship between permanent neutrality and collective security see Boleslaw A. Boczek, "Permanent Neutrality and Collective Security: The Case of Switzerland and the United Nations Sanctions against Southern Rhodesia," *Case Western Reserve Journal of International Law 1*, no. 2 (1969): 75-104.

[49]See, for example, Alfred Verdross, "Austria's Permanent Neutrality and the United Nations Organization," *American Journal of International Law* 50 (January 1956): 61, 66-67; J. Kunz, "Austria's Permanent Neutrality," ibid. 50 (1956): 418, 424; Karl Zemanek, "Neutral Austria in the United Nations," *International Organization* 15 (1961): 408-12; H. F. Köck, "A Permanently Neutral State in the United Nations," *Cornell International Law Journal* 6 (1973): 137; Hanspeter Neuhold, "Permanent Neutrality and Non-Alignment: Similarities and Differences," *Österreichische Zeitschrift*

für Aussenpolitik 18 (1978): 79, 82.

[50]Reply of the Austrian government to the Security Council, 28 February 1967, UN Doc. 8/7795 (1967).

[51]See the speech of Austrian Foreign Minister Willibald Pahr in 1983, "Austria between the Block Systems," p. 52.

[52]Under this status the Council of the League of Nations released Switzerland from participating in sanctions going beyond economic and financial measures, under Article 18(1) of the Covenant. For this Swiss experiment in "differential" or "qualified" neutrality (1920-1938) and its failure on the occasion of the sanctions against Italy in 1935 see Boczek, "Permanent Neutrality and Collective Security," pp. 97-99.

[53]*International Court of Justice Yearbook* (1947-48): 30, 31.

[54]However, Switzerland attached permanent neutrality reservations when joining some of the specialized agencies, for example, the International Atomic Energy Agency and International Maritime Organization (then IMOC). Boczek, "Permanent Neutrality and Collective Security," p. 101.

[55]*International Herald Tribune*, 17 March 1986.

[56]"Swiss Conception," see note 14.

[57]See Bindschedler, "Neutralitätspolitik und Sicherheitspolitik," p. 343.

[58]A precedent to this effect is provided by Belgium which, then a permanently neutral state, informed France and Great Britain of the German Schlieffen Plan and initiated secret talks with the general staffs of these two guarantor powers. Verosta, *Die dauernde Neutralität*, p. 85.

[59]The practice of Swiss cantons of supplying whole regiments to foreign powers did not even cease after 1815 and lasted until 1859. Verosta, *Die dauernde Neutralität*, pp. 83-84.

[60]Ibid.

[61]This problem is examined in Ingemar Dörfer, "Arms Dependencies of the Neutrals," Paper at the 25th Annual Convention of the International Studies Association, Atlanta, 1984.

[62]At that time, Sweden was forced by German threats of cutting off arms deliveries to grant Germany certain concessions incompatible with the law of neutrality. Woker, *Die skandinavischen Neutralen*, p. 82.

[63]Ibid., p. 77.

[64]Hans Vogel, "Switzerland and the New Cold War," Paper at the 25th Annual Convention of the International Studies Association, Atlanta, 1984, p. 14. See also Dörfer, "Arms Dependencies of the Neutrals."

[65]For example, Austria, which has its own arms industry, tries to purchase needed weapons and equipment from other neutrals. In 1985, Austria had two arms purchase agreements with Sweden. The *Military Balance, 1985-1986* (London: International Institute for Strategic Studies, 1985), p. 174. Finland produces only light weapons and in its procurement

policy seeks a balance between East and West. It also tries as much as possible to channel procurement to Switzerland and Sweden. Woker, *Die skandinawischen Neutralen*, p. 42. Still, in the period 1986-1990, Finland will buy weapons from the Soviet Union, worth $433 million. *International Herald Tribune*, 25 March 1986. See also *Military Balance, 1986-1987*, p. 209.

[66]Sweden does export some weapons to the United States, Denmark, and Norway. *Military Balance, 1986-1987*, p. 209; *Military Balance, 1985-1986*, pp. 174-77. Switzerland also exports military equipment to NATO countries. For example, Turkey is the main customer of the Oerlikon-Bührle combined air defense and antitank missile (ADAT) system, a collaborative effort with an American corporation (Martin-Marietta). "Guns for Neutrality," *The Economist*, 28 March 1986. Canada also purchased ADAT systems valued at $713 million. *Military Balance, 1986-1987*, p. 209.

[67]Article 11 of the Swiss penal law on war materiel of 30 June 1972 prohibits such exports, which could impair Switzerland's efforts in the humanitarian and development assistance areas. See Luzius Wildhaber, "Swiss Neutrality on the East-West Axis," in Birnbaum and Neuhold, eds., *Neutrality and Non-Alignment in Europe*, pp. 34-35. However, foreign subsidiaries of Swiss companies are free of Swiss restrictions. There are also other ways of avoiding the regulations governing arms exports. "Guns for Neutrality," pp. 59-60. For the Finnish restrictions on arms exports see Väyrynen and Pajunen, "The Neutrality of Finland," p. 162. Austrian law bans exports conflicting with Austria's permanent neutrality obligations. Neuhold, "Permanent Neutrality and Non-Alignment," p. 88. The export of *Kürassier* tanks to Chile's Pinochet regime was opposed on moral grounds by Austrian public opinion and had to be abandoned by the government. Ibid.

[68]Under Article 13 of the treaty, Austria is not allowed to possess (in addition to nuclear and other weapons of mass destruction) certain types of guided missiles and guns, torpedoes, and some other weapons. Finland is still subject to numerical limitations on its armed forces (and prohibition of possessing nuclear and other weapons of mass destruction), but in 1963 it was allowed by the other signatory powers of the 1947 Peace Treaty, *United Nations Treaty Series* 48:203, to possess defensive guided missiles. Woker, *Die skandinawischwen Neutralen*, pp. 40-44.

[69]For the contrary opinion see Göther Handl, "Zur Frage der Vereinbarkeit von Rüstungsbeschränkung und dauernder Neutralität," *Österreichische Zeitschrift für Aussenpolitik* 9, no. 4 (1969):211-27.

[70]However, the Soviet position is that possession of nuclear weapons is incompatible with permanent neutrality. See *Kurs mezhdunarodnovo prava* [A course of international law], (Moscow: Nauka, 1967), p. 143.

[71]See Jerome Garris, "Sweden's Debate on the Proliferation of Nuclear Weapons," *Cooperation and Conflict* 3, no. 2 (1973): 189. See also generally Woker, *Die skandinawischen Neutralen*, pp. 78-79.

[72]For Sweden, see George H. Quester, "Sweden and Nuclear Non-Proliferation Treaty," *Cooperation and Conflict* 3, no. 1 (1970): 52. For Switzerland, see Vogel, "Switzerland and the New Cold War," p. 12.

[73]See the speech of Austrian Foreign Minister Willibald Pahr, "Austria between the Block System," pp. 52-53. For the Swiss view see Bindschedler, "Neutralitätspolitik und Sicherheitspolitik," pp. 353-54. The Swedish government also has warned against arms control measures destabilizing the balance of power. Sweden's defense doctrine is based on the assumption that if a balance of power exists between the two blocs, the aggressor is unlikely to have very large forces available for operations against a marginal target such as Sweden. See Nils Andrén, "Sweden, Neutrality, Defence and Disarmament," in Neuhold and Thalberg, eds., *European Neutrals in International Affairs*, pp. 39-48. The European neutrals' position on arms control is examined in Hanspeter Neuhold, "The European Neutrals and Arms Control," in Karl Birnbaum, ed., *Arms Control in Europe: Problems and Prospects* (Vienna: Braumüller, 1980), Laxenburg Papers, p. 95.

[74]Woker, *Die skandinawischen Neutralen*, p. 48. See also Alexander Marschan, "Finlands Position gegenüber EFTA und EWG," *Aussenpolitik* 19, no. 4 (1968): 206.

[75]"Swiss Conception," p. 197.

[76]Stephen Verosta, "L'union douanière envisagée entre la France et la Belgique en 1841-1843 incompatible avec le statut de la neutralité permanente," *Mélanges Fernand Denousse--Les progrès du droit de gens* (Paris, 1979), pp. 149-54. The case of Luxembourg which, though neutralized, was permitted to continue its membership in the German customs union (*Zollverein*) provides an exception. It involved a very small and demilitarized state whose membership would not have endangered its independence and the European balance of power. Verosta, *Die dauernde Neutralität*, p. 87.

[77]*Permanent Court of International Justice Advisory Opinions, Reports*, Series A/B, no. 41 (1931).

[78]See the literature referred to in Verosta, *Die dauernde Neutralität*, 88n.82, and H. Eek, "Neutrality and the European Communities," in *Legal Problems of an Enlarged Community* (London, 1972); H. Eek, "Neutralitet, neutralitetspolitik och EEC," *Svensk Juristtidning* 56, no. 1 (1971): 1-21; Hans Mayrzedt and Hans Christoph Binswanger, eds., *Die Neutralen in der Europäischen Integration: Kontroversen-Konfrontationen-Alternativen* (Vienna: BraumÜller, 1970); U. Plessow, *Neutralität und Assoziation mit der EWG* (Cologne: Heymann, 1967); M. Schweitzer, *Dauernde Neutralität und europä-*

ische Integration (Vienna: Springer, 1977). For Switzerland see Alois Riklin and W. Zeller, "Verhältnis der Schweiz zu den Europäischen Gemeinschaften," in Alois Riklin, Hans Haug, and Hans Christoph Binswanger, eds., *Handbuch der schweizerischen Aussenpolitik* (Bern: Haupt, 1975), pp. 474-90; A. Borras Rodríguez, "La neutralización de la Suiza y sus relaciones con la Comunidad Económica Europea," *Anuario de derecho internacional* [Pamplona] 2 (1975): 303-23. For Austria see F. Esterpauer and H. Hinterleitner, eds., *Die Europäische Gemeinschaft und Österreich* (Vienna: Braumüller, 1977); Friedl Weiss, "Austria's Permanent Neutrality in European Integration," in *Legal Issues of European Integration* (Deventer, The Netherlands: Kluwer, 1977), pp. 87-127. For the Swedish position see, for example, Woker, *Die skandinawischen Neutralen*, pp. 88-91.

[79]Neuhold, "Permanent Neutrality in Contemporary International Relations," p. 21.

[80]Woker, *Die skandinawischen Neutralen*, p. 49.

[81]Ibid. It is worthwhile to note that Finland is not even a member of the Council of Europe.

[82]Neuhold, "Permanent Neutrality in Contemporary International Relations," p. 14.

[83]Some studies of the European neutrals exclude Ireland from their scope. See, for example, Birnbaum and Neuhold, eds., *Neutrality and Non-Alignment in Europe*; Neuhold and Thalberg, eds., *European Neutrals in International Affairs*. For inquiries into the legal and political status of Ireland see Ronan Fanning, "Irish Neutrality--An Historical Review," *Irish Studies in International Affairs* 1, no. 3 (1982): 27-38; Dennis Driscoll, "Is Ireland Really 'Neutral'?" *Irish Studies in International Affairs* 1, no. 3 (1982): 55-61; Gerard M. M. MacSweeney, "Irish Neutrality and International Law," *The Irish Law Times and Solicitors' Journal* 2, no. 8 (1984): 143-50; Raymond James Raymond, "Irish Neutrality: Ideology or Pragmatism?" *International Affairs* [London] 60, no. 1 (1983-84): 31-40; Trevor C. Salmon, "Irish Neutrality--A Policy in Course of Evolution?" *NATO Review* 32, no. 1 (1981): 27; Trevor C. Salmon, "Neutrality and the Irish Republic: Myth or Reality?" *Round Table*, no. 290 (April 1984); Patrick Keatinge, *A Singular Stance: Irish Neutrality in the 1980s* (Dublin: Institute of Public Administration, 1984).

[84]Peter Lyon, "Neutrality and the Emergence of the Concept of Neutralism," *Review of Politics* 22, no. 2 (1960): 255-68. For a more extended treatment see Peter Lyon, *Neutralism* (Leicester: Leicester University Press, 1963).

[85]This is a view attributed to Secretary of State John Foster Dulles. Lyon, *Neutralism*, p. 67. See also the position entertained initially by President Dwight Eisenhower that no nation has the right to be "neutral as

between right and wrong and decency and indecency." White House Press Release, 7 June 1956, in Whiteman, *Digest of International Law* 1:359.

[86]Joint Statement by Tito and Nehru, 23 December 1954, in Whiteman, *Digest of International Law* 1:363.

[87]See Theodore L. Shay, "Non-Alignment Sí, Neutralism No," *Review of Politics* 30, no. 2 (1968):228-45.

[88]Yugoslavia's constitution and legislation do not mention nonalignment, but the policy of nonalignment is referred to in resolutions of the Tenth and Eleventh Congresses of the League of Communists of Yugoslavia. Vladimir Bilandzic and Stanko Nick, "The Policy of Non-Alignment of Yugoslavia," in Birnbaum and Neuhold, eds., *Neutrality and Non-Alignment in Europe*, pp. 168, 170. Cyprus de facto consists of two states, although the Turkish Republic of Northern Cyprus is recognized diplomatically only by Turkey. Greek Cyprus is a member of the nonaligned group of nations. Malta, in 1980, proclaimed a status of neutrality "strictly founded on the principles of non-alignment." See Declaration of Neutrality, Preamble, in *International Legal Materials* 21, no. 2 (1982): 397.

[89]That is how the Albanians view the policies of the nonaligned states, and for once there is agreement between them and Western analysts. See Boleslaw A. Boczek, "Albania," in this volume. A convenient source of primary materials on nonalignment is Odette Jankowitsch and Karl P. Sauvant, eds., *The Third World without Superpowers: The Collected Documents of the Non-Aligned Countries*, 4 vols. (Dobbs Ferry, NY: Oceana, 1978). Among numerous studies of nonalignment, for example, Ljubivoje Acimovic, ed., *Non-Alignment in the World Today: International Symposium* (Belgrade: Institute of International Politics and Economics, 1969); D. W. Burton, ed., *Non-Alignment* (London: André Deutsch, 1966); C. V. Crabb, *The Elephants and the Grass: A Study of Non-Alignment* (New York: Praeger, 1965); L. W. Martin, ed., *Neutralism and Non-Alignment: The New States in World Affairs* (New York: Praeger, 1962); Leo Mates, *Non-Alignment: Theory and Current Policy* (Dobbs Ferry, NY: Oceana, 1972); Peter Willetts, *The Non-Aligned Movement* (London: Pinter, 1978).

[90]Documents of the Sixth Conference of Non-Aligned Countries, Havana, 1979, quoted in Bilandzic and Nick, "The Policy of Non-Alignment of Yugoslavia," p. 172.

[91]Bilandzic and Nick, "The Policy of Non-Alignment of Yugoslavia," pp. 173, 195. For participation of the European neutrals and other guest countries in the nonaligned conference in the years 1961-1979, see Table 1 in Harto Hakovirta, "Effects of Non-Alignment on Neutrality in Europe: An Analysis and Appraisal," *Cooperation and Conflict* 18, no. 1 (1983): 57, 62.

[92]Bilandzic and Nick, "The Policy of Non-Alignment of Yugoslavia," p. 172.

[93]See Milan Sahovic, "L'institutionalisation des non-alignés," *Annuaire français de droit international* 23 (1977): 187-96.

[94]For a comparative analysis of the two concepts and groups of states see Neuhold, "Permanent Neutrality and Non-Alignment"; Daniel Frei, "Neutrality and Non-Alignment: Convergences and Contrasts," *Korea and World Affairs* 3, no. 3 (1979): 275-86.

[95]It is interesting to note that in 1954, prior to the emergence of nonalignment as a crystallized ideology, Yugoslavia considered the idea of a Balkan alliance with Greece and Turkey. Willetts, *Non-Aligned Movement,* p. 4.

[96]*Military Balance, 1986-1987,* p. 80.

[97]Declaration of Neutrality, *International Legal Materials,* para. 2(e). However, building such ships for a superpower is not forbidden. Statement by Maltese Prime Minister Don Mintoff, referred to in Ronzitti, "Malta's Permanent Neutrality," 188n p. 62.

[98]Ronzitti, "Malta's Permanent Neutrality," p. 180.

[99]Declaration of Neutrality, *International Legal Materials* 21, no. 2 (1982), para. 2(b)(c)(d). For example, in 1980, Malta employed six North Koreans to train its armed forces. *Times* (London), 4 December 1980.

[100]For Swiss relations with the nonaligned countries and attitudes on NIEO see Caratsch, "The Permanent Neutrality of Switzerland," pp. 32-33. For Austria see Hanspeter Neuhold, "Austrian Neutrality on the North-South Axis," in Birnbaum and Neuhold, eds., *Neutrality and Non-Alignment in Europe,* pp. 81, 84-86; Hans-Georg Rudofsky, "Austria's Relations with the Non-Aligned States," in Birnbaum and Neuhold, eds., *Neutrality and Non-Alignment in Europe,* pp. 102-6; and Paul Luif, *Die Bewegung der blockfreien Staaten und Österreich* (Vienna: Braumüller, 1981). For Sweden see Frank Belfrage, "The Neutrality of Sweden: The North-South Dimension," in Birnbaum and Neuhold, eds., *Neutrality and Non-Alignment in Europe,* pp. 123-26.

[101]Lateran Treaty, Art. 29(2). Vatican City took part in the Conference on Security and Cooperation in Europe as a member of the neutral and nonaligned (n+n) group and was a guest at conferences of the non-aligned states.

[102]Woker, *Die skandinawischen Neutralen,* pp. 33-37.

[103]See Rosenau, "The Study of Foreign Policy," p. 19.

[104]Pahr, "Austria between the Block Systems," pp. 52-53.

[105]This interesting question is analyzed in detail in Frei, *Dimensionen neutraler Politik,* pp. 50-53. See also the discussion of the effects of polarization and depolarization on neutrality in Hakovirta, "The International System and Neutrality in Europe 1946-1980-1990," pp. 40-41.

[106]For example, the events of 1848 improved the position of Switzerland in the European system. A "tense" balance of power offers the best conditions for a neutral state. See Frei, *Dimensionen neutraler Politik*, p. 51.

[107]Speech of Austrian Foreign Minister Willibald Pahr in 1983, "Austria between the Block Systems," p. 53.

[108]Ibid.

[109]On the other hand, it is interesting to note that, in the case of Switzerland, religious heterogeneity contributed to the strengthening of its neutrality policy during the Thirty Years' War (1618-48). By pursuing such a policy the Swiss Confederation avoided internal religious conflict which, to a certain extent, threatened Switzerland itself. See Frei, *Dimensionen neutraler Politik*, p. 186.

SWITZERLAND

Mark R. Rubin and Laurent Wehrli

Ever since the 1983 publication of John McPhee's two-part article on the Swiss army, "La Place de la Concorde Suisse," in *The New Yorker*,[1] there has been a growing awareness and interest among the non-Swiss general public in the phenomenon represented by the Swiss Confederation and its unique defense establishment. Swiss neutrality and security matters have long been subjects of scholarly interest, and it would seem fair to say that a rather high degree of international awareness exists about Switzerland's status as a neutral. What is less evident, however, is the degree to which the public is aware of the formidable military apparatus which the Swiss have created to ensure their continued existence as a democratic and neutral nation in the maelstrom of superpower politics.

Indeed, the reactions one habitually elicits when discussing the Swiss military would tend to indicate a high degree of ignorance about such matters. Nevertheless, since the publication of McPhee's article and book, general interest in Switzerland and its defense forces appears to have increased, and the Information Service of the Federal Military Department has experienced a considerable increase in requests for information about the army.[2] Contrary to what might be expected, the Swiss authorities are particularly forthcoming in providing information about their defense forces, inasmuch as they consider widespread knowledge of their dissuasive capabilities to be an integral part of their defense plan.

This study will examine the Swiss concept of "general defense."[3] Because neutrality is the quintessential feature of Swiss foreign policy[4] and because thinking on the subject has evolved over several centuries, it is impossible to treat defense policy in any but the narrowest sense without taking neutrality into serious account. Consequently, the historical evolution of Swiss neutrality will be considered before questions of contemporary security policy.

FROM RÜTLI TO THE AFFIRMATION OF NEUTRALITY

The history of the Swiss Confederation is generally considered to begin in 1291 with the Rütli Oaths, a covenant concluded among the three *Waldstätten,* or rustic communities, of Uri, Schwyz, and Unterwalden, located on the northern approaches to the Saint Gotthard Pass, in response to an attempt by the House of Hapsburg to impose its political authority on them. The pact contained mutual military assistance provisions, as well as agreements to accept no foreign judges and to submit to arbitration any internal conflicts among the three cantons. Although Switzerland traces its roots back to Rütli, the resulting confederation, which in time would add other cantons to its number, was far from being a state in the modern sense of the word, since it did not provide for any central governing authority.

From its very beginnings, the political fortunes of Switzerland have largely been tributary to three factors, which worked together to bring about the policy of neutrality: 1) a lack of political cohesion inherent in the early stages of the Confederation and the frequently manifested internal dissension which arose from it; 2) a key geographical situation in central Europe, which historically caused it to become involved, willingly or not, in its neighbors' affairs; and 3) a continuing preoccupation with questions of security and defense, as originally manifested in the Rütli Oaths and as reinforced by the cantons' repeated military entanglement in European politics.

The Reformation was a key element of change in sixteenth-century Europe. It was particularly so in Switzerland, where it brought about crucial changes in the internal cohesion of the Confederation, which had by then expanded to thirteen cantons. Because of the political independence of its constituent parts, Switzerland did not have an official religion like most centralized states. It is not surprising, therefore, that this new, divisive element in the tenuous relationships between cantons would lead to armed conflict and would leave its impression until the middle of the nineteenth century.

The Thirty Years' War (1618-1648), which pitted Protestants and Catholics against each other in all of central Europe, stirred up a lively interest in Switzerland, where the cantons took sides along religious lines with one or the other camp. In spite of their dissensions and their desires to help their coreligionists, the cantons had the wisdom once again to proclaim the neutrality of the Confederation, thus confirming the decision taken in 1515 after their defeat at Marignano by the French. The Federal Diet understood the importance of Switzerland's staying out of the conflict which, because of the forces at work in the different alliances and of the different benefits that were anticipated by all involved, was literally to set Europe afire. Had that not been the case, national cohesion would have given way to division into two separate religious groups. Active neutrality was in this case extremely advantageous, for Switzerland was the only country in devastated Central Europe to remain intact. Consequently, it was in the position to sell great quantities of merchandise, including armaments, to the belligerents.

During this time, the judicial concept of neutrality evolved further. At the beginning of the war, neutrality meant that the Confederation did not participate in the conflict. That notion was flawed, on the one hand, because Swiss soldiers were engaged in the service of different belligerents under the terms of agreements[5] existing between foreign states and the cantons, and, on the other, because Switzerland was incapable of keeping belligerents from violating its territory. Little by little, the Confederation refined the notion of neutrality so that in 1624, in order to resolve the problems caused by frequent incursions of foreign troops using the assistance of coreligionist cantons to cross Swiss territory, the Confederation began conscripting federal troops and stationing them at its borders.

In 1647, at the urging of the Protestant cantons, the Confederation adopted the "Défensional de Wyl," a defensive alliance which stipulated that each canton maintain 12,000 men and a reserve at the disposal of a council composed of Protestants and Catholics. This pact sanctioned the principle of armed neutrality through an alliance for the common protection of the national borders. Later on, in 1663, the use of Swiss regiments in the service of foreign states during offensive wars would be forbidden and, in 1674, perpetual armed neutrality would become official policy. The 1648 treaties of Westphalia, which ended the Thirty Years' War, solemnly recognized the independence of the Confederation.

The affirmation of neutrality during the Thirty Years' War yielded four principal benefits for the Confederation. First, it was spared the difficult and bloody battles that pitted the belligerents against each other. Second, its unqualified sovereignty was recognized, thus freeing it from the trusteeship of the Holy Roman Empire. Third, the events of the war's first few years resulted in the recognition of the rights and obligations of neutral states. And fourth, the development of the concept of neutrality which took place during this difficult period allowed the members of the Confederation to recognize the defects in their defensive organization and to transform the neutrality which had sprung from Marignano into the notion of perpetual and armed neutrality, thus raising it to the level of national policy.

Nevertheless, religious animosities within the Confederation had not disappeared. To the contrary, they persisted, aggravating internal problems and preventing Switzerland from having a strong foreign policy of neutrality. Thus, in 1668, during the wars which took place under Louis XIV, it lost its territories in Franche-Comté as well as several of the dependencies of the diocese of Basel. The Confederation also was unable to keep foreign troops out of its territory, and its international reputation was compromised to the point that the two principal European powers, France and the Empire, hesitated to recognize Helvetian neutrality, fearing that the Swiss would be unable to defend their own territory.

In the Treaty of Utrecht of 1714, which brought peace back to Europe and to Switzerland, the Confederation obtained a second international recognition of its independence and of its neutrality. By according a place to the Swiss in the Utrecht negotiations, the great powers of the day demonstrated their intention to have a strong and neutral Switzerland in the heart of Europe, where it would assume the role of a buffer state.

The French Revolution would have repercussions in Switzerland. In a few cantons, revolutionary demonstrations sprang up, but they were quickly repressed by the aristocratic local governments. Following these failures, numerous revolutionaries took refuge in France. In 1792, Swiss Guards were massacred in Paris at the Tuileries and a revolutionary government took power in Geneva. The privileged relationship which had existed between the Confederation and France since 1516 was broken off. Switzerland once again proclaimed its neutrality while the European monarchies were calling on it to ally itself with them against the new French Republic.

A general weakening of national cohesion helped to make the 1798 French invasion of Switzerland possible. The Directory wanted to occupy Switzerland for strategic, financial, and political reasons. Along the lines of the French model, a so-called "Helvetian Republic one and indivisible" was created. In fact, it was little more than a puppet state occupied by the French military and obliged to enter into a military alliance with France. The French army, at first accepted as a liberator, quickly became hated, and a good deal of popular unrest led to several attempted revolts against the French occupation.   They were all brutally put down, but Napoleon, then First Consul, understood the importance of a reform which would calm the situation, and on 19 February 1803 he decreed the Act of Mediation.   Switzerland once again became a confederation, now of nineteen cantons, but a few territories, including Geneva, became French.   The apparent neutrality confirmed by the Act of Mediation was, however, contradicted by the requirement that the Swiss furnish Napoleon with a permanent contingent of some 16,000 soldiers.   Over a period of time, about 80,000 Swiss died as a result of that obligation.

On the economic front, the cantons suffered from the continental blockade, and the industrial infrastructure, patiently put in place during the eighteenth century, was destroyed, especially in the business of weaving.[6]   The Empire had allowed the Confederation to return to a more peaceful situation, but a profound change had taken place.   Nevertheless, the war of 1799 had demonstrated to all of the belligerents the difficulty of conducting battles in the alpine regions of Switzerland.

In spite of its obvious negative effects, the experience of the French Revolution did educate the Confederation about further improving its notion of neutrality and of how to implement it.   The first lesson learned was that continuing religious and social strife would always lead to the same errors: calling upon a foreign power to settle domestic problems and then having to suffer the intervention that inevitably followed, a process serving only the interests of the foreign power.   The second was that a strong defense was absolutely essential to the maintenance of national integrity.   The neutral state could not avoid war and occupation simply by seeking to avoid foreign conflicts.   Additionally, economic sacrifices, refused in the past, would be necessary in order to organize and maintain an army adequate to the task of defending Switzerland.[7]   The third lesson came from the institutions created by Napoleon's Act of Mediation, which pushed Switzerland toward the development of an authentic federal state.   The central authority was given increased power for national questions, thus strengthening Switzerland's viability.   Nonetheless, in 1814, allied troops crossed Swiss territory to attack France in spite of the Diet's 1813 proclamation of neutrality. Napoleon's forces fell in April 1814.

However, when Napoleon landed in France in March 1815 and once again threatened the allies, war began anew.   During the

Hundred Days, the Swiss Diet proclaimed neither neutrality nor the will to defend the Confederation. It even went so far as to allow the allies free passage across Switzerland in an attempt to win their good graces. That latter action dealt a serious blow to neutrality, since Swiss troops followed the allied armies into France, where, although small in numbers, they were able to recover the territories around Geneva which had been annexed by the French in 1798. With the Peace of Paris, following Napoleon's final defeat, the great powers formally recognized and guaranteed the neutrality of Switzerland and the inviolability of its territory,[8] thus formalizing the decisions made earlier at the Congress of Vienna, modified as a function of the Hundred Days. Henceforth the Confederation would have three new cantons--Geneva, Valais, and Neuchâtel--and would have the advantage of customs-free zones in the French areas surrounding Geneva. The federal institutions established by the Act of Mediation were almost completely dismantled. The old Diet was reinstated, albeit with greater powers in the area of foreign affairs and with an army and a military budget.

The Congress of Vienna and the Peace of Paris were extremely beneficial to the Confederation. Unlike some countries which had had neutrality forced on them, Switzerland wanted to be neutral.[9] The decisions of Vienna and Paris legitimized the foreign policy maintained by the Swiss since their declarations of neutrality during the Thirty Years' War. The characteristics of Swiss neutrality-- perpetual, armed, recognized, and guaranteed--entered common law and were written into legal texts, thus becoming the bases of Swiss foreign policy.

During the years that followed 1815, the Federal Pact did not allow Switzerland to elaborate a viable military policy. The federal army consisted merely of contingents that met for joint maneuvers a few days per year. By instituting a regular training program, however, General Guillaume-Henri Dufour was able gradually to build up a corps of officers. By the middle of the nineteenth century, the Diet could count on an army of 100,000 men and well-trained officers who could be mobilized at short notice.

In 1830 liberalism made great progress in the Confederation, thanks to the success of the July Revolution in France and the presence of so many revolutionaries in Switzerland. Half the cantons reformed their constitutions in more democratic directions, abolished all the old feudal tithes, and guaranteed basic political rights. Liberal ideas were quickly overtaken by radical ones of a more centralized, democratic, and nondenominational Switzerland.

As these ideas matured in several cantons, the Diet gained the means to put its policies into practice, at least as far as its foreign policy was concerned. That enabled it to resist the attempts by European powers to intervene on domestic questions such as, for example, the right of asylum for European revolutionaries.

Although Switzerland would not experience the disruption of the 1848 revolutions, it did suffer through domestic rebellion in 1847 by an alliance of conservative Catholic cantons (the *Sonderbund*). When the mainly Protestant Diet attempted to dissolve the conservative coalition in July 1847, Switzerland was torn by a veritable civil war (the *Sonderbund* War). General Dufour quickly mobilized the federal army and put down the revolt in a few days, with relatively little bloodshed. The major Catholic powers supporting the *Sonderbund* did not even have the time to intervene. The Diet then dissolved the alliance and obliged the Catholic cantons to pay a war indemnity. They returned to the Diet at the end of 1847. Thus, the mid-nineteenth century saw the return of a powerful Switzerland, able to defend its decisions and to maintain its internal cohesion.

In September 1848 a new constitution was approved which changed Switzerland's status from that of a confederation of states to a federative state, thus increasing the power of central authority. At last the Confederation was equipped with a real executive body, the Federal Council, separate from the legislative and judiciary bodies. The army became a strong federal unit under the command of the Council alone; in case of war, the Council would delegate its military power to a general appointed by the legislative body. This constitution of 1848, revised in 1874 to reinforce federal power and to give wider democratic control (by means of the referendum and of the popular initiative), is still in force. It has had enormous influence on the development of Swiss neutrality, as it protects the country to a very considerable extent from foreign influence. As they had imposed the Federal Pact of 1815, the major powers in 1848 thought they could have a hand in drawing up the new constitution, but the Diet refused categorically. In a very firm note dated 18 June 1848, it averted forever the specter of a protectorate with which the great powers had threatened the Confederation for over thirty years. The Revolution of 1848 in Paris and the fall of Metternich in Austria gave the major powers no chance to react.

From 1848 onward, the legal concept of neutrality was complete: foreign governments were no longer permitted to raise troops in Switzerland, foreign armies were forbidden passage over Swiss territory, the right to trade with neutral countries in times of armed conflict was upheld, the rights of asylum and political internment were clarified, and the supplying of arms or military equipment to countries at war was forbidden. Gradually all of these concepts entered international law. (They were recognized and codified in 1907 during the Hague Convention on the Laws of War.[10]) Having bolstered its sovereignty and neutrality, Switzerland remained outside all the European wars of the second half of the nineteenth century. The constitution of 1848 ushered in an era of peace and prosperity for the cantons, eliminated customs barriers between them, and allowed Switzerland to enjoy considerable economic development from the end of the nineteenth century onward. The Confederation was, therefore, able to enter the twentieth century more united and better equipped to survive the maelstrom that was to come.

NEUTRALITY IN THE TWENTIETH CENTURY

The First World War was a test for the unity of the Confederation, for it highlighted the linguistic and cultural--and therefore social--factionalism contained within the country. As soon as hostilities broke out, the Federal Council informed all the belligerents that Switzerland remained neutral and was determined to defend itself.[11] But, whereas the federal state proclaimed its neutrality, the Swiss people were clearly divided by their preference for the belligerent whose language they shared. This split between the French- and German-speaking Swiss, cleverly nurtured by foreign propaganda, was the gravest danger to national cohesion, but the solidarity of the army and the single-mindedness of the federal authorities prevented the situation from degenerating. Attempts by the belligerents to persuade Switzerland to abandon its neutral status and to participate in the conflict were firmly rejected.

By the end of World War I, restrictions, price increases, and the presence of revolutionaries such as Lenin had contributed to a climate of social agitation. The Socialist party declared a national strike in November 1918. The army had to intervene to maintain the economy, but the Swiss situation calmed rapidly, unlike that in other countries. Peace had returned to the continent, the linguistic and cultural oppositions lost their edge, and the financial markets were returning to normal. Those were all very good reasons to explain why social conflict had ceased to preoccupy the Swiss; they preferred to share in the new prosperity. Thus, the armed neutrality of Switzerland emerged reinforced from the First World War.[12]

After hostilities had ceased, the question of Switzerland's joining the League of Nations once again raised the problem of the Confederation's neutrality receiving international recognition. The Declaration of London, on 13 February 1920, gave Switzerland the particular status of "neutral state."[13]   It would not be able to participate in any military sanctions that the League might impose, but it would be allowed to apply economic sanctions. It went from the status of total, strict neutrality to one of differential neutrality. The Swiss subsequently voted to join the League by a very slim majority. As it was, problems cropped up and came to a head during the Italo-Ethiopian war in 1935.[14]   Realizing that it was impossible to maintain differential neutrality during the troubled 1930s, the Federal Council decided to return to armed, integral neutrality in 1938.   Although the Great Depression was a severe blow to the Swiss economy and industry, many scarce resources were sacrificed to improve military readiness.

Even before the beginning of hostilities in World War II, the Swiss learned about German maps which cavalierly showed Switzerland as a newly incorporated part of the new Reich.[15]   On 31 August 1939, the day before Germany invaded Poland, the Federal Council issued a declaration of neutrality very similar to its proclamation at the outbreak of the First World War,[16] thus demonstrating its determination to take seriously all of the obligations implied by its status as an armed neutral. The collapse of France in June 1940 meant that Switzerland was completely surrounded by Axis forces. Under General Henri Guisan, the Swiss army reacted to the threat of invasion by creating the national redoubt in the heart of the Alps.

Swiss neutrality also was put to the test by ruthless economic warfare, difficulties in obtaining foodstuffs, numerous overflights of the national territory by enemy aircraft, and pressure from the Germans, accompanied by more or less overt threats. Further, the German delegation in Bern repeatedly protested the attitude of the Swiss press, which it considered "hostile to the Reich." The Federal Council rejected those protests on the grounds that a neutral state cannot, even in time of war, be required to observe moral neutrality. Whereas a certain fringe of the population tended to support the Axis forces, the vast majority of Swiss favored the Allies.[17]   Thus, the problems of national cohesion were less acute than during World War I. Toward the end of World War II, it appeared that Swiss territory might be violated by Allied troops advancing toward Germany from the south and wishing to take a shortcut south of Basel, but the collapse of the Third Reich warded off this last danger.

Thus, in the space of a single generation, Switzerland succeeded in preserving its territorial integrity through two world wars. During World War I, a declaration of neutrality, the reminder of the 1815 guarantees made to the Confederation in Vienna and Paris, and the presence of the army along the national borders had barely sufficed to prevent the fighting from spreading into Switzerland. During World War II, the same three factors no longer proved adequate. By constantly drawing attention to its diplomacy and to its military preparedness, however, the Confederation managed to persuade the belligerents that an invasion of Switzerland would prove far too costly for the anticipated benefits. A strong army, a government whose power was deeply rooted in the people, and the geographical and financial situation of the Confederation all supplied strong dissuasive arguments for potential invaders. Moreover, a defensible and well-defended neutral state in the center of Europe provided all sides with a valuable refuge for capital and intelligence and a convenient international meeting place.

After the Second World War, the question of whether Switzerland should join the United Nations arose. As the UN founding powers made it quite clear that there was to be no room for neutral states, the Confederation gave up the idea of joining. The fact is that those powers found it suspicious, if not actually morally reprehensible, that neutral states--and particularly Switzerland--should have managed not to participate in the struggle against the Third Reich and Hitler. Neutrality seemed to be the height of national egotism. To those feelings were added the widespread belief, in Allied diplomatic circles,[18] that neutrality was an outdated concept in the age of the atom: in the case of nuclear warfare, it could hardly be applied.

By its determination to retain its perpetual armed neutrality and to remain outside the United Nations, Switzerland ran the risk, in the early postwar years, of finding itself diplomatically isolated. The Confederation's foreign policy sought therefore to avoid any such isolation by engaging in international cooperation wherever that was compatible with the principles of neutrality.[19] With that end in view, Switzerland delegated a permanent observer to the United Nations and became a full member of most of the specialized agencies created under its aegis, except a few such as the World

Bank and the International Monetary Fund. During the 1970s a movement developed in Switzerland in favor of joining the United Nations, with the argument that the organization had developed from a defensive alliance of the victorious countries into an international forum. That proposal was--and still is--the subject of much heated debate among the Swiss. The questions of continuing international recognition of their neutrality, of possible participation in international economic or military sanctions, of financial contributions, and of the very usefulness of what General de Gaulle called "the thing,"[20] are among the numerous questions that make the Swiss undecided about joining. The Federal Council has proposed[21] that the country should follow the example of Austria in proclaiming the neutrality of Switzerland to all UN member nations, since neutrality is not recognized by the UN Charter. Such a declaration would have the advantage of enabling Switzerland to abstain, in the name of neutrality, from economic or military sanctions. On 16 March 1986, the Swiss voted down a referendum to allow the Confederation to apply for UN membership by a margin of three to one.[22]

Parallel to its international involvement in the specialized agencies of the United Nations, the Swiss have debated the extent to which their country should cooperate with the European organizations that came into being during the postwar years. There is clearly no question of Switzerland joining in military or politico-military groups such as the European Defense Community, the Western European Union, or the Atlantic Alliance. On the other hand, the Confederation has joined several economic, social, scientific, cultural, and legal organizations such as the Organization for Economic Cooperation and Development (1947), the European Free Trade Association (1959), and the Council of Europe (1963). Participation in these organizations is seen to be compatible with neutrality, for the decisions they make do not impinge on national sovereignty or neutrality. This participation has helped the Confederation to experience rapid economic expansion, to the point where it now enjoys one of the highest standards of living in the world. In 1972 the Confederation signed free-trade agreements with the European Economic Community (EEC), its most important commercial partner. This was the limit of Swiss involvement with the EEC, given the long-term supranational principles aspired to by the organization.

Today, Switzerland participates actively in international affairs. In accordance with its policy of neutrality, it tries to maintain good channels of communication with major political and cultural constituencies in the world through its humanitarian missions, its willingness to serve as an international mediator, and its proposals, together with those of other neutral and nonaligned nations, for improving world peace. It has become a major setting for international business and the home of numerous international organizations. Finally, Switzerland has managed over the years to modify the way in which neutrality is perceived by other states. Looked on with skepticism in 1945, Swiss neutrality is now better understood and accepted as a useful and even necessary element in today's world.

Security Implications of Swiss Neutrality in the 1980s[23]

Switzerland is a nation of great diversity. On one level, it is a small, landlocked country of some 16,000 square miles, yet its residents speak four different languages, and they are divided into two religious groups of roughly equal size. It has a policy of perpetual, strict neutrality, both politically and militarily, yet it is, at the same time, clearly a member of the Western cultural community[24] and has a resolutely capitalist economy.

In spite of its numerous cultural diversities, though, Switzerland is a smoothly run country whose democratic political institutions have a long and honorable history. Although it is not the present purpose to make invidious comparisons, it is interesting to contrast the Swiss consensus with the strife found in other multicultural countries such as Belgium and Canada. It is a basic tenet of Swiss political philosophy that, in order to make government more responsive to the people, who remain sovereign, authority should be kept at the lowest level of government possible. Consequently, while organized as a federal state, Switzerland is in fact a relatively loose confederation of its twenty-six highly autonomous cantons, which themselves comprise a large number of somewhat autonomous local governments. In this scheme, the people can (and frequently do), at virtually any time, launch initiative petitions or call for referenda on a large variety of issues. Nevertheless, with all of the seeming potential for chaos, the system appears not only to work, but to work very well.

Although Switzerland is a neutral, it is important not to forget that it is, culturally and economically, very much a member of the Western community. It is geographically surrounded (except for the small portion of its eastern border with Austria) by NATO countries and imports most of its military equipment from those countries.[25] It seems clear, as noted by George Schwab in his 1969 article on Switzerland's tactical nuclear weapons policy, that in the event of a major East-West nuclear confrontation in Europe, Switzerland's future would be under the NATO nuclear umbrella.[26] The same logic probably would apply in the event of a conventional war once Swiss neutrality had been violated.   Those assumptions, though, should neither surprise anyone nor should they in any way be considered to disparage the seriousness of Swiss neutrality, which can only be a viable policy as long as it has not been violated.   In its 27 June 1973 report on Swiss security policy, the Federal Council states:

> From the moment that Switzerland is forced into a war, it stops being neutral and all of the military and foreign-policy limitations implied by neutrality cease being operative.   We are then *free* to collaborate, militarily or not with the adversary of our aggressor; in such a case, our combat potential should earn a solid position for us in eventual negotiations as well as appreciable participation in any joint decisions.[27]

The Swiss historically have taken their neutrality very seriously, and current events demonstrate that their concern in that regard has not diminished.   It must not, though, be forgotten that their country is an armed neutral and, as such, is presumed to be ready to defend both its neutrality and its territory against external threats.   Nevertheless, Switzerland has in recent times been taken to task by the Soviet Union for the closeness of its ties with NATO. An article appearing in the official Soviet organ, *Izvestia*, criticized a training exercise in Sardinia for Swiss pilots, saying that "it is not difficult to imagine who was the enemy programmed into the electronic equipment of NATO."[28]   Another article, appearing in *Red Star*, commented that Swiss-American relations had intensified to the point that Switzerland had assumed the "role of a potential [U.S.] ally."[29]   Interestingly enough, Yuri Karelov, writing in a prestigious Soviet journal, tells of a conversation between General Secretary Mikhail Gorbachev and then Swiss President Kurt Furgler in which the former "noted that on the strength of its traditional neutrality Switzerland could do a great deal to further the development of the European process, to arrange a productive East-West dialogue, strengthen detente and confidence." Karelov does not report Furgler's response.[30]

In an intermediate report on security policy dated 3 December 1979, the Federal Council defined six specific threats constituting the perceived danger to national security: the international political situation, the military threat, the economic threat, espionage, terrorism, and subversion.[31] Although there is considerable overlap in those areas, they generally deal with such matters as: 1) the evolution of relations between the United States and the Soviet Union, 2) the arms race, 3) the economic recession, 4) the dilatory implementation of the Helsinki Final Act, 5) the Middle East situation and the use of petroleum as a weapon, 6) the balance of power between NATO and the Warsaw Treaty Organization (WTO), 7) new developments in armaments (nuclear, air, conventional, and electronic), 8) the economic pressures that could be exerted on Switzerland (which is heavily dependent on imports of all sorts),[32] and 9) the general areas of espionage, terrorism, and subversion. All of those complex issues must be taken into account by Swiss strategic planners.

Swiss military authorities have defined six *cas stratégiques*, or strategic situations, which take the various elements threatening their national security into account. They are: 1) the "normal" case, characterized by "relative" peace; 2) the "crisis" case, characterized by heightened tension and serious upheavals; 3) the "protection of neutrality" case, which posits the outbreak of hostilities in Europe; 4) the "defense" case, in which those hostilities escalate to an attack on Swiss territory; 5) the "catastrophe" case, reached when an invader had carried out significant destruction within the country; and 6) the "occupation" case, involving enemy occupation of a part of Switzerland.[33] In order to deal with the various strategic situations described, the centerpiece of Swiss defensive strategy is a military depending almost entirely on a rapidly mobilizable militia force.

It has been said that Switzerland does not have, but rather is, an army.[34] There is much truth in that seemingly flippant statement, as can be seen from the fact that it is generally considered possible to mobilize the national defense forces of some 625,000 men within forty-eight hours; if the paramilitary civil defense forces are counted, that number increases to some 1,100,000. Also, because of Switzerland's staggered system of military training, there are generally about 18,500 recruits and soldiers of various sorts on active duty for training at any given time.[35] Considering that the country's regular army is extremely small, consisting of some 600 career officers and 900 career noncommissioned officers (primarily instructors),[36] such a capability obviously requires a considerable infrastructure.

Article 18, §1, of the federal constitution tersely states that "every Swiss is liable to military service."[37]   As currently implemented, every male Swiss citizen must serve in the militia from age twenty through age fifty (fifty-five for officers).   Typically, at age twenty, a new recruit will spend 118 days in a basic training school, after which he will be assigned to a unit in the general area of his residence.   From ages twenty-one to thirty-two, he will belong to the part of the army called the *Elite*, which means that on eight occasions he will be sent for twenty-day "refresher" courses; from ages thirty-three to forty-two, he will belong to the *Landwehr* and will be sent to three thirteen-day "complementary" courses; finally, from ages forty-three to fifty, he will belong to the *Landsturm* and attend two six-day *Landsturm* courses.   After that, his military obligation, as such, will be over and he will be transferred to the civil defense forces until age sixty.   Counting the mandatory personal equipment inspections and rifle training sessions, a Swiss can expect to spend about 363 days satisfying his military obligation. Those who become noncommissioned or commissioned officers can expect to spend increasingly and substantially greater amounts of time, depending upon how far they advance in the hierarchy.

Military service in Switzerland is truly universal, at least for men, with exemptions being given only in the case of physical disability, and even then at the price of a military exemption tax of 3 percent on the individual's net earnings.   Furthermore, the Swiss traditionally have taken a dim view of conscientious objectors, who are relatively few in number and are regularly handled through the military justice system.   The policy of generally assigning soldiers to units near their homes has the multiple advantages of minimizing mobilization time, favoring unit cohesion, providing added incentive to protect the unit's assigned territory, and, especially in the country's many mountainous regions, ensuring a high degree of familiarity with the local terrain.

In accordance with the basic Swiss position of neutrality, the army has a primarily defensive and dissuasive mission.   The Federal Council's *Rapport sur la politique de sécurité* states that the mission of the army is fundamentally to prevent war by letting any potential adversary know that a military aggression against Switzerland would be extremely costly in terms of time, men, and materiel and that it would be impossible to effect a surprise occupation of Switzerland, since the country possesses both the will and means to fight immediately and effectively. The goal of that policy is to temper any hope that a potential adversary might entertain of attaining operational objectives in a short time and at a reasonable cost. In the event of an attack on Switzerland, the army would have the threefold mission of defending Swiss territory "from the border," preventing the adversary from attaining its operational objectives, and maintaining at least a part of the national territory under the Confederation's sovereignty.[38]

The dissuasive portion of the military's mission is aided to a very considerable extent by the country's physical geography. Nearly 70 percent of the terrain is mountainous (Jura and Alps); the remaining 30 percent, the plateau, does not lend itself to conventional military operations because it is riddled with forest and urban areas, cut by rivers and hills, and blocked off at each end by Lakes Constance and Geneva.[39] Furthermore, the country has been provided with a formidable system of potential highway obstructions in the form of some 2,000 permanently mined roadways, bridges, tunnels, and even pine forests; in the event of an attack, key points in the Swiss highway and road network could quickly be blown up, thus rendering it virtually unusable. There also exists an extensive infrastructure of military installations, including some 2,000 fortified positions,[40] some 4,000 antitank obstacles, sufficient underground shelters for about 130,000 men, a dozen underground air bases, military hospitals with a total of 25,000 beds, about 600 storage installations for military rations and supplies (one ton for each soldier), 80 kilometers of underground munitions storehouses,[41] and some 2,700 buildings where various mobilization equipment is stored. Most of those facilities are located in deep underground caverns, hollowed out of rock, thus offering excellent protection and concealment. It would indeed appear that the Swiss policy of a "high entry price" for potential aggressors is not an empty threat.

At first glance the cost for maintaining such a system would seem to be considerable, and in many ways it is. Even if the total number of days of military service required of a Swiss, as shown above, is not excessively high, those days are spread out over thirty or thirty-five years, thus obliging the citizen-soldier to plan the better part of his adult life around his military obligations. There are rewards, however, especially for those who pursue advancement in the system. As John McPhee notes: "In contrast to all other countries, there is in Switzerland a positive correlation between military rank and economic leadership generally. . . . Chemical companies, insurance companies, construction companies are under the command of majors, colonels, brigadiers."[42]   The financial cost, although only 2.1 percent of gross domestic product, is none-theless a very elevated 21.3 percent of total government spending, a figure exceeded among NATO, WTO, and other European nations only by the United States (27.8 percent) and by the Federal Republic of Germany (22.3 percent).[43]

A Viable Policy?

Although the overall picture seems to be positive, it is not without its problems.   First are those of the purely military variety. Whatever may be its state of readiness, Switzerland is still a small country which ultimately could be overrun by a larger, more power-ful aggressor.   Assuming such an eventuality, which presupposes a general conflict in Europe, it is difficult to say to what extent the defensive scenarios foreseen would be effective, although it seems likely that they would, for a time at least, enjoy some measure of success.   Furthermore, Switzerland is as subject as any other coun-try to nuclear attack or to the effects of such an attack on a neighboring state.   Because of its geographic position, and even if it were not itself attacked, it would be exposed, under the best of circumstances, to a great deal of radioactive fallout in the event of a nuclear strike on NATO.

Swiss military planners are keenly aware of the dangers facing them.   Their principal defense against conventional attack is ul-timately the high price that a potential aggressor would have to pay to conquer Switzerland.   That threat is substantially backed up by the army and seconded by the country's topography.   Implicit in their philosophy is the rather plausible belief that the army would be able to take quick advantage of the difficult, but familiar, ter-rain.   In fact, the ultimate response to the most dire of the "strate-gic situations," that of partial occupation, would be retreat to a presumably impenetrable national redoubt in the Alps.

The Swiss army does not have a nuclear capability.   Strategic planning, therefore, for the contingency of a European nuclear war is essentially limited to the country's extensive network of nuclear shelters, which, as of 1 January 1984, could house or accommodate 5.5 million persons.[44]

What are the possibilities of an attack on Switzerland? The country clearly lies directly in a potential attack route leading from Czechoslovakia through Austria to Switzerland and Western Europe.[45] In realistic terms, however, they are probably quite slim. Barring a major conflict in Europe between the WTO and NATO, considered rather unlikely by most Swiss military planners, it is difficult to think that anyone would have any reason, either political or military, to attack Switzerland.[46] Furthermore, it seems to be in everyone's interest to have Switzerland--particularly Geneva--as a neutral meeting place for international meetings between adversaries. A Switzerland forced to give up its neutrality after an armed attack could no longer serve that essential diplomatic function and would, at least for a time, be a formidable opponent. Also, whatever strategic advantage could be gained from occupation of or from passage through Swiss territory would likely be outweighed by both the cost involved in capturing and in maintaining it and by the opprobrium it would elicit from the international community. Finally, the damage done to the international financial system by any interruption of normal banking operations in Switzerland would be so paralyzing and widespread that no one would benefit from it.

Mention has been made of the Swiss civil defense organization. Although not a part of the military, it does work closely together with the army in the framework of the general defense concept and has been designated to deal with any crisis situation of military, natural, or other origin. The *Protection civile*, responsible for the operation of the nuclear shelters, has put together contingency plans of great thoroughness and complexity. An example of such efforts is the wooden-lath partitions found in the basements of many modern Swiss apartment buildings, where they ostensibly serve the banal purpose of separating and securing building residents' storage areas. All of the pieces of wood in those partitions, however, are carefully inventoried and can, on very short notice, be converted into bunk beds, should an emergency arise. The civil defense forces have large underground installations which include sheltered hospitals and dormitories, as well as facilities for command and communications posts and emergency vehicle storage and maintenance. The activities of the army and of the civil defense forces are closely coordinated.

It would appear that Switzerland's reputation as a well-run, neat country is equally applicable to its defense establishment. Indeed, it is difficult to spend any time observing the Swiss military without being impressed by the thoroughness of its planning and the quality of its equipment and training. One is left with the impression that this country has developed a system which is perfectly adapted to its national character--at least to the extent that things human admit of perfection--and that perhaps Voltaire's best-of-all-possible worlds is more than a chimera.

The Helvetian Consensus?

Switzerland is not, however, a utopia. The human element is always to be reckoned with, and even a well-ordered society is subject to Robert Burns's maxim about the best-laid schemes of mice and men. An interesting example of that phenomenon is to be found in figures supplied by the Federal Military Department, which show that the number of convictions by courts-martial for refusing military service has climbed, during the reporting period 1970-1984, from a low of 175 in 1970 to a high of 790 in 1984, an increase of about 350 percent. A lower peak of 545 had been reached in 1974, but by 1980 the number had dropped again to 355. Perhaps not altogether unsurprisingly, the analysis of those convictions shows a generally rising trend toward objection to military service for religious reasons, while political motivation has remained a relatively minor factor, coming significantly behind ethical and "other" grounds. Part of that circumstance may stem from the fact that conscientious objectors for religious reasons are generally better treated than those who claim other, especially political, grounds. It finally should be noted that although the number of such convictions has risen significantly, when the 1984 figure of 790 convictions is compared with the 40,648 recruits inducted into active duty for training during the same year,[47] the rate of 2 percent is still very low.

One notes also an ongoing undercurrent of criticism about defense policy, albeit at a rather low level. One example of that phenomenon is the Pilatus PC-7 affair, which attracted a certain amount of international attention during late 1984 and early 1985, and which is of particular interest here because of its implications for questions of Swiss neutrality. The PC-7 is a "fully aerobatic two-seat training aircraft, powered by a 410 kW (550 shp) Pratt & Whitney Canada PT6A-25A turboprop engine."[48] An article appearing in the 19 October 1984 number of L'Express reported that Pilatus, part of the Oerlikon-Bührle group, had concluded a contract with Iran in 1983 for eighty PC-7 aircraft. As of the writing of the article, forty-one of them had been delivered. The transaction did not seem to contravene Swiss law, which forbids "the sale of military materiel, arms, and munitions to countries at war or located in a zone of major conflict," since as delivered, in its civilian version, the PC-7 could scarcely be considered to fall under any of the prohibited categories.

What was less evident, according to the article, was that the plane, already capable of landing and taking off from short, unimproved runways, is easily modified into a military version which can be equipped with an impressive arsenal of rockets, bombs, machine guns, and other weapons. The PC-7 is considered to be one of the most effective multipurpose aircraft currently on the world market. In all events, according to *L'Express,* the Iranians were using their converted PC-7s to repress revolts in Kurdistan. Under such conditions, the legality of their export from Switzerland, and the propriety of their sale to Iran by a neutral power, is much less clear.[49] Official discussion on the matter was closed by a decision of the Federal Council, taken on 11 March 1985, to the effect that the "PC-7 cannot be considered as war materiel in the sense of the federal edict governing its export. Moreover, it would be inappropriate to modify the legislation in question in order to subject this aircraft to export restrictions."[50] The same article goes on to imply that economic considerations were not completely foreign to the Council's decision.

What is at issue here is, in fact, a highly complex problem. In keeping with its neutral stance, to say nothing of economic imperatives, Switzerland would like to procure as much of its military materiel as possible from domestic sources. Clearly, though, it is impossible to maintain a viable armaments industry without achieving economies of scale far beyond the needs of the Swiss military forces. Thus, as is the case in France, for example, the necessity of exporting arms is evident. Unlike France, however, Switzerland is a perpetual neutral, whence the dilemma in which it found itself during the PC-7 affair and in which it is likely to find itself again and again unless the question is resolved once and for all in a direct manner. The Swiss have not been particularly forthcoming on the issue. Indeed, reactions such as the one attributed in the *L'Express* article to Georges André Chevallaz, then head of the Federal Military Department (that is, minister of defense), are, unfortunately, not uncommon: "Under these conditions even a baby carriage can be considered as an offensive arm. It suffices to fill it with plastic explosive."[51]

Much of the current domestic criticism of Swiss security policy revolves around the belief that largely because of a certain national self-satisfaction, it is not sufficiently responsive to external realities. Hans Vogel argues that Swiss postwar security policy is grounded in tradition (rather than in threat analysis) and in the belief that it is legitimate, both morally, because of its defensive character, and absolutely, because of its perceived effectiveness in forestalling invasions during World Wars I and II.[52] A recently published article based on an interview with the noted Swiss historian, J. R. von Sali, would seem to corroborate such a general theory. Von Sali expresses surprise at his compatriots' conservatism and attributes it to their conviction that, having been spared by war, they have no obligation to participate in world affairs. It is as if, he says, they believed themselves to be living in 1914.[53]

The question of Swiss self-image and how that is translated into political decisions leads logically to the last question to be treated here, that of membership in the United Nations. As has already been mentioned, the Swiss recently defeated a referendum, by a surprising three-to-one margin, which would have cleared the way for full membership in the organization. The results of the vote are especially significant to the extent that the government had conducted an intensive publicity campaign in favor of membership. An article appearing in *The Economist* claims quite plausibly that the reason for the vote,

> apart from a feeling that to be entangled in the arguments of the UN's General Assembly would produce little advantage to anybody, seems to have been a desire not to put even the slightest question-mark over Switzerland's policy of permanent and strict armed neutrality. The decision of the Swiss not to get involved in anybody else's quarrels, from here until kingdom come, dates back to the sixteenth century. Is it compatible with taking part in the activities of the UN in New York? No, think most Swiss.[54]

Perhaps more interesting than the simple fact of the referendum's defeat are the decisiveness of the refusal, the fact that it came in spite of the government's campaign in favor of UN membership, and the fact that the participation rate in the vote was 50 percent, compared to the 35 percent normally achieved in such elections.[55] There is good reason to believe that many Swiss voters reacted negatively to what they considered the unseemly intervention of the government in this matter.

As may be imagined, a good deal of newsprint and talk was expended during the period preceding the referendum in discussing the pros and cons of full UN membership. The basic position of those opposing was that belonging to the United Nations would put Switzerland in a position where, under the terms of the UN Charter, it would be impossible to refuse participation in sanctions of various sorts that might be decided upon by the Security Council under the UN system of collective security. Of particular concern was the provision (Article 2, §5) which obliges members to participate in preventive or enforcement actions undertaken by the United Nations and to abstain from providing assistance to states against whom such actions may be directed. It was thought by many Swiss that assumption of such obligations would be totally incompatible with their policy of neutrality.[56]

The other argument against membership was that as a neutral, and a nonmember of the United Nations, Switzerland was better able to offer its good offices as an intermediary in resolving international conflicts. Roger Gallopin, former general director of the International Committee of the Red Cross, for example, dismissed the "rhetoric about the supposed isolation of Switzerland" and maintained that "it is in the best interest of the international community and of Switzerland that the latter abstain from becoming a member of the General Assembly."[57] The country would, it was argued, lose some of its prestige and credibility by joining the organization. That position was opposed by most of the large political parties, including the Socialists and Christian Democrats, who maintained that membership would, on the contrary, reinforce Switzerland's position in that respect. It was pointed out that since the end of the Second World War, Switzerland was being called upon less and less to furnish its good offices in such international disputes while neutrals who were also UN members, such as Austria and Sweden, were being asked increasingly to provide such services. The danger for Switzerland, they believed, lay in the sin of conceit: "The country which thinks that others cannot do without it is mistaken."[58] Curiously enough, in this election, there was a very significant difference between the position of the political parties at the national level, most of which were urging a positive vote, and the same parties at the cantonal and local levels, which opted for rejection.

Perhaps, though, the remark made at least partially in jest in *The Economist* article cited above--that entanglement in the General Assembly's arguments would be of little advantage to anybody--was determinative for many voters in the election. There is reason to believe that many Swiss were more influenced by such practical reasoning than by the somewhat abstract, intellectual arguments cited above. What is clear is that the results of the referendum reflect the fact that neutrality as a national policy has become so ingrained in the thinking of Swiss voters that it will be a long time before any proposal to modify it, in even the slightest way, will have the remotest chance of success. There is, moreover, little reason to think that the average Swiss voter has a more profound understanding of the complexities of that policy than do those of other countries of the different issues facing them. That being the case, it is probably true that a certain element of hubris is involved.

In conclusion, it is probably safe to assume that neither Switzerland's status as a neutral nor its way of implementing that status on the level of national security policy is likely to change significantly in the foreseeable future. In the final analysis, that prospect, while perhaps disheartening to critics of the current policy, and while perhaps an indictment of certain Swiss values, makes an important contribution to the international situation. The age of modern warfare has undoubtedly made Switzerland's historic role as a buffer state largely symbolic; nevertheless, the status it derives from its neutrality, and above all, from its political and economic stability make it an important feature of the contemporary international scene. In today's world, where the adversarial relationship between the superpowers has to some degree become one of the more stable aspects of international politics, the likelihood that Swiss policy will remain unchanged is particularly reassuring to both sides.

NOTES

[1]This long article appeared in the 31 October 1983 (pp. 50-117) and in the 7 November 1983 (pp. 55-112) issues of *The New Yorker*. The text was subsequently published as a book under the same title (New York: Farrar, Straus, and Giroux, 1984). It has enjoyed considerable success both in English and foreign-language versions and has attracted considerable attention in Switzerland.

[2]See Paul Widmer, "A Renewed Interest in Switzerland's Neutrality," *Wall Street Journal* (European ed.), 2 July 1984. More recently, an excellent comprehensive article on Switzerland by John J. Putman, "Switzerland: The Clockwork Country," appeared in *National Geographic* 169, no. 1 (January 1986): 96-126. The information about inquiries to the Information Section was conveyed through conversations with representatives of the Federal Military Department. It is appropriate to acknowledge the kind collaboration of the Military Department, and particularly of Messrs. Daniel Margot and Etienne Reichel of the Information Section, in arranging visits, interviews, and briefings, in supplying printed materials, and in generally furnishing all possible assistance. The authors also would like to express their sincere thanks to Michel Cluzel, Chantal Ostorero, Monique Savoy, and Professor G. P. Winnington for their invaluable assistance.

[3]"General defense" is the English translation of the French *défense générale*, or of the German *Gesamtverteidigung*. Unless otherwise indicated, all translations are by the authors.

[4]Among the sixteen specific duties assigned by the constitution to the Federal Council (the executive of the federal government) is the following: "It sees to the external security of Switzerland and to the maintenance of its independence and of its neutrality." (*Constitution fédérale de la Confédération suisse*, 29 May 1874, art. 102, §9.) Indeed, the third "strategic case" foreseen in Swiss military doctrine is that of the "protection of neutrality," which would involve the outbreak of hostilities in Europe, but without any direct Swiss involvement.

[5]These agreements were binding treaties between the cantons and foreign states which wished to have Swiss troops in their service. Swiss soldiers fighting for foreign governments were, therefore, not mercenaries in the strict sense of the word, since they were in fact in the service of their cantons.

[6]The textile industry depended heavily on Great Britain for its supply of wool; its sales of finished goods were widely exported to all of Europe and to North America.

[7]Maintaining a troop of 30,000 men cost about 10 million (1790) Swiss francs, while the treasury of Bern alone held some 200 million francs at the time. See Colonel EMG Daniel Reichel, "La Défense militaire de la neutralité suisse, hier et aujourd'hui--quelques considérations" (Bern: Service historique de l'armée, 1982): 8.

[8]Emanuel Diez, *Neutrality* (Bern: Département fédéral des affaires étrangères, 1985), pp. 11-12.

[9]Lucien Cramer, *Notre neutralité: Autrefois et aujourd'hui* (Geneva: Sanor, 1916), pp. 66-70.

[10]*Le droit de la guerre, le droit de la neutralité*, vol. 4 of *Répertoire suisse de droit international public* (Basel: Helbing und Lichtenhahn, 1975).

[11]Diez, *Neutrality*, p. 13.

[12]For general historical background see Roland Russieux, *La Suisse de l'entre-deux guerres* (Lausanne: Payot, 1974); and Hans Ulrich Jost, "Menace et repliement (1914-1945)," in *Nouvelle histoire de la Suisse et des Suisses* (Lausanne: Payot, 1983), pp. 91-178.

[13]Diez, *Neutrality*, pp. 14-16.

[14]Participating in the sanctions imposed against Italy by the League of Nations in fact stripped Switzerland of its neutral status.

[15]James Murray Luck, *A History of Switzerland* (Palo Alto, CA: Society for the Promotion of Science and Scholarship, 1985), p. 803.

[16]Ibid.

[17]Only 1,250 Swiss volunteered for SS service, and 1,500 Swiss civilians worked in Germany for the Nazi propaganda services. In Switzerland, the "fronts" (pro-Nazi parties) never attracted very many members. Their strength in Basel, for example, never went beyond 4,000. See, among others, Edgar Bonjour, *Histoire de la neutralité suisse: Quatre siècles de politique extérieure fédérale* (Neuchâtel: La Baconnière, 1970), 4:455-56.

[18]Diez, *Neutrality*, p. 23.

[19]For further information on this topic see, among others, Bernard Dutoit, *La Neutralité suisse à l'heure européenne* (Paris: Pichon-Durand, 1962); Peter Hofacher, "Wehrbereitschaft und Neutralität der Schweiz, Neutralitätsrechtliche Aspekte einer Atomwaffenbeschaffung und einer 'militärischen' Zusammenarbeit mit anderen Staaten," in *Allgemeine Schweitzerischen Militär Zeitschrift* 2 (1967): 65-69; Georges Perrin, *La Neutralité permanente de la Suisse et les organisations internationales* (Heule [Belgium]: U.G.A., 1964); and Dietrich Schindler et al., eds., *Dokumente zur Schweizerischen Neutralität seit 1945, Berichte und Stellungnahmen der Schweizerischen Bundesbehörden zu Frage der Neutralität, 1945-1983* (Bern and Stuttgart: Haupt, 1984).

[20]See Daniel Colard, "L'ONU a quarante ans: Réflexions pour un bilan," *Défense nationale* (February 1986): 68.

[21]On 21 December 1981 in the *Message concernant l'adhésion de la Suisse à l'Organisation des Nations Unies (ONU), Conseil fédéral* (Bern: Office fédéral des imprimés, 1981), p. 82.

[22]*Sélection hebdomadaire du journal "Le Monde,"* 13-19 March 1986. The actual vote was 1,591,428 against UN membership and 511,548 for it.

[23]Much of the information contained in this section was gathered during visits to Swiss military and civil defense installations and through conversations with officers and members of the Swiss military and civil defense forces. The authors wish to express their thanks to those in-

dividuals for the frank and open manner in which they were willing to cooperate in the present research.

[24]Hans Vogel, "Switzerland and the New Cold War: International and Domestic Determinants of Swiss Security Policy," in Bengt Sundelius, ed., *The Neutral Democracies and the New Cold War* (Boulder, CO: Westview Press, 1987), p. 107.

[25]Jean-Jacques Chouet, "Querelle d'Allemand en Russe," *Tribune de Genève*, 26 July 1985. Colonel Chouet notes that the principal criterion in selecting arms to be purchased is that of technical quality. He also adds that "it is clear that our [armaments] suppliers are in the west rather than in the east. After the excellent G-13 wheeled tank destroyers acquired from Czechoslovakia before the Soviet intervention there, communist Europe is no longer among those suppliers. It is not Switzerland's fault, but the USSR's, which only arms states in its sphere of influence or likely to serve its purposes." Vogel also remarks that "the almost total reliance on NATO technology is a delicate handicap to Swiss neutrality. In order to maintain credible neutrality in peace and war, Switzerland purchases western technology, wherever possible, in the form of contract licenses." "Switzerland in the New Cold War," p. 105.

[26]George Schwab, "Switzerland's Tactical Nuclear Weapons Policy," *Orbis* 13, no. 3 (Fall 1969): 914.

[27]Switzerland. *Rapport du Conseil fédéral à l'Assemblée fédérale sur la politique de sécurité de la Suisse (Conception de la défense générale)*, 27 June 1973, p. 40 (henceforth referred to as *Rapport sur la politique de sécurité*).

[28]Quoted in "La Suisse neutre . . . du même côté," *Tribune de Genève*, 1 February 1985.

[29]Quoted in "Un allié de l'OTAN," *24 Heures* (Lausanne), 17 July 1985, as well as in "USSR Condemns Swiss-US Military Ties," *Jane's Defence Weekly* 4, no. 4 (17 August 1985): 296.

[30]Yuri Karelov, "The Smaller Countries of Europe in the Modern World," *International Affairs* 2 (1986): 65-66.

[31]Switzerland. *Rapport intermédiaire concernant la politique de sécurité*, 3 December 1979, p. 4 (henceforth referred to as *Rapport intermédiaire*).

[32]Switzerland imports 100 percent of its raw materials, 82 percent of its energy, 45 percent of its food, and 27 percent of its manpower (*Introduction à la défense générale* [Bern: Office central de la défense, 1984], p. 7).

[33]*Rapport sur la politique de sécurité*, p. 14.

[34]Bénédikt Cramer, "Dissuasion infra-nucléaire," *Cahiers d'études stratégiques* (Paris), no. 4 (1984): 20-21, cited in *Introduction à la défense générale*, p. 16.

[35]*The Military Balance, 1986-1987* (London: International Institute for Strategic Studies, 1986), pp. 86-87.

[36]*Aperçu de l'armée suisse* (Neuchâtel: Denis Borel, 1984), p. 13. *The Military Balance, 1986-1987* also states the permanent strength of Swiss military professionals to be fifteen hundred. It is nevertheless true, as stated rather obliquely in the *Aperçu de l'armée suisse*, that the actual number of professional soldiers must be higher. In addition to the fifteen hundred instructors, there is also discussion of high-level employees of the army general staff and of commanders of divisions and equivalent units, all of whom are career officers. The precise number of officers involved is unclear.

[37]Switzerland. *Constitution fédérale de la Confédération suisse*, in *Constitution fédérale; Code civil suisse*, 4th ed. (Geneva: Chapalay & Mottier, n.d.), p. 4.

[38]*Rapport sur la politique de sécurité*, p. 25.

[39]See Gustav Däniker, "The Swiss Model of Conventional Defense," *Armed Forces Journal International* (July 1984): 33-43.

[40]Armed with 400 artillery pieces, 600 antitank guns, 250 antiaircraft guns, and 1,800 machine guns (*Aperçu de l'armée suisse*, p. 19).

[41]There appears to be some confusion about the length of these underground ammunition chambers. The (probably erroneous) figure given in the *Aperçu de l'armée suisse* is thirty kilometers (about 18.75 miles); an overhead slide used for briefings by the Federal Military Department, however, indicates the length to be in excess of eighty kilometers (about 50 miles). That latter figure also is confirmed by General Däniker's excellent article, cited above. The discrepancy is probably owing to a typographical error.

[42]McPhee, *La Place de la Concorde Suisse*, p. 57.

[43]*Military Balance, 1986-1987*, p. 212. Figures cited are for 1984.

[44]*Introduction à la défense générale*, p. 22.

[45]Armed neutrality assumes that an equally vigilant military eye be turned toward the threat presented by either side. While Swiss military planners have contingency plans covering attacks from virtually all sides, it would seem that those dealing with attacks from the east and northeast are the subject of the most attention.

[46]The *Rapport sur la politique de sécurité* states that a direct attack against Switzerland, supported by means of massive destruction, seems unlikely (p. 12).

[47]Figures on court-martial convictions and inductions are from overhead slides used for briefings by the Federal Military Department.

[48]John W. R. Taylor, ed., *Jane's All the World's Aircraft*, 1985-86 ed. (London: Jane's, 1985), p. 208.

[49]Safa Haeri, "Un Monomoteur au-dessus de tout soupçon," *L'Express*, no. 1736 (19 October 1984): 45.

[50]"Exportable sans autre," *24 Heures*, 12 March 1985.

[51]Haeri, "Un Monomoteur au-dessus de tout soupçon," p. 45.

[52]Vogel, "Switzerland and the New Cold War," p. 98.

[53]Pierre-André Stauffer, "Les Etats-Unis boudent l'Europe, c'est notre chance; Entretien avec Jean-Rodolphe de Salis," *L'Hebdo* 1 (30 December 1986): 10.

[54]"Guns for Neutrality," *The Economist* (28 March 1986): 49-50.

[55]"Swiss Vote by Wide Margin Not to Join U.N.," *New York Times*, 17 March 1986.

[56]*Charter of the United Nations and Statute of the International Court of Justice* (New York: United Nations, n.d.): 4. For an exhaustive treatment of this question see also Boleslaw A. Boczek, "Permanent Neutrality and Collective Security: The Case of Switzerland and the United Nations Sanctions against Southern Rhodesia," *Case Western Reserve Journal of International Law* 1, no. 2 (Spring 1969): 75-104.

[57]"Dernier recours," *Tribune de Genève*, 10 October 1985.

[58]"Il vaut mieux aller à l'ONU!" *La Suisse*, 14 January 1986.

SWEDEN

John Logue[1]

The increasing military pressure on the Nordic area following the end of superpower detente is likely to reduce the credibility of international action as a means toward furthering Swedish security. Swedish foreign policy stands the risk of going through a similar process of contraction such as occurred before 1939: from the solidaristic internationalism of the twenties, to an attempt to formulate a regional concept of security following the breakdown of the sanctions system of the League of Nations, and finally, in the neutral isolation of the war years, to an interpretation of the national interest so narrow that even Sweden's Nordic neighbors felt a sense of betrayal.

--Arne Ruth[2]

Since the "whiskey on the rocks" incident, when astonished Swedish fishermen found a Soviet *Whiskey* class submarine aground just outside the Swedish naval base at Karlskrona on 28 October 1981, Sweden's policy of nonalignment in times of peace and neutrality in times of war has been the subject of unaccustomed foreign attention and domestic discussion. Developed in the aftermath of the Napoleonic Wars, Swedish policy has rested on an unusual degree of realism about the military capacity of small powers. The Swedes have long reasoned that self-protection required at least rough parity with any force likely to be fielded against them. This has led them to maintain a relatively large military establishment. Today Sweden has, for example, more than twice as many combat aircraft as Denmark and Norway combined, and about two thirds as many as Britain or the Federal Republic of Germany. Although these high levels of military preparedness are maintained simultaneously with active promotion of international disarmament, Swedes find no incongruity in this situation. While armed neutrality has saddled them for practically all the postwar period with a proportionally heavier military budget than that of their Nordic neighbors, it also has stood the country in good stead.

The rapid development of military technology in the last quarter century has dramatically raised the costs of sustaining a credible defense. As long as détente between the United States and the Soviet Union continued, the problems raised by this situation did not seem particularly salient. The Nordic area was a region of low tension because of Swedish and Finnish nonalignment, despite the fact that the contiguous Kola Peninsula had become the base for three-fifths of the Soviet submarine-based nuclear force. With the collapse of détente, it became more difficult to ignore the obvious: the policy that had served Sweden well for 170 years was again under pressure.

Before beginning a detailed discussion, three basic parameters of Swedish nonalignment should be mentioned. The first is the obvious: the country's geographic placement on the periphery of Europe. The Scandinavian peninsula, which it shares with Norway, offers no highroad to conquest elsewhere. Indeed, much of it is impassable. Sweden's location, unquestionably, has been the principal factor sustaining its neutrality: to attack Sweden produces few strategic advantages.

Second, Swedish neutrality differs from that of other European neutrals like Switzerland, Austria, and Finland in having no basis in international treaties or bilateral agreements. The Swedish policy of nonalignment in peace, aiming at neutrality in war, is the nation's security policy, self-proclaimed and self-maintained. As such, it is grounded in a realism that seems almost cynical to outsiders. Although other powers have clearly benefited from that policy, it has evolved out of Sweden's interests, not those of its neighbors, yet it must be credible if it is to serve as a guarantee of what has come to be called "the Nordic balance"--the political and military balance between NATO and the Soviet Union on the northern flank of Europe which has maintained that region as one of relatively low tension. That credibility is not only a result of military strength but also of political will, and it rests in no small measure on massive popular support. After the Normandy invasion was a clear success, when it might have seemed opportune to join the Allies, polls indicated that Swedes reaffirmed their support for neutrality by 96 percent to 1 percent.[3] The preservation of that neutrality is one of the few basic tenets of Swedish policy on which all parties and nine-tenths of the voters agreed.

Third, although Swedish neutrality has existed since 1815, its outward reach has waxed and waned in response to international and domestic pressure. At its flood tide, Swedes sought to extend their neutrality to the Nordic countries generally and took an active role in the promotion of international cooperation and disarmament outside the region. At its ebb, Sweden's neutrality was isolationist, and Swedes perceived their responsibilities to stop at their own borders. The reason is simple enough. While neutrality since the triumph of the democratic popular movements at the end of World War I clearly has had strong moral overtones, its overriding aim has been identical with the neutrality of predemocratic days: to keep Sweden out of war.

PREHISTORY OF SWEDISH NEUTRALITY

There was a time when Sweden was as bellicose as any other European power. From its rebellion against Denmark under Gustav Vasa in 1521 until the Treaty of Nystad in 1721, Sweden was at war as often as it was not. In the period from Gustav II Adolf's[4] entry into the Thirty Years' War in 1630 until Karl XII's defeat at Poltava in 1709, Sweden was numbered among the European great powers. During that three-quarters of a century, the Baltic was little more than a Swedish lake, and the country was regularly entangled in alliances of its own and others' making. Subsequently, from the Treaty of Nystad to the end of the Napoleonic Wars, Swedish dreams of recovering the lost empire continued sporadically to shape the nation's policies. That 1815 would mark a watershed--the advent of more than 170 years of peace--certainly could not have been predicted on the basis of Swedish behavior prior to that date.

The Swedish state that entered the European arena under Gustav Vasa (1496-1560; king 1523-1560) was small in population and relatively backward economically, yet it had several notable advantages. The feudal legacy in Sweden was weak; half the land in 1520 was owned by peasant farmers. The new state's establishment coincided with the Reformation, and the Crown was the prime beneficiary of the seizure of Church lands which provided the spoils necessary to solidify secular loyalty to the new regime. Starting from scratch, Gustav Vasa laid the foundations for what was, by the standards of his times, a modern state administration; that administration was perfected by his grandson Gustav II Adolf (1594-1632; king 1611-

1632) and his highly capable chancellor, Axel Oxenstierna. The virtual Swedish monopoly on European copper production and Swedish customs duties on the Russian and, after the 1620s, the Polish Baltic trade provided a firm financial basis for the state.

The relative efficiency of the state administration and its openness to new ideas and technology[5] explain much of Swedish military prowess in the century between Gustav II Adolf's accession to the throne in 1611 and Karl XII's defeat by the Russians at Poltava in 1709. Although the population in 1630 was only about 1.5 million--roughly 900,000 in Sweden, 375,000 in Finland, and 225,000 in the Baltic provinces[6]--the Swedish state was able to muster, in Gustav II Adolf's day, a conscripted army of 70,000, supplied by a highly efficient state-sponsored defense industry at home.[7] Moreover, despite his use of mercenaries to good effect in Germany, Gustav Adolf was convinced of the superiority of national troops. The reform of the conscription system under Karl XI (king 1680-1697) produced a regular army of about 40,000 and a navy of about 11,000 (the Karlskrona naval base was opened during his reign). Karl XII (1682-1718; king 1697-1718) would use it to raise army after army.

For a century the edge in modernity of administration and military production gave competent kings the wherewithal to make Sweden a great power, despite the general backwardness of the economy and society. But in time Sweden's opponents, notably the Russians under Peter the Great, undertook their own reforms. By Poltava, the size of population clearly told. Karl could raise fresh armies, but so too could the Russians.

The Peace of Nystad in 1721 crowned Sweden's defeat by the Russians in the Great Northern War. Sweden was forced to surrender its Baltic provinces; beside the core of the kingdom in Sweden and Finland, it retained only a small part of Pomerania. Karl XII's wars left the country battered and impoverished. Casualties, Russian raids, and hunger cost Sweden and Finland one-eighth of their population. The obvious disaster of Karl XII's military adventures convinced the nobility of the need to avoid a repetition, and they took steps to establish a constitutional regime upon Karl's death in 1718. For half a century the royal fixation on recovering Sweden's territorial losses in the east was stymied by a strong parliament and by regular foreign intrigue and bribery there. The "age of freedom," as this period of parliamentary supremacy was known, lasted until Gustav III (1746-1792; king 1771-1792) staged a royal coup d'état in 1772 immediately after ascending the throne.

Gustav III's and Gustav IV Adolf's attempts to replay their predecessors' foreign wars started in farce and ended in tragedy. In 1788, Gustav III took advantage of the outbreak of Russo-Turkish hostilities to take Sweden to war against its eastern neighbor. He circumvented the Riksdag's prohibition against waging aggressive war by dressing a detachment of Swedish troops in Cossack uniforms borrowed from the Royal Opera and attacking one of his own border posts in Finland. Gustav III got the war he sought but produced a virtual mutiny among Finnish officers; his response in attacking the nobility led to his assassination in 1792. The war was badly mismanaged, but Sweden escaped disaster by winning a major naval victory at Svensksund, off Finland, in July 1790.

His son and successor Gustav IV Adolf (1778-1837; king 1792-1809) followed him in attempting to emulate Gustav II Adolf and Karl XII. Gustav IV Adolf was easily drawn into the war on the Continent, marching out of Swedish Pomerania in 1805, but his army was defeated in 1806 by French Marshal Bernadotte. Worse was to come. Within months after Napoleon and Alexander's meeting at Tilsit gave the latter a free hand, Alexander turned on his erstwhile ally and attacked Finland. Although the Swedes were capable of fielding there an army that was not notably inferior to the Russian forces available in that arena, disastrous mismanagement quickly lost Finland. The fighting continued and before the end, Russian troops took the Åland Islands and parts of northern Sweden. Finally, in desperation, Georg Adlersparre, one of the Swedish commanders on the Norwegian front, reached an agreement with the Danes (who were fighting on the Russian side) which permitted him to disengage, march on Stockholm, depose Gustav IV Adolf, reestablish a constitutional regime, and make peace.

The military coup d'état of 1809 changed more than the personnel of government. Under the pressure of the war with Russia, a new constitution was hastily drafted which divided powers between the monarchy and the Estates General and circumscribed royal powers. Gustav IV Adolf's uncle, Duke Karl (1748-1818; king 1809-1818), who served as regent until the constitution was approved, was promptly elected king under it. Karl XIII was old, feeble (though he would reign until 1818), and lacked an heir. The Swedes first turned to Danish Prince Christian August, commander of the Danish forces in Norway, who had tacitly supported the overthrow of Gustav IV Adolf. He was proclaimed crown prince in 1809 but died the following year of a fall from his horse, apparently caused by a stroke, although poison was widely suspected at the time. The Swedes then elected as their crown prince Jean-Baptiste Bernadotte (1763-1844; king, as Karl XIV Johan, 1818-1844), the French marshal who had defeated Gustav's army in Germany in 1806. The choice was a dramatic break with tradition: Bernadotte was a lawyer's son. He was, however, in effect, also a member of Napoleon's family. His wife, Désirée Clary, was the sister of Joseph Bonaparte's wife, and Désirée had been Napoleon's first fiancée. Bernadotte's selection was dictated by the desire for a French alliance to recover Finland.

That was not to be. Bernadotte demonstrated the flexibility that made him the only one of Napoleon's family to retain his throne. He converted to Lutheranism while passing through Denmark en route to Sweden, took the name Karl Johan, and was adopted by Karl XIII as his son. Without the fixation of his predecessors on the historical boundaries of Sweden-Finland or on Sweden's possessions in Germany, Karl Johan moved quickly to reverse the Swedish orientation from east to west. With the excuse provided by the French occupation of Pomerania in January 1812, Karl Johan denounced the Swedish-French alliance and negotiated instead a pact with Alexander which promised Norway, part of Denmark since 1380, to Sweden. With Napoleon's defeat in Russia, Prussia and England were induced to recognize Sweden's claim to Norway in order to persuade Karl Johan to join the battle on the Continent. The campaign culminated in October 1813 at Leipzig, where Karl Johan led one of the three allied armies against his former commander. Turning north, he forced Denmark, which was still inopportunely allied with Napoleon, out of the war, and by the Treaty of Kiel (1814) took Norway in exchange for Swedish Pomerania and the Norwegian portion of the Danish national debt.

The Norwegians, who had not been consulted, demonstrated little enthusiasm for the Swedish plans, drafted their own constitution, elected a Danish prince as king, and prepared to resist. But Karl Johan moved rapidly against Norway, and, after a brief campaign, made a generous settlement in which he accepted a loose union that restricted the rights of the king relative to the Norwegian parliament far more than the new Swedish constitution did.

Karl Johan escaped the obligation to turn Pomerania over to Denmark by arguing that the Danes had not surrendered Norway peaceably, but he had the judgment to sell Pomerania promptly to the Prussians. The loss of Finland and the disposal of Sweden's continental outpost removed what had been the two principal sources of Swedish involvement in foreign wars from 1660 to 1815.

Now Sweden occupied the entire Scandinavian peninsula, and its one remaining land border (with Russian Finland in the north) was in a thinly populated area that made it an unlikely source of conflict. The stage was set for neutrality.

DEVELOPMENT OF SWEDISH NEUTRALITY

Neutrality by Accident

Since the end of the Napoleonic Wars, Sweden has avoided war, a record matched in Europe only by Switzerland. Today, Swedish nonalignment in peace and neutrality in war is a policy sanctified by more than 170 years of peace. It is so much a part of the national tradition as to be beyond political dispute; almost alone among significant Swedish policies, neutrality enjoys the support of all parties and major interest groups. Yet that development was hardly a foregone conclusion in 1815. In fact, Swedish nonalignment of the postwar period was preceded by a century and a quarter in which Sweden avoided alliances and involvement in wars more by a combination of the caution and opportunism of its leaders and the fear of domestic opposition (with a substantial admixture of good fortune) than out of any clarity in vision or policy.

The development of security policy through the nineteenth century in Sweden reflected some very basic changes in military realities. At the beginning of the century, the possibility of Sweden's winning a war against Russia, assuming that the latter was fighting on some second front too, lay within the bounds of sane calculation. The Swedes were badly beaten in 1808-09, but that was more a product of Gustav IV Adolf's incompetence than of numerical inferiority; the army fielded by the Swedes was essentially the equal of the one the Russians committed. That Sweden avoided war with Russia after 1814 was not the result of principled neutrality. It rather reflected Karl Johan's caution in the early part of the century, especially in 1834 during the Near East crisis between Britain and Russia,[8] and the fact that the British and French refused to commit themselves during the Crimean War to Swedish recovery of Finland in order to bring Sweden into the war on the allied side.

The Swedish attitude toward military adventures on the Continent changed as well. Sweden and Norway did provide troops for the defense of Denmark proper (but not Schleswig) in 1848; they were used as a peace-keeping force in Schleswig after the armistice in 1849. But that commitment of Swedish troops to defend Denmark's borders was not matched despite royal promises in 1864, and the Danes were left to face the Austrians and Prussians alone. Swedish intervention was not even suggested subsequently during the Austro-Prussian War in 1866 or during the Franco-Prussian War. With German unification, the military equation had clearly shifted against Sweden, and, in time, Oscar II (1829-1907; king 1872-1907) came to admire the new German state. Moreover, Swedish neutrality in the last quarter of the century took on a decidedly pro-German cast. The Germans reciprocated by offering aid against the threatened Norwegian rebellion, which finally came to a head in 1905 after some two decades of rising tension when the Norwegian parliament unilaterally--and unanimously--declared the union dissolved. There was strong sentiment in Sweden to use its superior military strength to reestablish the union. The Norwegians mobilized, but again caution prevailed: Crown Prince Gustav (1858-1950; king, as Gustav V, 1907-1950) urged recognition of Norwegian independence, and the Social Democrats threatened a general strike if the government resorted to force. Under strong domestic pressure, the Swedish government eventually opted against military intervention and conceded Norwegian independence.

The domestic political situation changed as much as the military equation in the latter half of the nineteenth century. Although Sweden remained backward industrially relative to the Continent, the same sorts of social forces were building up, and the same political demands were made. The refusal by the government to support the king blocked Swedish intervention in the war between the Danes and Prussia and Austria in 1864. The replacement of the old Estates General with a modern, bicameral parliament in 1866 and the rapid growth in representation, first for the Liberals and then for the Social Democrats, increased pressure within Parliament and outside it to avoid military adventures. Both Liberals and Social Democrats opposed military spending which, as they saw it, strengthened the hands of their opponents, the dominant Conservatives. While the Swedish military might not be very useful against the Russians or Germans, they feared that it was eminently useful against Swedish democrats. The impact of the Liberal-Social Democratic pressure from below is clearest in 1905, when the threat of a general strike against the application of Swedish military force in Norway played a significant role in deterring Swedish use of arms.

The Norwegians subsequently were able to establish their independence. Thus, by the turn of the century, the power to determine issues of war and peace was passing out of the hands of the king and his Conservative advisers and into a far broader circle.

During the twenty years before World War I the debate about military preparedness became entangled in the struggle for political democracy. Despite its long parliamentary tradition, Sweden was not a democracy. Restricted suffrage and an upper house indirectly elected by a system that gave property owners multiple votes guaranteed political power to a tiny, well-to-do minority. It seemed briefly in 1901 that Conservatives would accept a broader suffrage in return for Liberal support for their defense measures, but ultimately universal military service was legislated in that year without universal suffrage. Conservatives received approval for fortifications in the north of the country at the turn of the century and a major naval construction program a decade later. The Liberal government stopped the so-called F-boat battleship program in 1911, but the *Sverige* was finished by popular subscription. Both left and right mobilized massive demonstrations to support their respective sides in the defense issue, and Liberal Prime Minister Karl Staaff was forced from office in the aftermath of a Conservative demonstration in 1914. If there was consensus in any area of Swedish politics, this was not it.

Neutrality by Design

Between 1815 and the turn of the century, Sweden had stayed out of war more by luck, accident, and inertia than by principle. If there is any common denominator for Swedish declarations of neutrality during that period, it was that neutrality was the opportune choice. But the rapidly growing strength of the democratic parties produced a sea change in the early years of this century. The acceptance of Norwegian independence became a harbinger of the future policy of neutrality, even when military adventures might have seemed opportune.

In 1912, during the intermittent crises in the Balkans and North Africa that preceded World War I, Sweden joined Denmark and Norway in affirming its commitment to neutrality. When war broke out in 1914, Sweden first unilaterally reaffirmed its neutrality on 3 August and then again, together with Norway, on 8 August. Even so, Sweden barely escaped involvement. On 9 August the Russian

Baltic fleet sailed from Helsinki to attack the Swedish fleet. The Russians had no faith in Swedish protestations of neutrality and assumed such declarations were probably a cover for preparing common action with Germany, but they recalled the fleet at the halfway point. It was deemed better for Russia to wait and see than to guarantee Swedish involvement on the German side through a preemptive strike.

Russian fears were not groundless. Pro-German sentiment in Sweden proved strong among the nobility and seems to have been shared by Gustav V. Germany represented a bastion of conservative values not unlike Sweden's, while Russia remained the hereditary enemy. Moreover, the Germans held out the possibility of restoring Finland to Sweden. However, domestic opposition was also strong. Although the Conservatives beat the Liberals soundly in the first election in 1914, the Social Democrats continued to gain strength and, in the second election in 1914, passed the Conservatives to become the largest party in the lower house. As the war on the Continent continued, the political tide in Sweden swept leftward as the disruptions of normal economic activity and food shortages took their toll. In the election of 1917, before universal suffrage was implemented, the Conservatives lost one-third of their seats in the lower house, and a revolutionary left Socialist party--the *Vänster-socialisterna*--polled one vote in twelve. Thus, German pressure on Sweden to enter the war on the German side failed in 1915 and again in December 1917, when the Bolshevik Revolution offered the Swedes a free hand in the Åland Islands.

Sweden came through the war with its productive capacity intact and with substantial export earnings. It had rearmed, for the outbreak of the war had put an end to the dispute about linking defense to reforms. Sweden also achieved full political democracy when the Russian, German, and Austrian revolutions of 1917-18 made the handwriting on the wall clear to all but the most recalcitrant conservatives. The reforms of 1918-1921 finally established universal and equal suffrage in the elections to both houses of Parliament. The consequence of these changes was to tilt the balance of political power to the popular forces--Liberals, Agrarians, and Social Democrats--who were antimilitarists by tradition. They saw neutrality not only as opportune, but it was also their preferred course.

In that crucial period in which the modern political system was being established in Sweden, the cultural nationalism of the democratic movement--liberal, farm, and labor--came into conflict with the military nationalism of the old ruling class. The democratic popular movements feared, realistically, that the army was more suitable for use against domestic than foreign opponents. The democrats claimed nationalism for their own and derided the delusions of chauvinistic military grandeur that still filled the minds of conservatives.[9] For the left, patriotism, common sense, and democratic aspirations all argued for neutrality and disarmament. For the right, from the vantage point of hindsight, neutrality had been an astonishing success; the apparently realistic alternative, the German alliance, would have brought defeat and, presumably, revolution in its wake. The lesson was reasonably clear.

Sweden passed quickly from the control of a conservative, nondemocratic regime into an egalitarian, Social Democratic one, with only a brief Liberal interlude. While the first purely Social Democratic government formed in Sweden lasted only a matter of months in 1920, more stable Social Democratic governments held power from 1921 to 1923 and from 1924 to 1926. In 1932, Social Democrats returned to power and remained there alone or in coalition until 1976, yielding office only for two months in the summer of 1936. It was an unparalleled record of longevity in democratic government. For Swedish Social Democrats, like their party comrades elsewhere at the time, promoting disarmament and international cooperation and avoiding capitalistic alliances were cornerstones of proper working-class foreign policy.

Sweden began the interwar period with an early version of what has since become known as the "policy of active neutrality." This policy, which represented the flood tide of the extension of Swedish neutrality, sought to modify the international environment by promoting the relaxation of tensions and international cooperation. This role was not, however, easily adopted initially. The vote divided on joining the League of Nations, but the pro-League group won, in part because of the erroneous assumption that American membership was inevitable. There was an initial fear that League membership would commit Sweden to military sanctions--the League, after all, had grown out of a wartime alliance--and Sweden specifically ruled out that option in 1924; that the League would prove incapable of military action was not foreseen. The Social Democrats quickly ascertained the opportunities presented by the League and sent topflight delegates: Hjalmar Branting, the party's leader and prime minister, was the Swedish delegate until 1925, and he was followed by Östen Undén, who served for twenty-five years in the cabinet, principally as foreign minister after World War II.[10]

The new Swedish policy also involved support for international arbitration as a means of settling disputes among nations. The first example, the Åland Islands case, hardly reassured the Swedes. The islands in the Gulf of Bothnia had been part of Sweden until the loss of Finland to Russia in 1809, and they were of strategic importance both to newly independent Finland and to Sweden. The population was almost entirely Swedish and, in 1919, 95 percent voted in favor of reunification. Finland responded by sending troops. Both Finland and Sweden agreed to the League's binding arbitration, the former reluctantly, the latter enthusiastically. When the League's special commission awarded Åland to Finland, Swedish disgust was unconcealed.[11] Yet Sweden persisted in being an outstanding supporter of the League and its efforts to settle disputes by peaceful means. What real defense, Swedish leaders argued, did small nations have other than strengthening international law? When Conservative Foreign Minister Carl Hederstierna in 1923 advocated a Swedish-Finnish defense agreement directed against the Soviet Union, he was forced from office.

Had the rest of the world emulated the Nordic area (Denmark and Norway also accepted international adjudication of their quarrel over the ownership of East Greenland[12]), the interwar period would have been far more peaceful. But it was not, and the collective security system of the League broke down as the organization proved unable to impose effective sanctions on aggressors. By the time the Scandinavian countries finally withdrew from the sanction system in disgust in 1938, the League's hopes for maintaining peace were in shambles.

After the Nazis' assumption of power in 1933, the Swedish government gradually retreated from the international arena to explore narrower alternatives, including a regional Scandinavian defense union proposed by the Danish government out of concern with developments south of its border. The additional possibility of Swedish-Finnish military cooperation to protect the Åland Islands became the subject of serious negotiations. However, in 1937, in the face of rapid German rearmament, the Danes withdrew their support of a Scandinavian defense pact, which Prime Minister Thorvald Stauning, who had made the original proposal, now called utopian and likely to decrease Danish security by the implicit threat such a pact posed to Germany. Instead of collective security, the Scandinavian countries reaffirmed their individual neutrality in a jointly drafted declaration in the spring of 1938, but pressure quickly increased.

In the aftermath of the Austrian *Anschluss* and the Munich agreement, the Nazis pressed all the Scandinavian countries for nonaggression pacts. The Danes signed, the Social Democratic-Radical Liberal government having long concluded that Denmark was indefensible. Norway was more defensible but equally unprepared. Only Sweden and Finland, which had undertaken rearmament in the 1930s after the sharp arms reduction of the 1920s, were in any way prepared militarily for what was to come, but the proposed Swedish-Finnish pact for the defense of the Åland Islands, which would have linked them militarily, foundered on Soviet opposition in 1939.

The Ribbentrop-Molotov pact in August 1939 freed the Soviets to develop a better defensive perimeter in the west. In September the USSR forced the Baltic states to agree to Soviet bases on their territory. In October similar Soviet demands for military bases in Finland, in return for Soviet territorial concessions, were met by Finnish rejection. The three Scandinavian states offered the Finns rhetorical support, but when the Soviets invaded at the end of November, Denmark and Norway proclaimed their neutrality in the struggle. Sweden, however, declared itself a nonbelligerent and pursued a policy that one director of the Swedish Institute of International Affairs would describe as "nonbelligerent interventionism";[13] Sweden resupplied the Finns from its military stores and permitted Swedish volunteers to join in the fray. Again the Swedish role, which the Soviet Union protested bitterly as anything but neutral, was cautious: while the Swedes had permitted the transit of British and French weapons to the Finns, on 3 March 1940, they rejected a British and French query as to whether the transit of troops to Finland would be permitted. The rationale was to prevent Scandinavia (and Sweden) from being a theater of war for outside powers.

The threat to Swedish neutrality posed by the Winter War was removed by Finnish defeat and the peace of March 1940. A worse danger followed promptly. On the morning of 9 April, German troops invaded both Denmark and Norway. Denmark fell quickly, but the Norwegians fought on for two months in the north with British aid. Again public sentiment in Sweden demanded support, and again the government equivocated. The danger of a Nazi invasion was perceived to be immediate.

Despite rapid rearmament in 1939,[14] Sweden's ability to defend itself against the Germans in 1940 was strictly limited. As a consequence, after the fall of France, the Swedish interpretation of the meaning of neutrality was flexible and pro-German. Neutrality, as Wilhelm Carlgren puts it, "covered all measures which served to keep Sweden out of war, whether or not they were consistent with the rules of neutrality in international law."[15] Sweden became a route for resupplying German troops in northern Norway. After 22 June 1941, Finland reopened hostilities, using the opportunity provided by the German invasion of the Soviet Union to try to recover what it had lost in 1940. Sweden not only permitted German supplies to be transported across its territory to the Finnish-Soviet front, but it also allowed an entire German division to cross from Norway to Finland.

This was the cause of immense controversy within Sweden's national unity coalition government, which included Liberals and Conservatives as well as Agrarians and Social Democrats. The Social Democrats were generally opposed, but they bowed to the views of their coalition partners and King Gustav's threat to abdicate "rather than risk war by saying no."[16] While the Swedes excused the act as being a one-time concession to Germany which served to support the Finns, it was similar to what they had earlier refused to let the British do. The ultimate difference, however, was the realistic fear that the alternative to agreement would be a German attack. In the first years of the war, the Swedish government permitted German troop transports to sail through its territorial waters and German planes to use its air space. Swedish industry supplied Germany with key war materiel as well as civilian goods and extended economic aid and credit to Finland.

Only after the German defeats in 1943 in North Africa and at Stalingrad did the Swedish position begin to change. Sweden reduced its trade with Germany, provided sanctuary for Norwegian and Danish resistance groups, and, as the war moved toward an end, trained Danish and Norwegian security forces who would play a role in the liberation of their respective countries. Swedish humanitarian aid included sheltering the entire Danish Jewish community, 35,000 Estonian refugees, and 70,000 Finnish children; toward the end of the war, Count Folke Bernadotte arranged the transportation to Sweden of some 19,000 Danish and Norwegian prisoners in Nazi concentration camps.

The German surrender in May 1945 brought a national collective sigh of relief. Although Sweden's pursuit of international collective security and, subsequently, of a regional defense pact in the interwar period had been in vain, through its isolated neutrality it escaped war and the accompanying destruction. Indeed, the national industrial base had expanded, and the end of the war ushered in an era of unparalleled prosperity that derived, in no small measure, from Swedish exports to devastated Europe. The Swedes drew the obvious conclusions that neutrality had served them well and that it had been preserved by a combination of military preparedness and flexibility in policy.

A NEUTRAL NORDEN?[17]

The Nordic world of June 1945 was very different from that of June 1939. To the east, Finland had fought two wars against the Soviet Union; while the first had been forced upon it, the second had been chosen in alliance with the Germans. Although Finland had lost both, it nonetheless had saved its independence through a successful effort to stop the Soviet offensive in summer 1944 and a timely separate armistice in September 1944, which the Swedes, as intermediaries, had encouraged. Its scope for independence in foreign and military policy was, however, strictly circumscribed by the terms of the armistice, which included stationing Soviet troops at the Finnish base at Porkkala. To the west and south, Norway and Denmark had been occupied despite their neutrality and had become unwilling participants on the Allied side; finally Iceland, which had been part of Denmark since 1380, used the opportunity presented by its occupation by the British and Americans to proclaim its independence in 1944. The various Resistance groups that had grown up in Norway and Denmark had close ties either to Great Britain or to the Soviet Union. Neutral Scandinavia had been caught in a web of foreign entanglements neither of its making nor choosing. Only Sweden had escaped.

In the immediate aftermath of the war, the Swedes sought to restore the nonaligned status quo ante in the Nordic area within the new world order that was expected. In 1946, Sweden followed its Scandinavian neighbors into the United Nations. It was the Swedish hope, as it was in other countries, that this broadening of the wartime Allied coalition would be able to maintain the peace as the League had not. This time, after all, the United States had joined. Sweden was enthusiastic in its support, in part because of the role of Trygve Lie, the Norwegian Social Democrat who served as the first UN secretary-general, and took an active role in early UN efforts to reduce tension.[18]

But as tensions rose in 1946-47, postwar hopes dissipated. The proclamation of the Truman Doctrine, the Marshall Plan and its rejection in the East, and the hardening lines of division in Germany were all disturbing. The parallels to the prewar period were frightening. When British Foreign Secretary Ernest Bevin suggested in January 1948 the need for a European alliance extending beyond Britain's closest neighbors, he touched off a major foreign policy debate in the Scandinavian countries. Should nonalignment be maintained? Östen Undén, the Swedish foreign minister, replied with alacrity in the Riksdag that "we do not want, through prior commitments, to deprive ourselves of the right and possibility of remaining outside a new war."[19] The Danes and Norwegians initially pursued parallel courses, but the Communist coup d'état in Czechoslovakia at the end of February and increasing Soviet pressure on Finland (that finally resulted in the Finno-Soviet Treaty of 1948) made the maintenance of neutrality by individual nations seem increasingly precarious. The signing of the Brussels Pact by France, Britain, Belgium, the Netherlands, and Luxembourg on 17 March 1948 marked the formal resurrection of the old system of military alliances.

On 1 May 1948, as the Social Democratic party leaders then in office in all three countries made the traditional May Day addresses (Danish Prime Minister Hans Hedtoft stressed the need to preserve a common Scandinavian foreign policy), Sweden proposed an independent Scandinavian defense agreement in a private communication to the Danes and the Norwegians. For Sweden, the aim essentially was to adapt nonalignment to the new context. Unarmed, isolated national neutrality had demonstrated its limits on 9 April 1940. Armed neutrality, however, had kept Sweden out of war. While the Swedes doubted the defensibility of Denmark and specifically excluded the possibility of a bilateral Swedish-Danish pact in 1949, a reasonably armed Swedish-Norwegian agreement might have protected Norway in 1940. A Scandinavian pact might keep all three out of another war. Sweden had emerged from World War II with substantial military capacity; its air force, for instance, was second only in Europe to Britain's. It seemed plausible that expanding Swedish armed neutrality to a regional pact might be a viable mechanism for confining East-West tensions to occupied Central Europe and for lessening the likelihood of serious Soviet pressure on Finland.

In the effort to create a Scandinavian defense pact, the chief protagonists were the Norwegian Labor and Swedish Social Democratic governments. While their policies in domestic affairs, ideologies, and bases of support were similar, their experiences during the war were fundamentally different. The Norwegian experience--occupation, resistance, and a government-in-exile in London--left the Norwegian Labor government with a healthy respect for great powers, both as friends and enemies. The Swedes emerged from their wartime experience with the conviction that neutrality was eminently sustainable, provided that the government was astute and the country well armed.

Negotiations between the Scandinavian countries in the fall of 1948 took place under outside pressure. Denmark and Norway were given to understand that they would be invited to join an Atlantic pact. The discussions between the three countries started without a public avowal of the Swedish premise that neutrality was the sine qua non for a Scandinavian pact; the Norwegians were not eager to compromise themselves vis-à-vis possible membership in an Atlantic alliance. The Danes expressed support for a Scandinavian agreement, even suggesting to Bevin that an invitation to join the Atlantic alliance was untimely while negotiations continued, but the Norwegians were more dubious of the viability of such an agreement in a world bifurcated between East and West with Scandinavia in between.

On 5 and 6 January 1949, the three countries' prime ministers and foreign and defense ministers met in Karlstad. The proposal before them called for establishing a regional defense pact within the framework provided by Article 52 of the UN Charter with a military buildup in Denmark and Norway, the modernization of Swedish forces, and coordination of defense planning and production. A résumé released by the Danish Foreign Ministry in 1968 divulged the negotiators' basic premise that the pact would have a deterrent effect both by making potential aggressors consider the power of the pact and by making outside support more likely in the event the group was the target of aggression.[20]

The Swedish government insisted at Karlstad that none of the pact's members should be linked to any other alliance, but foreign sources of weapons were vital to the military viability of the project. The U.S. government announced on 14 January that countries allied formally to the United States would have first priority in acquiring American weapons. At the negotiations in Copenhagen on 22-24 January 1949, the Norwegians insisted that Scandinavian security should be approached within the context of the general question of Western defense. A Scandinavian pact was viable, in their view, only if linked to the Atlantic alliance. The latter was precisely what was unacceptable to the Swedes. Negotiations collapsed. February found Norwegian Foreign Minister Halvard Lange in Washington to discuss Norwegian membership in NATO, and the Danish foreign minister followed suit. In April they were back again to sign the North Atlantic Treaty. General Scandinavian neutrality was a thing of the past.[21] The Swedes once again found themselves in splendid, isolated neutrality between the blocs.

MAINTAINING SWEDISH NONALIGNMENT

In the new configuration, with Norway and Denmark in NATO and Finland linked to the Soviet Union through the Treaty of Friendship, Cooperation, and Mutual Assistance of 1948,[22] Sweden alone remained completely nonaligned. Where the Nordic countries had pursued parallel courses before the war, there were now three divergent paths.[23] Yet, while the Nordic countries had accommodated themselves to a bipolar world, they retained a strong degree of community even in diversity and considerable allegiance to their traditional nonalignment which Swedish policy sought to encourage. Thus Norway, while an eager founding member of NATO, rejected stationing foreign troops on Norwegian soil at the time it joined; Denmark followed its lead in 1953. Both Denmark and Norway rejected stationing nuclear weapons on their territory and renounced their development; Sweden has done the same. While Norway is the only NATO country to share a border in Europe with the Soviet Union--and the Norwegian border is close to the key Soviet naval installations on the Kola Peninsula--it has only minimal forces close to it. Svalbard, which is part of Norway, is demilitarized under the treaty of 1920 and, while under Norwegian administration, has a substantial Russian community; after the war, Norway required that the United States vacate its radio station on Jan Mayen, another Norwegian arctic island. The Åland Islands are demilitarized by an international agreement of 1921. And the Faeroe Islands, which are part of Denmark, have a radar station that is part of NATO's early warning system, but no foreign NATO personnel.

The Soviet Union also has demonstrated restraint in the region. The Red Army liberated both northern Norway and Bornholm from the German occupation and then withdrew. While the Finnish armistice of 1944 turned a military base in Porkkala over to the Soviets and Finland was linked with the USSR by treaty in 1948, the Soviets relinquished the major naval base of Porkkala in 1955 and have had no troops in Finland since. When the Soviets pressed in 1961 for military consultations with the Finns, President Urho Kekkonen argued against the idea. The Finnish position was backed by the Swedes and by Norwegian threats to permit the stationing of foreign troops on its soil in peacetime, invoking the need to preserve the Nordic balance.[24]

What has come to be called the Nordic balance refers to the fact that, since the beginning of the Cold War, the Nordic area has been one of low tension and relatively low force levels. In the early part of the period, that condition was a consequence of the marginal importance of the region to the United States and the USSR, as well as of the substantial force the Swedes could field. More recently, the importance of the region has increased dramatically with the Soviet naval buildup in the Kola Peninsula. There has been an accompanying increase in Soviet ground forces in the area, but their number and armaments seem more appropriate to the defense of the naval facilities on Kola than to offensive action.[25] The Soviet Kola facilities would, however, permit rapid deployment of significant offensive strength, and past low force levels provide no certainty that future troop buildups will not occur.

That there is a Nordic balance rests upon three interrelated factors. The first is the great-power common interest in maintaining the Nordic region as a low-tension area. The Soviet Union has more to lose than to gain from promoting a military buildup in the north, for that would threaten its major naval bases. While that, presumably, would be to NATO's advantage, there is no Norwegian interest in encouraging an arms race on its own soil that would endanger its security, nor is reducing Norwegian loyalty to NATO in the interest of the alliance. The second is the extraordinary stability of democracy in all of the Nordic countries. Domestic stability guarantees no sudden changes of alliance, no reversals that could alter the balance in the north. Finally, the linchpin is the crucial role played by Sweden's armed nonalignment. Sweden is a buffer between NATO and Finland which provides reasonable security to the Soviets that an independent Finland poses no threat to their security. The credibility of Sweden's nonalignment and neutrality are a guarantee that permits Finnish independence. Swedish officers speak of Swedish armed nonalignment as being "a strong stabilizing factor in the North,"[26] and it even draws what seem to be sincere accolades from the Soviets.[27]

Defense Policy

As the Swedes began to rearm in the late 1930s, their strategic doctrine called for matching potential aggressors in every way possible. The Germans never put the Swedes to the test, but, as far as the 1942-1945 period is concerned, the Swedes could with reason attribute this to the deterrent effect of their rapid rearmament. Their air force, in particular, became a potent force.

The strategy of unlimited defense remained the foundation of Swedish military thinking into the 1960s. Its realism, however, was affected by two factors: 1) the development of nuclear weapons, and 2) the changing Swedish conception of the military threat it faced. In the first decade of the Cold War, Swedish defense planners prepared for an isolated attack, rather like the Finnish-Soviet Winter War. Meeting any potential aggressor on an equal footing required a Swedish nuclear force. "All military considerations speak unanimously and strongly for acquisition of atomic weapons," judged the military high command in 1957, "so long as we must reckon that an attacker could use them."[28] Although nuclear weapons were judged vital for credible neutrality in war, the cost of developing and maintaining a serious nuclear force was a worrisome consideration. Sweden was, after all, a small power, though a technologically advanced one. Developing a nuclear force sufficient to be credible vis-à-vis a Soviet attack would be extraordinarily expensive and would make sharp cuts in Swedish conventional forces unavoidable. That policy decision might, in its turn, increase the likelihood of a conventional attack, decreasing national security instead of increasing it, unless Sweden proposed to meet a conventional attack with an immediate nuclear response--obviously suicidal. Ultimately, the air force itself opted against going nuclear, principally out of concern with the impact of the cost of an atomic weapons program on vital modernization of its capacity.[29]

In the 1950s the Swedes basically regarded nuclear weapons as only quantitatively different from conventional arms. As time passed, it became increasingly clear that there was a qualitative difference as well. The escalation of a conventional war to a nuclear one threatened the existence of civilization as we knew it; hence, the first use of nuclear weapons became a political, not a military, choice. By 1968 the government's defense committee had come to reason that a Swedish nuclear force offered no increment in security: if Sweden would not be the first to use nuclear weapons, then such weapons could not be used to deter a conventional attack; it was highly unlikely that it would be the object of another nation's first use of nuclear weapons (against which a Swedish nuclear force might actually be a deterrent); and a Swedish nuclear force could not be an effective counter to a massive nuclear attack in a general nuclear war. So Sweden attached its signature to the nonproliferation treaty in 1968. It has subsequently been an advocate of successive proposals for nuclear-free zones in the Baltic area, which would constrain the deployment of nuclear weapons by the nuclear powers.

Moreover, by the early 1960s, Swedish perceptions of the potential military threat had changed. With the development of ICBMs, the usefulness of Swedish territory to either superpower diminished; the likelihood of facing alone a superpower bent on improving its defensive perimeter seemed increasingly small. Instead, Swedish defense planners reasoned that the only realistic military threat to their country would occur in the context of a general European conflict, in which any power attacking Sweden could devote only a small portion of its resources to a Swedish campaign. In that circumstance, Swedish strength should be sufficient simply to make an attack on the country more costly for a potential aggressor than any benefits that power might derive from conquering it. Swedes assume that superpower objectives can be achieved without use of Swedish territory. Control of their territory and air space would be a convenience, but not a necessity. Their aim, therefore, is to keep the cost of acquiring that convenience above its value.[30]

As a consequence of a changed threat perception, Swedish defense strategists developed a more limited conception of the aims of the defense forces. Today, defense doctrine calls for a combination of conventional peripheral and territorial defense sufficient to make taking Sweden more troublesome than worthwhile for any likely aggressor. To this end Sweden spends a bigger portion of its gross national product, or GNP (an average of 3.5 percent in recent years), on its armed forces than any other European neutral except Yugoslavia. Its expenditures exceeded those of many NATO countries, including its immediate neighbors, for many years, but in the mid-1980s Norwegian expenditures as a proportion of GNP surpassed the Swedish level.

Swedish armed forces consist of an active-duty force of about 65,000 (1984), which serves both as a training force for conscripts and as a cadre for full mobilization. The conscription and reserve system are designed to permit mobilization of up to 850,000 men within seventy-two hours, not an unimpressive figure in a population of 8.3 million.   Of the army's mobilized strength of about 700,000, 300,000 are committed to field forces to provide a forward defense. Of those remaining, 300,000 are assigned to territorial units and 100,000 to the home guard; their obligation is that of territorial defense.   While official doctrine calls for stopping any invading force quickly and pushing it back over Sweden's borders, the decentralized nature of the preparedness system permits the easy dispersion of army units important to territorial defense.   The Swedish navy is designed principally for coastal defense, while the air force, which has absorbed the lion's share of defense spending and new technology, currently has about 400 combat aircraft and substantial peripheral defense capacity.[31]

The military is backed by a substantial civilian defense effort which includes a shelter and evacuation program,   sometimes described as "the most extensive nuclear shelter programme in the world,"[32] and an economic defense program which attempts to stockpile key supplies that would be cut off in wartime.   Oil stocks, for example, are designed to last for a year with rationing.   Again, the stress is on maintaining the credibility of Swedish neutrality in war.

The most likely threats to Swedish neutrality in wartime are today considered to stem from the importance of the Kola bases and fleet to the Soviet Union.   The Soviet interest in northern Norway in any general war is obvious: NATO bases there control access to the North Atlantic and threaten the Kola bases.   The only efficient land route west is to strike across northern Finland and Sweden.   A public debate of this question in 1981 exposed the open secret that, in such a circumstance, Sweden assumes that it will receive assistance from NATO; moreover, it was learned that plans existed for Swedish air interdiction of a Soviet advance across Finland once Sweden had been attacked.   While nonalignment precludes discussion in peacetime of assistance, neutrality would not preclude actual assistance in war should Sweden be attacked.[33] The largest Swedish maneuver since World War II was conducted in 1982 in this area of northern Sweden.   Some observers would argue, however, that the growth of Soviet amphibious landing capacity in the Northern Fleet has reduced the likelihood of a Soviet strike across northern Sweden in the event of war, although control of Swedish air space would remain important.

An equally serious threat to Swedish neutrality, though not to its territory, is the likelihood of Soviet and NATO violations of its air space, primarily by overflights of bombers and attack aircraft, but also by NATO's firing cruise missiles at the Soviet Kola bases across Swedish and Finnish air space. Swedes fear that the temptation for the latter violation of their neutrality will prove almost irresistible. Hence, current Swedish defense planning calls for developing a defense against this threat as well.[34]

Self-Sufficiency in Materiel

The Swedish policy of neutrality has rested not only on the ability to field a substantial military force, but it has also required that Sweden be able to supply that force independently in war. The country has never been completely self-sufficient in military production and has been dependent on foreign raw materials and fuel, but until World War I its defense industry, including Bofors and state workshops, was adequate to meet national needs. The changes in military technology and strategy in the interwar period, however, rapidly undermined Swedish capacity, since the country was dependent on foreign suppliers of tanks and aircraft. One of the key problems in rearmament, especially between 1938 and 1942, was the creation of that production capacity.[35] While that problem was solved during the latter part of the war, accelerating postwar changes in military technology with the rapid increase in sophistication and escalating costs have threatened continued self-sufficiency.

The most striking demonstration of the difficulties of combining self-sufficiency and high performance with affordable cost to date has been the decade-long discussion of whether Sweden should build its own replacement for the *Viggen*, its chief combat plane, or buy one abroad. The decision, ultimately made in 1982, was to replace the *Viggen* with a Swedish-built aircraft, the JAS-39 (*Gripen*).[36] However, the *Gripen* program strains national capacity both technologically and financially. Close to a third of its components will be foreign-made, despite the efforts to put together the strongest Swedish consortium possible. Estimates of the cost of the program are as high as Skr 30 billion, and it is likely to force cuts in other areas of defense spending.[37] Costs could be lowered if the production run were longer, but that, in turn, would require substantial foreign sales which Sweden, as a neutral, has difficulty making. It may be, as Johan Jørgen Holst suspects, "the last combat aircraft developed by Sweden."[38]

The *Gripen* has a number of advantages. A STOL aircraft, it is able to operate from the small airports and rural roads of northern Sweden, no small advantage given likely war scenarios. While Swedes could get more planes for their money by buying them abroad, the perception of defense production capacity is worth a good deal in maintaining the credibility of the country's neutrality, especially against the threat of a wartime embargo like that imposed by the United States against Sweden in 1940. Although 15 percent of Swedish defense contracts are, in fact, let abroad, Sweden does have sufficient production capacity to supply itself with reasonably sophisticated equipment should it be cut off from foreign suppliers for an extended period, as it was during World War II. While some defense contractors, like Bofors, are highly competitive in the international market, the maintenance of domestic technological and production capacity requires continuous investment along the lines of the JAS program.

The costs, however, are high. The number of active-duty troops, naval vessels, and combat aircraft declined as the costs of new technology were paid within the constraint of constant or declining real defense budgets. The training period for the majority of conscripts has been cut from ten to seven-and-one-half months. In some areas, such as antisubmarine warfare, the decline has become a positive embarrassment. The Swedes have traded quantity for quality, but potential opponents have improved their quality as well.

Nonalignment Is More than Military Policy

Security policy is only one facet of Swedish nonalignment. The Swedes have taken a leading role in international organizations, not least because they could play the role of the honest broker between East and West and, increasingly, between North and South. It is no accident that Sweden has furnished more than its share of UN leaders, including Dag Hammarskjöld, and that Swedish troops have been regular participants in UN peace-keeping forces; commitment to the United Nations remains a cornerstone of Swedish foreign policy, not because the Swedes are unrealistic about the organization but because it represents one of the few avenues of hope for small, neutral states. Efforts in promoting arms control and confidence-building measures fall in the same category, as does the willingness to attempt to mediate the most intractable disputes--witness Olof Palme's attempt at mediation in the Iraq-Iran war.

Considerations of nonalignment have shaped relations to regional organizations. Sweden has been an active participant in the Nordic Council since it was formed in 1952 on a Danish initiative; Finland was able to join in 1955 during the relaxation in the aftermath of Stalin's death. The Nordic Council has created a common labor market (1954), a passport union (1954), a technology and industrial development fund (1972), and an investment bank (1975), among other measures of functional integration; it involves no military entanglements, however. Sweden rejected the idea of membership in the European Community as irreconcilable with its neutrality, but neither the European Free Trade Association (EFTA) nor the abortive attempts to establish a Nordic Common Market offered a permanent alternative to association with the European Community; Sweden finally negotiated a trade agreement with the EEC.

The long, involved discussion in Sweden of what sort of relations with the EEC might be compatible with Swedish neutrality is a fairly extreme example of the concern with maintaining the credibility of that neutrality. It is reasonably obvious that full EEC membership does not place many restrictions on the foreign policies of France or Britain or even neutral Ireland, but that peacetime reality had less effect on Swedish policy than possible crisis scenarios. And since the Soviet Union judged the EEC dangerous company for neutral Finland (which ultimately established formally comparable ties simultaneously with the EEC and COMECON), then Swedish-EEC relations could not be considered without regard to that fact.[39] The credibility of neutrality is, like beauty, in the eye of the beholder.

A final aspect of Swedish neutrality has been its increasing focus on the Third World. Its nonaligned stance has been taken seriously in the Third World in no small measure because Sweden, among industrial democracies, was the most outspoken opponent of the U.S. policy in Vietnam. It has thus been able to serve as a bridge between North and South. It is one of the few countries to provide development aid at the level mandated by the United Nations. While it is certainly true that Swedish companies have followed in the wake of Swedish development programs, Swedish aid has, to an unusual extent, been focused on grass-roots development. More than any other aspect of the country's foreign policy, development aid has been influenced by the basic Social Democratic preoccupation with the creation of popular organization from below. It is also characteristic that the Swedes have provided aid to revolutionary movements and regimes, including the MPLA in Angola, Frelimo in Mozambique, PAIGC in Guinea-Bissau, and the Sandinistas in Nicaragua, and to ongoing liberation movements, such as the African National Congress in South Africa, as well as to firmly established, moderate governments.

Maintaining Neutrality Today

The regular probing of Swedish reactions by submarines, presumably Soviet, over the last five years has induced a degree of hysteria among journalists who came to see it as pressure to "Finlandize" Sweden. If that was the Soviet aim, it reflected exceptional miscalculation. The result of the submarine incursions was increased government spending for antisubmarine warfare capacity and a surge in popular support for higher defense spending. Far from being intimidated, polls suggest that the Swedish population shows a higher will to resist militarily today than in the 1970s--a higher will to resist, incidentally, than in the United States or the United Kingdom.[40] Given the importance attached to mobilization and in-depth territorial defense in Swedish defense thinking, a high level of popular support is vital to the credibility of Swedish neutrality, and the government has sought to promote that by maintaining as high a degree of consensus on defense as possible. In the context of the sharp disagreements on defense policy that existed prior to World War II, the relatively consensual nature of postwar defense policymaking is the more impressive. The submarine incursions reestablished broad support for higher levels of defense spending which were controversial in the 1970s.

Nor has the pressure been sufficient to induce Sweden to retreat from its internationalism. Its neutrality has been independent, but it remains internationalistic in orientation. The pessimism of Arne Ruth, expressed earlier, seems unconfirmed by events. If Sweden's international profile seems lower under Ingvar Carlsson than under Palme, it is a difference of person, more than of policy. Sweden's pursuit of active neutrality has been as vigorous in the Nordic area as in the arena of international organizations and in its development policies in the Third World.

There is no question that the rapid growth of the Soviet navy has made Swedish (and Norwegian and Danish) territorial waters of greater interest.   But in a historical perspective, the submarine visitations are a minor, if blatant, irritant; there have been equivalent threats to Swedish neutrality with some regularity in the past. In fact, Sweden has previously enjoyed only two extended periods as peaceful as the last forty years: from 1815 to 1853, and again from 1865 to 1914.   While one should never overestimate one's security when living on an international fault line, Sweden clearly has been fortunate.

The Swedes would argue that good fortune accrues to those who help themselves.   Their neutrality has been relatively heavily armed.   That has obviously not been enough to deter submarine incursions, but that particular kind of peacetime violation was not foreseen, and it will take time to acquire the materiel and personnel to counter those incursions.   The focus of Swedish defense spending was not to keep submarines out of its territorial waters in peacetime, but to enable Sweden to withstand an attack or invasion during a war among the big powers.   The aim was simple: to make the costs of an attack on Sweden outweigh the benefits for any potential aggressor.

Can Sweden's deterrent actually deter a marginal attack? Fortunately, the country has not been put to the test, but the guiding principle in Swedish neutrality has never been to deter so much as to avoid the need to deter.   Today, such policy requires not the maneuvering of monarchs but the credibility of Swedish nonalignment in peace and neutrality in war.   That objective is provided by a reasonably strong defense, a stable national consensus around neutrality, and the consistent government effort to assure any potential belligerent both that Sweden is not going to enter the conflict on the other side (and hence need not be attacked) and that an attack on Sweden costs more than it is worth.   It is the consistency and credibility of this policy that has created the Nordic balance, and that balance, in its turn, has created around Sweden a low-tension area in which neutrality is easily maintained.   In no small measure Sweden has achieved the aims of minimizing great-power confrontation in the Nordic region, the intent of the abortive Nordic Defense Pact, through its unilateral action.

NOTES

[1] It is a pleasure to thank Michael Lytle, Bernt Schiller, Bengt Sundelius, Ulf Olsson, and Krister Wahlbäck for their comments on this paper and also the Lyman L. Lemnitzer Center for NATO Studies, Kent State University, for its support.

[2] Arne Ruth, "The Second New Nation," *Daedalus* 113, no. 2 (Spring 1984): 75. Ruth is editor-in-chief of *Dagens Nyheter*.

[3] Elis Håsted, ed., *"Gallup" och den svenska väljarkåren* (Uppsala: Hugo Gebers Förlag, 1950), pp. 228-29.

[4] Both Gustav II Adolf and Karl XII played a sufficient role on the world stage to have their names anglicized as Gustavus Adolphus and Charles XII, respectively. That has not been true of other Swedish kings. For the sake of consistency, I have used the Swedish names throughout.

[5] Perhaps the most notable from a military point of view was the importation of Dutch and Walloon craftsmen under Gustav II Adolf to develop a munitions industry. Willem de Besche and Louis De Geer opened cannon factories in Finspaang and Norrköping, respectively, that supplied Gustav with the light artillery that was one of his advantages in the field during the Thirty Years' War. The evidence provided on the field of the quality of Swedish cannon made them an export item; Franklin Scott describes De Geer as "the Krupp of his day" (Franklin Scott, *Sweden: The Nation's History* [Minneapolis: University of Minnesota Press, 1977], p. 176). Between 1655 and 1662, Sweden produced 11,000 cannon and exported 9,000 of them.

[6] Population figures for the period should be taken with a grain of salt; the first official Swedish census was in 1750.

[7] In 1629-30, as Gustav II Adolf prepared his German campaign, the royal munitions works, managed by De Geer, produced 20,000 muskets, 13,670 pikes, and 4,700 suits of cavalry armor; Gustav II Adolf's expeditionary force consisted of 10,000 infantry and 3,000 cavalry (Scott, *Sweden*, pp. 175, 189).

[8] Krister Wahlbäck traces the development of Swedish neutrality to Karl Johan's memorandum of 4 January 1834, proclaiming Sweden's neutrality in this conflict to the British and Russian governments. (Krister Wahlbäck, *The Roots of Swedish Neutrality* [Stockholm: Swedish Institute, 1986], pp. 8-12.)

[9] For an example of the Social Democratic position see Zeth Höglund, Hannes Sköld, and Fredr. Ström, *Det befästa fattighuset* (1913; reprint Lund: Arkiv, 1979), which argues that "profit is the fatherland of the rich, just as it is their god. It is the only fatherland they will defend. . . .

The only patriotism worthy of the name is that of the working class" (p. 127).

[10]Undén served as foreign minister in the Social Democratic government from 1924 to 1926 and again from 1945 to 1962.

[11]For a detailed treatment of the Åland dispute see James Barros, *The Åland Islands Question: Its Settlement by the League of Nations* (New Haven: Yale University Press, 1968).

[12]The dispute came to a head after Norwegian expeditions occupied portions of East Greenland in 1930 and 1931. It was taken to the International Court, which awarded sovereignty over the disputed area to Denmark in 1933.

[13]Brita Skottsberg Åhman, in Henning Friis, ed., *Scandinavia between East and West* (Ithaca: Cornell University Press, 1950), p. 277.

[14]Swedish defense spending in 1939 was increased to eight times the 1938 level.

[15]Wilhelm Carlgren, *Swedish Foreign Policy during the Second World War* (London: Ernest Benn, 1977), p. 5. This originally appeared as *Svensk utrikespolitik 1939-1945* (Stockholm: Allmänna Förlaget, 1973).

[16]Stig Hadenius, Björn Molin, and Hans Wieslander, *Sverige efter 1900: En modern politisk historia*, rev. ed. (Stockholm: Aldus, 1972), p. 157. While there is some question about whether the king actually threatened to abdicate, there is no question that Social Democratic Prime Minister Per Albin Hansson used the king's alleged threat to force recalcitrant Social Democratic cabinet members into line.

[17]Scandinavia, as a geographic concept, includes Denmark, Norway, and Sweden. As a cultural concept, it includes Iceland and the Faeroe Islands as well. Norden (or the Nordic countries) is a geographic and political concept that encompasses both Scandinavia in its cultural sense and Finland.

[18]Perhaps the most notable case was the Swedish role in mediation in the Middle East where Count Folke Bernadotte (the nephew of Gustav V), who had transported Danish and Norwegian prisoners from the German camps to Sweden as head of the Swedish Red Cross, was assassinated by Zionist terrorists in September 1948. His mission is analyzed by Sune Persson, *Mediation and Assassination: Count Bernadotte's Mission to Palestine* (London: Ithaca Press, 1979).

[19]Speech to the Riksdag, 4 February 1948, as quoted in Barbara Haskel, *The Scandinavian Option: Opportunities and Opportunity Costs in Postwar Scandinavian Foreign Policies* (Oslo: Universitetsforlaget, 1976), p. 41.

[20]Udenrigsministeriet, *Dansk Sikkerhedspolitik 1948-66* (Copenhagen, 1968), vol. 2, app. 27 and 28, as quoted in Haskel, *Scandinavian Option*, pp. 45-46.

[21]For accounts of the efforts to establish a Scandinavian defense union see Haskel, *Scandinavian Option*, pp. 39-87; Geir Lundestad, *America, Scandinavia and the Cold War 1945-1949* (Oslo: Universitetsforlaget, 1980); and Krister Wahlbäck, *Norden och blockuppdelningen 1948-49* (Stockholm: Utrikespolitiska Institutet, 1973). Bernt Schiller argues provocatively that this attempt, like others to achieve Nordic unity in the military and economic fields, was a product of *incipient* outside pressure and failed, as the others did, when the outside pressure became manifest. (Bernt Schiller, "At Gun Point: A Critical Perspective on the Attempts of the Nordic Governments to Achieve Unity after the Second World War," *Scandinavian Journal of History* 9, no. 3 [1984]: 221-38.)

[22]Designed to prevent a repetition of the Continuation War, this treaty commits Finland to defend its territory against Germany or any state allied with Germany which seeks to attack the Soviet Union through Finland, with Soviet aid if needed, and requires Finnish-Soviet consultations when such an attack is threatened.

[23]See Johan Jørgen Holst, ed., *Five Roads to Nordic Security* (Oslo: Universitetsforlaget, 1973); and Nils Andrén, "Changing Strategic Perspectives in Northern Europe," in Bengt Sundelius, ed., *Foreign Policies of Northern Europe* (Boulder: Westview, 1982), pp. 73-106.

[24]For a good summary of the discussion of the concept of the Nordic balance see Tomas Ries, *The Nordic Dilemma in the 80's: Maintaining Regional Stability under New Strategic Conditions*, PSIS Occasional Papers, No. 1 (Geneva: Programme for Strategic and International Security Studies, 1982), pp. 5-24.

[25]See Jon L. Lellenberg, "The Military Balance," in Johan Jørgen Holst, Kenneth Hunt, and Anders C. Sjaastad, eds., *Deterrence and Defense in the North* (Oslo: Universitetsforlaget, 1985), pp. 41-65. Lellenberg was director, Northern Region (European and NATO Policy), in the Office of the Assistant Secretary of Defense for International Security Policy at the time he wrote this piece. Moreover, the Norwegian edition of the International Institute for Stategic Studies (IISS), *Militærbalansen, 1985-1986* (Oslo: Det norske Atlanterhavskomité, 1985), which adds a special section on military forces in Northern Europe (pp. 128-43), concludes that the Soviet forces regularly stationed on the Kola Peninsula have a capacity for only "a limited attack against targets in Finnmark [the part of Norway bordering the USSR] . . . [which] would give such modest military advantages that it is doubtful that it is worth the risk for the Soviet Union in terms of countermeasures from NATO" (p. 139).

[26]Einar Lyth, *Den nordiska balansen* (Stockholm: Utrikespolitiska Institutet, 1977), p. 23.

[27]Consider, for example, O. K. Timashkova's comment that "Sweden's non-alignment policy favourably influences the foreign-policy actions of other Nordic countries. For example, though Denmark and Norway are NATO members, they rejected the deployment of nuclear weapons on their territory largely under the influence of their neighbours' peaceable policy." (*Scandinavian Social Democracy Today* [Moscow: Progress Publishers, 1981], p. 193.) For an examination of the changing Soviet views see Bo Petersson, "Changes of Wind or Winds of Change? Soviet Views on Finnish and Swedish Neutrality in the Postwar Era," *Nordic Journal of Soviet and East European Studies* 2, no. 1 (1986): 61-85.

[28]As quoted by Gunnar Jervas, "Sverige, Norden och kärnvapen," in Bertel Heurlin, ed., *Kernevåbenpolitik i Norden* (Copenhagen: Det Sikkerheds- og nedrustningspolitiske Udvalg, 1983), p. 58. For a magisterial discussion of changing Swedish policy toward nuclear weapons see Wilhelm Agrell, *Alliansfrihet och atombomber: Kontinuitet och förändring i den svenska forsvarsdoktrinen från 1945 till 1982* (Stockholm: Liber, 1985).

[29]See Agrell, *Alliansfrihet och atombomber*, pp. 289-330.

[30]For a concise discussion of Swedish threat perception and the "marginal attack doctrine" see Nils Andrén, *Säkerhetspolitik* (Stockholm: Utrikespolitiska Institutet, 1984), pp. 89-99. The marginal attack doctrine has been repeatedly reaffirmed by the parlimentary defense committee reports, most recently in 1985. There has, however, been increasing concern that Soviet interest in Swedish air bases might make an "opening attack" on Sweden in the event of war attractive to the Soviet Union. See Gunnar Jervas, *Sweden between the Power Blocs: A New Strategic Position?* (Stockholm: Swedish Institute, 1986), pp. 16-26.

[31]*Militærbalansen, 1985-1986*, pp. 77-78, 137.

[32]Adam Roberts, *A Nation in Arms*, 2d ed. (New York: St. Martin's, 1986), p. 102.

[33]See Erling Bjøl, *Nordens sikkerhet i 1980-årene* (Oslo: Den norske Atlanterhavskomité, 1986), pp. 37-38.

[34]Ibid., p. 38.

[35]See Ulf Olsson, "The State and Industry in Swedish Rearmament," in Martin Fritz et al., *The Adaptable Nation: Essays in the Swedish Economy during the Second World War* (Stockholm: Almqvist & Wiksell, 1982).

[36]The debate about building or buying a successor to the *Viggen* is the subject of a case study in defense policymaking by William Taylor, "Sweden," in William Taylor and Paul M. Cole, eds., *Nordic Defense: Comparative Decision Making* (Lexington: Lexington Books, 1985), pp. 127-86. The decision to build the *Viggen* represented a comparable commitment in research, development, and government spending; it is the subject of a detailed study by Ingemar Dörfer, *System 37 Viggen: Arms, Technology*

and the Domestication of Glory (Oslo: Universitetsforlaget, 1973).

[37]Krister Wahlbäck, "Swedish Security Policy," *Political Life in Sweden*, no. 18 (October 1984): 10.

[38]Johan Jørgen Holst, "The Pattern of Nordic Security," *Daedalus* 113, no. 2 (Spring 1984): 207.

[39]This point of view, incidentally, also had the signal advantage that it enabled Swedish Social Democrats to escape the bloody battles about EEC membership that wounded their Danish and Norwegian equivalents in 1971-72. One should not ignore the value of neutrality in domestic party politics.

[40]See *Nordisk säkerhetspolitik i utvekling* (Stockholm: Centralförbundet Folk och Forsvar, 1983), p. 65; and Taylor, "Sweden," pp. 150-51.

IRELAND

Joseph P. O'Grady

As is the case with any nation, the foreign and national security policies of the Republic of Ireland have not been written in a vacuum, and any attempt to comprehend these policies must begin with an effort to understand the context in which they have been formed. Such a process in the case of Ireland quickly becomes complex, for its current policies have several deep-seated origins.

One of the profound influences on Irish national security policy is geography. Ireland is a relatively small island, west of a much larger island, which in turn lies off the northwest coast of Europe. The English came to dominate that larger island during the Middle Ages and eventually made it the center of an empire that placed England among the most powerful nations in the world.

This geopolitical positioning meant that the English would eventually come to dominate Ireland. They arrived as a conquering army in 1169 and managed for the next four hundred years to control an area around Dublin, known as the Pale. Changes in technology and the appearance of oceangoing vessels in the fifteenth and sixteenth centuries gave Ireland a clear strategic role in the defense of England. When the British built their empire upon those new developments, total control of Ireland became a fundamental necessity; thus began the process by which they would eventually come to influence every facet of Irish life.[1] That story, filled with enormous excesses on both sides, cannot be repeated here. It is sufficient merely to indicate that for the vast majority of the people who have lived in Ireland since 1169, their history is filled with attempts to expel British influence. The Irish had little real success in these efforts until early in the twentieth century.[2]

In 1913, Ireland's national aspirations took a turn for the better with the appearance of the Irish Volunteers. They, in turn, sparked the Easter Rebellion in 1916, which was followed in 1919 by the War of Independence. In the midst of that struggle, by passing the Government of Ireland Act of 1920, the British Parliament permitted northern Unionists, loyal to the British connection, to form a separate state in Ulster. The British and Irish next agreed to a truce and negotiated a treaty to end their war in the fall and early winter of 1921. The sequence of events led to the emergence of two Irelands. Northern Ireland remained a part of the United Kingdom and organized a government in Belfast. The Irish Free State created one in Dublin and became a new state within the British Commonwealth.[3]

These same developments also released social and political forces that immediately influenced the writing of Dublin's defense policy. First and foremost, the new government of the Irish Free State had to deal with the English-supported partition of the island. That situation and the events that flowed from it quickly became the fundamental concern of the Dublin government. It has remained so ever since.[4] The presence of a separate state of Northern Ireland, protected by British troops, also provided the Irish Republican Army (IRA) with a justification to remain as a force in local life. Originally created in 1919 to oppose British control of the island with armed force, the IRA has posed a threat not only to the British in Northern Ireland but also to the Dublin government.[5] Partition and the IRA effort to end it raised the question of how Dublin should formulate defense policies for a state holding membership in the British Commonwealth, but whose government and a sizable portion of the Irish people disagreed with a fundamental decision of London in a commonwealth dominated by it.

Another challenge for Ireland's new government was money. From the very beginning Dublin faced enormous financial difficulties that grew directly out of the basic nature of economic life in Ireland. It was a small country with few natural resources, limited population growth (the young constantly emigrated), and scant industry.[6] In such a setting the new government found its ability to raise revenue very restricted and its social and economic needs far beyond what its resources could provide. Each successive government in the 1920s and 1930s sought to eliminate all unnecessary expenditures, and each saw defense as an area that could accept budget reductions.[7]

Within this atmosphere, created by financial limitations and the open wound of partition, the Irish Free State had to establish diplomatic relations with the outside world. Signs of how the future Irish state would shape these relations had appeared during World War I, when London attempted to extend conscription to Ireland. The Irish political leadership reacted violently to that proposal. It preferred to stay out of Britain's wars, unless these conflicts might be used as a means to gain Ireland's freedom. What the Irish really said in 1917 was that once they gained their freedom, they would follow a policy of neutrality, at least in any future war that involved England.[8]

Michael Collins raised that specific issue during the fall 1921 treaty negotiations, but the English would not agree to such a policy. To ensure that the Dublin government would not become a strategic liability by following a policy of neutrality, London insisted that the treaty give the British the right to continue the occupation of certain strategic forts in the Irish Free State and to keep open certain port facilities for the British navy. Without these forts and port facilities, Britain's admirals argued, they would not be able to maintain control of the sea-lanes to the empire. In other words, the very security of the empire required a continued British presence in both parts of the new Ireland.[9] This presence not only placed limitations on Ireland's independence but also ensured that it would be unable to avoid going to war on England's side in a future conflict.

DEFENSE POLICIES PRIOR TO WORLD WAR II

In the years from 1921 to 1939, Irish governments formulated and executed defense policies within the context of four areas--geography, partition, financial limitations, and the desire for neutrality--while constantly bearing in mind the continuing economic and strategic relationship with Britain. The process began once the Dail, the lower house of the Irish Parliament, accepted the 1921 treaty with Britain on 13 January 1922 by a vote of 63 to 54. The treaty terms provided for a period of transition from English to Irish rule, but a civil war erupted between the pro- and anti-treaty forces in the summer of 1922. Consequently, the first defense policy of the new government was one of mere survival.[10] Only after the antitreaty forces faded into the countryside in the summer of 1923 did the government find time to address the formulation of a defense policy based upon broader guidelines, but even that effort was interrupted by a threatened military coup in March 1924.[11] The collapse of this effort ensured the supremacy of the civilian leadership over the army, and the government finally had the time to write its policy on defense.

Developing that first clear policy statement, however, was no easy task, and it was only one of many challenges facing the Dublin authorities. The process began when the government introduced the Temporary Defence Bill and submitted a Defence Estimate in 1923.[12] Concurrently, General Richard Mulcahy provided the first organizational scheme for the army.[13] In the following year the Ministers Act created the Department of Defence. With these organizational aspects of defense planning out of the way,[14] time was available to develop a statement on policy. The new defense staff then wrote a policy which the cabinet discussed on 13 November 1925. At that meeting they approved a plan for a small standing army, one that would not bankrupt the nation but that would nonetheless provide a base for an expanded force in an emergency.[15]

The army staff went about implementing these decisions, but quickly ran into problems. The first scheme clearly would not work, and a second effort followed in 1927.[16] The army leadership also concluded that it needed to know much more about the nature of modern warfare and, therefore, arranged for a special military mission to the United States in 1926. Members of that mission attended American military courses, collecting as much information as possible. They returned to Dublin with trunks filled with copies of every piece of paper issued to them as students at Forts Benning, Sill, and Leavenworth.[17] The manuals, course outlines, and examinations helped the Irish establish both a military college in 1930 and an army that accurately reflected developments in other armies around the world.[18] These concepts, in turn, had grown out of experiences during World War I with the introduction of the tank, airplane, and motor transport. All these developments confirmed what some of Ireland's military leaders had decided as early as 1922: their country needed an army which, though essentially an infantry force, would include artillery, engineer, signal, transportation, supply, air, medical, and military police units.[19]

Unfortunately, these major decisions were quickly followed by two problems--a shortage of both modern weapons and funds to buy them. The British had realized in 1922 that with the signing of the treaty and the Dublin government's decision to resist the antitreaty faction, by force if necessary, it was in their best interests to provide the new Irish army units with sufficient arms to win any civil war. Thus, Britain provided the new army with a store of arms that ensured the government sufficient power to survive its first major test. The supply levels, however, were neither adequate to threaten the British position in Ireland nor modern enough to avoid rapid obsolescence.[20]   Toward the end of the decade the need for new weapons became obvious.

Meanwhile, by 1927 the fledgling Irish politicians discovered that the management of a modern system of government was complex and expensive. Professionals in the Department of Finance realized in that year that revenues were falling behind budget estimates, and the government ordered an immediate reduction of expenditures.[21]   When the budget crisis of 1927 deepened in 1928, the administration of William Cosgrave found itself with inadequate funds to maintain basic services. Cuts had to be made somewhere. The civilian leadership soon focused upon the Department of Defence, which offered, in its estimation, the least vital government services. The only justification for an army rested upon threats to the existence of the state, and none existed in 1928. Budget reductions in that department appeared more acceptable than in other departments. Cuts in defense spending also would find favor among those groups which had feared a strong military in 1924 and had argued for the elimination of a standing military force.[22]   For these reasons the government mandated a decrease in military strength from sixteen battalions of infantry in 1927 to five by 1932.[23]   Worldwide depression assured that these cuts would remain for the immediate future.

The financial crisis of 1927, followed by the economic consequences of the Great Depression, resulted in a victory by the Fianna Fáil (the party formed by Eamon de Valera in 1926) in the election of 1932.[24]   Military policy at that moment rested upon Ireland's relationship to Britain as a member of the Commonwealth, financial restrictions, a policy of maintaining a small expandable force, and lack of a secure source of modern military supplies. De Valera did nothing to change those realities except to introduce the idea of a volunteer force to supplement the nation's military mobilization strength.[25]   Ireland maintained policies for a small-sized army, limited military budget, and a freeze on the purchase of new weapons up to 1939.

If de Valera's government did little to alter basic defense policy, it did much to change the atmosphere in which it was written. From the very beginning of his tenure, de Valera sought to reduce England's influence. His policies led to strained relations and an economic war with Britain that began shortly after he took office.[26] It ended in 1938 when "Dev" accepted a settlement of some outstanding financial questions. At the same time the British withdrew from their privileged defense positions in Ireland, thereby assuring the Irish that they could, if they so wished, remain neutral in any future war involving the British. That opportunity came in 1939 when, after Hitler attacked Poland, Britain and France declared war on Germany. Ireland immediately declared neutrality.[27]

DEFENSE POLICIES IN AN ERA OF RELATIVE ISOLATION, 1939-1952

Ireland's policy of neutrality provoked considerable pressures in the late spring and summer of 1940 from both Britain and the United States to permit the return of British forces to the old treaty forts, which they had left in 1938.[28] The de Valera government refused to accede to such pressures and organized the nation to defend itself against either a German or British invasion. The prime minister expanded the defense forces, found necessary arms, and aroused a vigilant citizenship to protect Ireland's neutrality. The combined prospect of the cost of military action against an aroused Ireland and the small military advantages to be gained from it doubtlessly dissuaded the Germans, British, and Americans from violating Irish neutrality during the war.[29]

At the end of World War II the Irish demobilized their wartime army and returned to their normal defense policy, which followed the guidelines established in 1925. The war, however, proved the necessity for a well-organized and well-equipped reserve force. That lesson caused de Valera's government to form the An Forsa Cosanta Aitiuil (FCA) in 1947 to fill that need,[30] but soon postwar economic problems took precedence over all other considerations.

The worldwide economic crisis struck Ireland in spite of its wartime political and military isolation because it still remained dependent upon its larger British neighbor. Consequently, whatever happened to Britain's economy had an impact upon the Irish state. World War II had virtually destroyed the system of economic relationships that had functioned within the "sterling bloc" prior to 1939. Britain had no money to stimulate trade within its old sphere of influence or to rebuild its economic infrastructure. Conditions in other areas of Europe were even worse. Ireland had not suffered from the destructive capability of modern weapons, but it could not hope for economic improvement if Britain and the rest of Europe did not recover from the effects of the war. Thus, in June 1947 when American Secretary of State George Marshall outlined what would become the European Recovery Program (better remembered as the Marshall Plan), Ireland immediately indicated a willingness to participate. Both the United States and Britain accepted that participation despite Irish neutrality during World War II, thus acknowledging Britain's heavy dependency upon Ireland for foodstuffs. A healthy Irish agricultural economy could only contribute to the restoration of a healthy "sterling bloc."[31]

This phase of Ireland's willingness to participate in European affairs, however, did not extend to the second major Western European cooperative effort in the postwar period, the formation of the North Atlantic Treaty Organization (NATO). The ongoing partition issue, vagaries of domestic politics, and the question of neutrality posed obstacles to a positive Irish response to the invitation to join NATO.

De Valera's Fianna Fáil party had lost the general election in 1948, sixteen years after first coming to power in 1932. A coalition government formed around the strength of Fine Gael, the descendant of the protreaty government of 1922-1932. The coalition had to prove to the electorate that it was just as strong on the partition question as Fianna Fáil. That issue and other considerations motivated it to take the final step toward independence: the formal proclamation of Ireland as a republic in April 1949.[32] In response to Ireland's departure from the Commonwealth, London passed the Northern Ireland Bill, in which it gave the government in Belfast what would become known as the famous "guarantee." The English would not permit the new Irish Republic to absorb Northern Ireland without the majority of the population in the north expressing voluntary assent for such a union.[33]

It was within the context of these sensitive issues that the question of NATO membership and the Irish government's negative decision arose. Officially, Dublin stated that it could not enter a military alliance of which Britain was a member while that country continued its occupation of the north, but others have argued that additional reasons prompted the decision.[34] Whatever the reason, the Irish did not join. Dublin committed itself to continue its policy of neutrality, a decision that led to another problem: the acquisition of arms.

Irish ability to gain access to modern military equipment naturally rested upon the availability of funds and the willingness of producers to sell arms. The British had readily provided an initial supply of arms in 1921-22, but the Irish had been unable to fund modernization in the 1930s. That failure left the Irish virtually unarmed on the eve of World War II and unable to purchase arms during the early years of the war. After considerable effort, the British did give them some weapons and equipment, but even with these additions by 1949 the Irish still possessed many obsolete arms.[35] The decision not to join NATO denied them a sure method of modernization.

Since this decision assured the continuation of arms shortages, the Irish sought aid from the United States in 1950. Such an effort, however, came at a most difficult time for Washington. In the spring of 1949 the United States oversaw the formation of NATO and assumed a commitment to help Western Europe rearm. In the summer of 1949 the Nationalist Chinese forces lost control of mainland China. Then, in September 1949, the Soviet Union exploded an atomic device. These events caused a full-scale review of Soviet-American relations that found expression in April 1950 with National Security Council document NSC-68, which called for a threefold increase in American military spending. Next, the North Koreans attacked South Korea in June 1950. The United States now suddenly found itself short of arms. The Korean conflict, the need to arm NATO, and the necessity to build U.S. forces to meet a possible Soviet threat constituted the list of priorities for arms distribution. Then the Chinese Communists intervened in Korea with large forces in late November 1950.

It was in this troubled world that the Irish made their request for arms. The Americans simply told them that available arms for the foreseeable future were needed in Korea and Western Europe.[36] There was nothing left for the Irish. The Americans would satisfy their own needs first and those of their allies second; that would clearly take some time.

The arms question came also at a period when the European Recovery Program was drawing to a close, and the whole question of American aid was undergoing change. What had begun in 1947 as a purely economic program gradually assumed military dimensions. This aspect became particularly true in 1951 with the passage of the Mutual Security Act, which required participating countries (if wishing to continue receiving aid) to agree to the purpose of that act: "to strengthen the mutual security and individual and collective defense of the free world."[37]

The implementation of this act created problems for Ireland. The newly elected government of de Valera refused to accept the suggested wording of a new agreement in late 1951 and early 1952 on the grounds that it would violate Irish neutrality. As a result,

American economic aid under the Marshall Plan ended in January 1952, and no other program took its place.[38] This decision also virtually killed any hope of arms assistance from the United States in the foreseeable future, at least until Ireland would change its mind about accepting the purpose of the Mutual Security Act.

DEFENSE POLICIES IN AN ERA OF INVOLVEMENT, 1953-1986

As a result of Irish decisions from 1949 to 1952, any effort at modernization of the military had to await a new source of supplies. It was not long, however, before Ireland made some purchases from Sweden in the fall of 1953.[39] These included some small arms and antitank and artillery weapons, which proved to be far superior to those the Irish army had been using. Dublin's success in procuring them set the pattern for future arms purchases up to the present. Ireland would deal with any supplier except the United States or the Soviet Union.

While the Irish government debated the country's membership in NATO and the continuation of U.S. aid, it also produced a permanent defense bill. After thirty years of discussion and delay, the Dail finally received the bill, which was carefully studied by the Special Joint Committee of the Irish Parliament. Extensive discussion resulted in a number of minor changes to the government's draft, and debate in the full house followed in the spring of 1954.[40] The new bill created a legal status for the armed forces and came just in time for another change in Ireland's international activities.

The return to relative isolationism that followed the refusals to enter NATO and to sign a new economic aid package with the United States did not last very long. Although Ireland had tried to join the United Nations as early as 1946, the Soviet Union exercised its veto power and continued to do so until late 1954. Ireland was finally able to enter the United Nations in 1955, ultimately taking advantage of the international opportunities on the world stage that such participation permitted.[41]

Two other events occurred that would open more opportunities for Ireland to play a wider role in world affairs. In 1958, de Valera finally retired from active politics, a juncture marking more than just a change of personalities at the top of Ireland's political structure. It also signified the passing of his definition of what Ireland should be: Gaelic, Catholic, rural, and pure.[42] This shift came just as Dr. James Whitaker, an economist in the Department of Finance, wrote a proposal for the introduction of long-term economic planning for the first time in Ireland's history. His plan called for a violent and rapid shift from the inward-looking isolationist, protectionist economic policies of the de Valera years. Whitaker proposed to open Ireland to the outside world, drawing it to Ireland with the help of tax incentives and government subsidies. His plan envisioned the country as a place for multinational corporations to build factories.[43]

While the combination of the entry into the United Nations, the end of the de Valera era, and the arrival of the Whitaker concept gradually caused the Irish to look toward the wider world for their future, the old issue of internal security once again surfaced to emphasize that the past would not go away. The IRA had been relatively quiet in the early post-World War II years, but it had not disappeared, as an occasional attack upon British forces in Northern Ireland demonstrated. By the mid-1950s, however, the IRA had once again increased its strength to the point where it could mount a sustained effort to drive the British out of Northern Ireland. In 1956 it opened the famous Border Campaign. For the next four years the IRA used the sanctuary of southern Ireland to mount armed raids across the border against British and Royal Ulster Constabulary (RUC) installations in the north. These attacks placed an added burden upon the Irish defense forces as they acted to suppress the IRA, but with little real success.[44]

While the internal security struggle captured the attention of the Irish military, the increasing involvement in UN affairs caused a major shift in both defense and foreign policy. In 1960 the UN staff asked the Irish government if it would be willing to participate in peace-keeping operations.[45] This request provoked an immediate and serious political debate, since such participation required a revision of the Permanent Defence Force Act of 1954. The required changes came quickly, however. It was determined that involvement in UN peace-keeping operations could only help the image of Ireland in other parts of the world and contribute to the expanding Irish economy. Peace-keeping activities also would increase Irish involvement in a broader range of foreign policy questions, something which both the professionals and the politicians in the Department of External Affairs sought. More importantly, the Irish agreed to accept such assignments for purely defense-related economic reasons. The United Nations paid the salaries of the troops involved, thereby reducing Irish defense costs. At the same time, weapons and equipment could be depreciated; the United Nations would cover the cost of replacement and thus provide for the modernization of equipment at minimum cost for Dublin. A peace-keeping effort also would have considerable impact upon the morale of the officers and men, who since World War II had found that their only real duty involved police, not military, work. Now they had a chance to work as a military unit in potentially explosive situations that would have nothing to do with Britain.[46]

The decision to accept the invitation of the United Nations brought considerable change to the Department of Defence during the 1960s, but that would not be the only significant development during this period. Increased economic activity brought an unprecedented degree of prosperity to Ireland, but prosperity, in turn, brought a clear shift in priorities. Once again demands on limited public funds forced cuts in some areas and, as in the past, the government responded to the end of the Border Campaign and the relative weakness of the IRA with reductions in the army. Total strength soon fell to 6,000 men. With 600 to 800 men per year assigned to UN duties, relatively few troops were left for home duties, but policy decisions did permit the Permanent Defence Force (PDF), for possibly the first time in its history, to be armed adequately with the kind of weapons and the range of equipment a balanced modern infantry force required.[47]

These developments in the early 1960s combined to provide Ireland by the end of the decade with a military force, backed by clearly defined policies, modern equipment, accepted traditions, good staff work, more than adequate educational facilities, and definite missions. The resultant sense of accomplishment in government and military circles came just as another major era in Irish history began.

The relative quiet that had characterized life in Northern Ireland since 1923 drew to a close in the mid-1960s with the Tricolor riots of 1964 in Belfast and the formation of the Northern Irish Civil Rights Movement during the following year.[48] The former represented the first riots in Belfast in thirty-one years, while the latter represented the essential desire of Roman Catholics in Northern Ireland for basic civil rights. Into that movement went the energies of most Catholics and fair-minded people in Ireland for the next four years, but in 1969 a peaceful civil rights march in Londonderry ended in bloodshed.[49] Another "Bloody Sunday" had entered the pages of Irish history, and the traditional defender of the Catholic minority in Ulster, the IRA, reappeared. Thus began the new "troubles." Catholics demanded basic civil rights; the government of Northern Ireland with the aid of the British army acted to suppress them. The IRA began a guerrilla war to destroy the government and to drive the "Brits" out, while protecting the Catholic nationalists whenever or wherever necessary against whatever enemy--the British army, the RUC, the "B" Specials, or the Unionist paramilitary forces.[50]

These new troubles placed serious strain upon Ireland's defense forces. The increased demand for patrol of the border, coupled with normal commitments at home and with the United Nations, soon exceeded the capabilities of the 6,000-man force. The army had to be increased, reserve units had to be employed, and the cost of defense grew, resulting in rising costs. At the height of the troubles in 1974, units had to be recalled from UN assignments.[51]

While the partition issue came to dominate life in Ireland and to complicate relations between London and Dublin in the years after 1969, another major change appeared when Ireland entered the European Economic Community (EEC). The close economic ties between it and Britain virtually forced the Irish to follow the British lead when London applied for entry into the EEC in the early 1960s. France under Charles de Gaulle blocked both applications at that time, and neither state was able to enter the EEC until January 1973.[52]

This new affiliation brought considerable economic change almost at once to the small island. But the impact upon its neutrality and defense policies would not clearly emerge until the end of 1975, when Belgian Prime Minister Leo Tindemans filed his report on what should constitute European Union. In that document Tindemans called for the development of community discussions on political and security matters.[53] Such a suggestion caused little reaction among the other members, for they were already members of NATO. The Irish, however, had refused the invitation to join that security agreement in 1949 and had continued their policy of neutrality, defined simply as the avoidance of any political or military alliance. Contrary to Irish interests, the movement toward integration in political and security matters gathered momentum after 1975, culminating in the vote of the European Parliament on 14 February 1984 to approve the Draft Treaty on the European Union. The European Council also decided to establish a high-level committee of personal representatives to report on the steps needed to move the European Community (EC) in the direction of real integration. The committee, under the leadership of Ireland's James Dooge, filed its report in March 1985 for consideration by the EC.

The possibility thus exists of Ireland's having to decide in the near future whether continued involvement in the EC requires participation in both political and security discussions.[54] If it does, will that involvement mean the abandonment of neutrality? Any such decision will undoubtedly have a profound effect upon both defense policy and economic life. If the consequences of losing EC aid are too great, then neutrality will end. On the other hand, if the Irish elect to leave the EC to save neutrality, serious economic consequences are likely.

CURRENT THREATS

Within the context of the factors most influencing its policy--geography, proximity to and economic dependence upon Britain, limited funds, partition, neutrality, the United Nations, and the European Community--the Republic of Ireland has established six specific roles for its defense forces: 1) to defend the state against external aggression, 2) to aid the civil power in maintaining public peace and internal security, 3) to aid Civil Defence, 4) to provide observers and units for UN peace-keeping efforts, 5) to protect the fishery industry, and 6) such other specific duties (search and rescue missions, helicopter ambulance service, escort services for money and arms transfers, protection of essential facilities) as the government may require.[55]

The most significant of those is the first, the defense of the state against invasion from the outside; but the only time Ireland actually faced such a real possibility was from May to July 1940, when Hitler was preparing for an invasion of Britain as a follow-up to his rapid defeat and humiliation of France; that, of course, never materialized. The same is true of potential threats from Britain or the United States. Anglo-American planners discussed the relative strategic value of accessibility to Irish airfields and ports in the antisubmarine war, but such discussions never reached the stage where an invasion of Ireland was seriously considered. Everyone agreed that the Irish would resist such an Allied move, thereby driving the price of the Irish facilities far beyond their worth in the U-boat battle of the North Atlantic.[56]

No German attack came in 1940 and no British or American invasion occurred in 1943 or 1944, when England served as the staging area for the assault upon Hitler's Europe and German submarines endangered the Atlantic sea-lanes. Consequently, it is unlikely that Britain or its NATO allies, with the current forward deployment strategy, have given serious consideration to an invasion of Ireland in a future war.[57]   The only other possibility for such an attack would have to come from the Soviet Union, but that could only develop after the Soviets had successfully destroyed NATO forces on the Continent and occupied the United Kingdom. Even then there would be no real need to invade Ireland.   Consequently, in the context of the current East-West struggle, geography has graciously placed Ireland beyond the main battle area of a future European war, thus diminishing significantly the threat of an invasion.[58]

There are individuals, however, who assert that Ireland still holds the same strategic value for Britain, and hence for the rest of NATO, that it had in the age of sailing vessels and submarine warfare.   It still controls sea-lanes across the North Atlantic. Some recent writers, therefore, have suggested that Ireland could play three roles in World War III: to assist in control of the North Atlantic, to serve as part of an air bridge from the United States to Europe, and to provide sites for electronic warfare.   But in an age filled with long-range missiles, nuclear submarines, airplanes refueled in flight, funds for the Strategic Defense Initiative, and plans for a suborbital airplane capable of flying from Washington to Japan in two hours, one has to wonder if technology has not bypassed Ireland in any future conflict between NATO and the Warsaw Pact. The potential roles for Ireland in such a conflict could only materialize in a lengthy conventional European war and, if such a situation did present itself, there would be other ways to accomplish those missions without Ireland.   The Irish made the price for invasion too high in World War II; they can surely do the same in any future conflict.[59]

Although Ireland lacks a positive strategic value for Britain and NATO, it still could become an object of invasion by them, if only to deny the geographic position it holds to a potential aggressor from the Soviet bloc.   Here the current crisis in Northern Ireland carries the seed for such a problematic situation.   In that struggle the IRA wants not only to drive the Brits out of Belfast but also, according to many of its supporters, to create a unified socialist Irish state. If that should happen, a government sympathetic to the Soviet Union might emerge in Ireland, thereby creating a serious challenge for NATO.   Would such a government create a strategic liability for the line of communications between the United States and Europe in the period prior to the outbreak of a major war?   If

NATO strategists answer that question with a yes, it could possibly lead to a NATO-approved invasion to deny the assistance that a friendly Irish government could render to the Soviet Union.[60]

Such a scenario ultimately rests upon the assumption that a pro-Communist government could emerge in Ireland as a result of either a British withdrawal from Northern Ireland in the face of IRA activities there or worsening economic conditions in the Republic. Such an assumption, however, would appear highly unlikely in a country as Roman Catholic as Ireland. The IRA has the capacity to embarrass British forces in Northern Ireland because it has the support of local Catholics who look upon it as their protector. But one has to doubt whether the IRA has the necessary support in the Republic to overthrow the present government and to create a unified Irish socialist state friendly to the Communist world.[61] Short of its ability to do that, it is difficult to see what set of circumstances would bring Britain or NATO to consider any serious attempt to invade Ireland.

Invasion from Britain and NATO or from the Soviet Union and the Warsaw Pact thus remains remote now or in any future war. Nonetheless, there still remains one problem that worries NATO officials whenever Ireland is discussed: their concern that the troubles in Northern Ireland can interfere with the vitality of the British contribution to the defense of Western Europe. They focus on the seemingly endless drain on Britain's manpower and economic health caused by the Irish problems. For most Europeans and Americans, that problem is a small sideshow on the world stage that only complicates London's ability to meet its strategic and tactical commitments to the defense of Western Europe.[62] NATO allies tend to view the troubles as a negative force in British life and would like to see the problem resolved in a manner that will permit London to concentrate its available wealth and power upon the real issues between East and West. Such sentiments would never generate enough interest to cause any of the NATO states to suggest direct military intervention, but they could cause some of those nations to urge England to get out from under that problem as quickly and as painlessly as possible.[63]

For all these reasons one can argue that Ireland faces little threat of invasion from the two major power blocs in the world today and that only in the troubles in the north can one find a potentially remote justification for invasion from outside. In other words, the Irish army, if it is preparing to fulfill its most important role, may be preparing for an invasion that will never come.

If the army's first mission appears somewhat improbable, its second role does not, because of the sensitive issues associated with partition. For the past sixty years both the Irish people and their governments have been virtually mesmerized by the dream of final unification. Even those who pretend to ignore the issue, or who honestly do not care, cannot avoid the impact of partition; it conditions so many aspects of Irish life. The threat to the Republic from the north, however, is not viewed in terms of a normal cross-border invasion by one sovereign state into another. The sovereign power in the north, the United Kingdom, has neither the plans (apart from standard contingency) nor the interest to invade the Republic. Moreover, the IRA and the loyalist paramilitary units do not have the capability or the intention of invading southward. But there is a justifiable fear that violence in the north, generated by IRA attacks upon police forces and the British army plus a loyalist reaction to those efforts, may spill over into the south in the form of terrorist activities by both the IRA and the loyalist paramilitary units. This possibility constitutes the only real threat to the Republic from outside the state, and it is one for which the Irish army must be ready.[64]

Unfortunately, that potential problem from the north also is linked directly to today's main internal subversive threat. The Republic has faced the possibility of the IRA attempting a revolution in the south since the Civil War in 1922-23. To counter that threat, governments from 1922 to the present have passed special-powers laws to control the IRA, but it nonetheless persists as a force in Irish life simply because the British remain in the north. Enough Catholics on both sides of the border want to permit the illegal army a life of its own.[65] How much of a threat it represents is open to debate, but that it exists is not. For that reason alone, the army in the Republic cannot ignore it.

In addition to these potential problems, the Dublin government also confronts the question of coastal defense. At first, the British Royal Navy assumed that responsibility, but Ireland acquired it in 1938 with the return of the ports. The Royal Navy with the assistance of the United States, however, continued to protect Ireland's coasts during World War II. When the war ended, Ireland formed a formal naval service of its own, but its work in peacetime was reduced to protecting the fishery industry.[66] That became a major task with the decision to extend the territorial waters limit to 200 miles for fishing purposes, increasing the area of responsibility for

Ireland's small navy to 136,000 square miles, an undertaking that has yet to be successfully managed.[67]

Dublin, therefore, has to deal with three realistic threats to its security: 1) violence may spill over from Northern Ireland, 2) the IRA may attempt a revolution, and 3) foreign fishermen may destroy the Irish fishing industry. Moreover, it has at least to consider the unlikely possibilities that the Soviet Union may attack Ireland and that NATO may act to deny the use of Ireland to the Soviet bloc prior to the outbreak of war, along with the highly improbable circumstance that, in an extended conventional European conflict, NATO forces may move to take over Ireland to keep sea-lanes open.

CURRENT POLICIES

Finances

Current financial limitations upon defense are as strict as ever, if not more so. In the estimated 1986 budget, social services expenditures, which include health, education, social welfare, housing, and subsidy payments, were at Irish £5.1 billion (in a total budget of £7.0 billion) and constituted 30.4 percent of the gross national product (GNP) for 1986. At the same time total security costs (courts, prisons, police, and defense forces) would reach £661 million in 1986, less than 10 percent of total government expenditures. The Ministry of Defence would spend £301 million, slightly more than the police, or 1.8 percent of the GNP. That amount is £172 million less than the cost of unemployment insurance. In terms of capital services, the problem is even more acute. The Department of Defence received £5.2 million in the 1986 estimate, out of a total capital budget exceeding £648 million, a figure amounting to a 31 percent increase over the 1985 allocation. The Department of Fisheries, however, would spend more (£5,813,000) in capital projects, as would the Department of Education (£85,600,000), while the Department of Environment (housing, water, sewage, roads) would spend £197,008,000. If the Department of Defence suffered from budget controls both before and after World War II, one can argue that the conditions of the 1980s rival those of the past.[68]

This lack of money, unfortunately, will not go away, at least for the foreseeable future. The economic boom that came to Ireland in the 1960s and continued into the 1970s, with the admission of

Ireland to the EEC, suffered serious setbacks as the 1980s approached. The oil crises of 1973 and 1979, resulting in a tenfold rise in the price per barrel, struck Ireland hard. The Fianna Fáil government that took office in 1977 decided to sustain economic activity on borrowed funds, but that policy did not solve the basic problems. It may have increased the number of public service jobs, but it also caused a major jump in the foreign debt to be serviced.[69]   After the somewhat frightening political experience of living through three general elections in less than eighteen months in 1981 and 1982--during which no government was able to develop a plan to solve the foreign debt--the coalition administration of Garrett Fitzgerald (Fine Gael and Labour) that took over in late 1982 did develop an economic plan for the future and submitted it in 1984 to the Dail, where it was approved.[70]

That plan proposed a policy of strict financial control of expenditures and heavy taxation to reduce the nation's foreign debt, but in September 1985 a government minister suggested that the policy would require an additional ten years of effort to get results. Some politicians have argued that Fitzgerald has not reduced the growth of the debt because of interest payments and deficit budgets.[71]   In such an atmosphere there is little hope for any large increase in expenditures for the Department of Defence, which will have to live within very severe constraints in the foreseeable future.

Geography

The military is also constrained by Ireland's geography. Because of the island setting, the government has the responsibility of protecting the approaches to the country, as well as the resources of the sea within its territorial jurisdiction. It must develop naval forces that can patrol 136,000 square miles of ocean and 1,190 miles of coastline, and it must provide military forces that can cover an island with a total area of 32,595 square miles.[72] Fortunately, one can drive from the east to the west in less than four hours and from north to south in less than eight. One would have to assume that the army could move rapidly from one place to the next, but upon reflection, the nature and condition of the road system will work against any such rapid disposition of large forces. Except for a few miles in the immediate Dublin area, there are few highways that can provide for a speedy displacement of major, large-sized units. Additionally, almost all roads, with rare exceptions, run right through the center of the towns, the vast majority of which are small villages with narrow nineteenth-century streets. Any knowledgeable and determined invader with the careful use of air power could virtually cripple large-scale military movements by turning these towns into roadblocks, thereby necessitating cross-country travel. Such tactics would at least slow the advance of military forces in most parts of the country and in some areas would virtually stop it.

Within the restrictions of force size, which financial resources alone will determine for the immediate future, the Irish must therefore develop plans to distribute troops throughout the island to cover likely landing sites and invasion routes. Concurrently, they must hold forces under central control to serve as a counterattack element to resist an enemy's main thrust. Such was the basic strategic plan developed by the general staff during the "Emergency" from 1939 to 1945. That plan concentrated the great bulk of the Irish forces in the southeast to face the German threat and in the Dublin area to confront the British menace. From present dispositions it would appear that a similar plan exists today. The army would meet the enemy with all available units. In case of the defeat of the regular and reserve forces, the state would resort to guerrilla warfare.[73]

Today's dispersion of forces is also prompted by the other peacetime missions assigned to the Permanent Defence Force. By distributing units throughout the island, men and equipment are readily available on short notice to assist the police in the internal security mission, to provide escort and installation security operations when requested, and to permit the integration of reserve units into the total force structure.[74]

Force Level and Organization

Within the existing parameters of financial limitations and geography, the government of Ireland today maintains a Permanent Defence Force of 13,668 men and women (as of 31 May 1985), a total Reserve Defence Force (RDF) of 9,699, and a civilian staff of 2,353, including those in the office of the Minister of Defence--all of which reflect slight reductions from fiscal year 1984. The figures on the PDF and RDF are below those levels established by law: 18,060 for the PDF (15,783 army, 1,172 air corps, and 1,105 naval service); and 22,214 for the RDF. In terms of the total population the current PDF strength represents only .04 percent and the RDF represents .03 percent.[75]

The total force is organized into the army headquarters and four territorial commands: Eastern, Southern, Western, and Curragh. Each of these commands is composed of a headquarters and command units (garrison-type troops, school personnel), an infantry brigade (two infantry battalions with support units), an FCA Command Group which controls all the reserve units in the geographic area, and some additional detachments. For the present land forces the equipment problems of the past have been somewhat eliminated, and the inventory includes Swedish, French, British, and Italian weapons systems. The policy today appears to be one of buying the best available equipment for the best price, except from the Soviet bloc.[76]

The real problem in equipment comes when one examines the air corps and the naval service. Equipping those forces has always been difficult, and the last modernization effort dates from the mid-1970s. In 1976, CM Fouga *Magisters*, originally built for service in the Belgian Congo, were acquired to replace old British *Vampires*, and in the following year ten Siai Marchetti SF-26-W *Warriors* arrived to replace the British *Chipmunks* and *Provosts*. Then in 1977 the air force leased and later purchased two Beechcraft (KA-200 *Super King Air*), for long-range surveillance in support of the naval mission, adding a third in 1980. Eight Cessna 172 Hand K models were also acquired for reconnaissance missions on the border. No helicopters were in service until 1964, when eight Aérospatiale *Alouette III*s were purchased. Plans are now under way to replace those craft with new French *Dauphines*.[77]

The total force of forty-one planes is used for training, transport, maritime patrol, VIP and liaison transportation, and support of the Garda (police). With the current inventory of aircraft and a total force of 881 personnel (31 May 1985), the current peacetime missions can be maintained except for complete coverage of the fishery protection mission, but one would have to question seriously the effectiveness of these forces in aerial combat.[78]

The same problems face the naval service. From its inception at the end of World War II into the early 1970s, it used British vessels, but these were retired starting in 1968 over a three-year period. To replace them, the government contracted with Verolme Cork Dockyard for ships designed especially for the fishery protection mission. Work did not begin on these vessels until 1971, and it was therefore necessary to purchase three coastal minesweepers built in the 1950s from the British. They were acquired in January and February 1971, and the naval service took delivery of the first Verolme ship, the *Deirdre*, in May 1972. Ireland's entrance into the EEC in the following year and the declaration of the 200-mile fishing limit in 1977 required a new training and support vessel and three additional fishery protection vessels from the Verolme yards between 1978 and 1980. Recently, the navy took possession of a new class of ship that will have a helicopter pad on board to provide more extensive coverage of the miles that have to be protected. Today, the vessels built at the Verolme yards patrol the offshore areas, while the three British minesweepers work on the inshore waters. With such a small force the Irish have great difficulty protecting their fishery industry. If these units cannot adequately fulfill their peacetime role, they surely will not be able to fulfill their wartime mission.[79]

THE FUTURE

The entire defense force is composed of volunteers. Only once, at the end of World War II, did the discussion of a "national service policy" arise, but nothing came from that suggestion. Not even during the Emergency did the government establish conscription, and there is no likelihood that such a policy could be implemented unless the nation faced a devastating defeat that would force the institution of a guerrilla war program.[80] The military also works under the general policy that Ireland has no aggressive interests and only wishes to remain as an "active" neutral in world affairs.

This policy of neutrality is, however, currently under serious attack from two quarters. One group continues to suggest that the British withdraw from Northern Ireland in exchange for Ireland's entrance into NATO. Such a fundamental change may have considerable support among professional soldiers and many politicians. It obviously would require the rapid acquisition of modern equipment, the expansion of the present forces, and possibly even the commitment of a full division in support of NATO operations. Some professionals have suggested that maybe two or three divisions could be formed, which would mean a fourfold increase in military manpower. Such a policy would clearly appeal to those politicians who look to army service as a way to reduce the high unemployment rate among Ireland's youth, especially if the cost could be picked up by the United States. The Irish do not have enough available cash; it is unclear whether the United States does.[81]

The neutrality-for-partition argument may be more wishful thinking than anything else, but the pressure from the other quarter, the European Community, that could end neutrality cannot be dismissed so lightly. The European drive toward real unity that produced the draft treaty of 14 February 1984 and the Dooge Report of March 1985 continued its momentum at the EC meetings in June 1985 in Milan and in December 1985 in Luxembourg. Since the demands for EC coordination have continued to grow in foreign policy decisions in 1986, Ireland may well have to decide between continued membership in the EC or neutrality.

Within the context of those pressures for ending its neutrality, Ireland continues its involvement in the UN peace-keeping forces both with observers and unit deployment in Lebanon, but some signs of concern for that work have appeared recently. In October 1986 at the United Nations, both Prime Minister Fitzgerald and Foreign Minister Peter Barry complained that the United Nations Interim Force in Lebanon (UNIFIL) could not fulfill its mission, but the Irish did not withdraw from the force and did agree to keep their commitment to the United Nations for the immediate future.[82]

Another recent development that has and will influence defense forces is the Hillsborough Anglo-Irish Agreement on Northern Ireland of 15 November 1985. It gave to the Dublin government a role in the affairs of Northern Ireland, including security questions. Unionists appear ready to do everything possible to reverse this role. The IRA also has condemned the agreement because the Dublin government has pledged not to use force to unify the island, to wait for a majority in the north to seek such unification, and to recognize British sovereignty for the present. Since both the nationalist and loyalist extremists have vowed to fight the agreement and have already increased their activities to discredit it, both the London and Dublin governments will probably have to increase their military and police forces in the area.[83]

As the Irish continue to participate in the peace-keeping effort in the Middle East and prepare for more border activities, concern for the effectiveness of present force levels will persist. The army element of the PDF can perform the police duties now assigned to it both in Lebanon and on the border, but it is difficult to imagine how it could fulfill its role to serve as the base for an expanded army since there does not appear to be any program in place to stockpile sufficient equipment or to prepare the trained manpower.

Even the efficiency of the current active reserve forces would have to be questioned because of the recent drop in numbers and the high turnover of personnel.   On 31 December 1983 the figure given in the Dail for the FCA was 16,361, but the budget request for 1985 allocated pay for only 9,000 troops.   More significantly, in the period from 1980 to 1983 the army enlisted 15,472 soldiers in the FCA, while discharging 21,905.[84]   Such a turnover in such a short period of time, coupled with a corresponding reduction in strength, will seriously affect efficiency.

If the reserve naval force is weak, the active force may also have some difficulties.   It currently has six vessels, but only three are capable of covering the 136,000 square miles of open sea necessary for fishery protection.   Total strength was 902 as of 31 May 1985.   The closing of the Verolme Cork Dockyard in early 1985 means that an expansion of the present fleet will require purchases. Furthermore, the current fleet is equipped with armaments useful only in police actions to control illegal fishing but not very helpful in modern naval warfare.   The naval reserve is in worse condition. As of 31 October 1984 the total strength of the force was 353, organized into two groups but equipped with only five rowing/sailing boats, one for each company, two yachts, and a leased motor launch.[85]

If the general reserve forces of the army and navy are questionable in terms of combat effectiveness and the active navy simply is not equipped for naval warfare on the high seas, one could hope that the air force is better off in this respect; it is not.   Most of today's planes are used for pilot training, transportation of all kinds (including VIP), maritime patrol, and aid to civilian authorities. The only really operational aircraft in a military sense are the Cessnas and *Alouettes* when they operate along the border, but they are not equipped for combat operations, nor are the pilots trained for such missions.   Only the Fouga *Magisters* are designated for a combat support role as the Light Strike Squadron, but they were designed in the late 1950s with a top speed of 540 knots, hardly the kind of speed to provide any degree of survivability on today's battlefield.[86]   As for the rest of the fleet, it is vulnerable even to armed terrorists with modern surface-to-air missiles.   And on top of everything else, even the land forces in a few years will have to think in terms of replacing their major end-items.[87]

The future of defense policy will depend upon a combination of pressures, some of which have influenced policymaking since 1921. Thus, geography will remain, as will the British, partition, and financial difficulties. The UN mission could change, but that would appear unlikely, for Ireland receives from it far more than it gives. Involvement with the European Community will be subjected to serious debate in the next few years, but again the reality of net gain for Ireland will probably preclude any withdrawal by the Irish.

Thus, only the policy of neutrality can change, perhaps as a result of what takes place in the north in terms of the implementation of the Hillsborough Agreement. Success there could remove the prime support of the neutrality policy. Such a development in combination with EC pressure could mean the abandonment of neutrality and the joining of NATO. If that happens and a war in Europe follows, Ireland will contribute to the anti-Soviet forces. If, on the other hand, neither relations with the north nor the EC pressures create an opportunity for the Irish to end their neutrality policy prior to the outbreak of another war, Ireland will stay out of the fighting, as it did in World War II.

NOTES

[1]John Bowle, *The Imperial Achievement: The Rise and Transformation of the British Empire* (Boston: Little Brown, 1974), pp. 198-299; Angus Calder, *Revolutionary Empire: The Rise of the English Speaking Empires from the Fifteenth Century to the 1780's* (New York: E. P. Dutton, 1981), pp. 36-64, 93-106.

[2]J. C. Beckett, *The Making of Modern Ireland, 1603-1923* (London: Faber and Faber, 1966), tells this part of the story.

[3]Ibid., pp. 435-54; Charles Townshend, *The British Campaign in Ireland, 1919-1921* (Oxford: Oxford University Press, 1975); Joseph Curran, *The Birth of the Irish Free State, 1921-1923* (University: University of Alabama Press, 1981), pp. 27-30, 132-46; Sheila Lawlor, *Britain and Ireland, 1914-1923* (Dublin: Gill and MacMillan), pp. 44-65, 99-145.

[4]Maurice Moynihan, *Speeches and Statements by Eamon de Valera, 1917-73* (Dublin: Gill and MacMillan, 1980), p. 628. In the index to these speeches the word partition has the longest list of references. The question has constantly reappeared in Irish life since 1920, and the current debate over the Anglo-Irish Agreement of 15 November 1985 only underlines the enormous problem that partition and the presence of British troops in Northern Ireland have created for both sides of the border.

[5]Bowyer Bell, *The Secret Army: The IRA, 1916-1970*, 2d ed. (Cambridge: MIT Press, 1980), pp. 73-141; Timothy Patrick Coogan, *The IRA* (London: Fantana Paperbacks, 1980), p. 38.

[6]Basil Chubb, *The Government and Politics of Ireland* (Stanford: Stanford University Press, 1982), pp. 2-4.

[7]Ronan Fanning, *The Irish Department of Finance, 1922-1958* (Dublin: Institute of Public Administration, 1978), tells the story of the influence of finances upon all government departments.   For the army problems that began in 1922, see pp. 42-56.   The story of the shortage of funds for defense was also a public issue.   See *The Irish Times*, 2 July 1924, 22 April 1927; "The Future of the Army," *An T-Oglach* 3 (January 1930):   19; "A Politician's View of the Problem of Defence," *An T-Oglach* 4 (March 1931): 13.   George O'Brien, "Defence and Opulence," *An T-Oglach* 4 (March 1931): 37.   Numerous references to the issue can also be found in reports filed by the American Military Attaché in London.   See 2633-18, 2633-20, Military Intelligence Division, 1917-41, War Department General Staff, Record Group 165, National Archives (hereafter cited as MID, WDGS, RG 165, NA).

[8]Lawlor, *Britain and Ireland*, pp. 26-27; The Earl of Longford and Thomas P. O'Neil, *Eamon de Valera* (London: Hutchinson, 1970), pp. 71-74; Moynihan, *Speeches by de Valera*, pp. 12-13.

[9]Minutes of Informal Conference, Naval Defence, 13 October 1921, Peace Negotiations, DC 2/304/4, I & II, Provisional Cabinet Papers, State Paper Office, Dublin (hereafter cited as SPOD).   See also Frank Pakenham, *Peace by Ordeal* (London: Sedgwick and Jackson, 1972), pp. 75, 233-35.

[10]For details see Calton Younger, *Ireland's Civil War* (London: Frederick Muller, 1968).

[11]Mary Ann Gianella Valiulis, *Almost a Rebellion, The Irish Army Mutiny of 1924* (Cork: Tower Books, 1985), pp. 51-84.

[12]*Dail Debates* 3 (1923), col. 1603; vol. 4 (1923), col. 1295.

[13]Chief of Staff to Defence Minister, 19 November 1923, S.3442A, Cabinet Minutes and Papers, SPOD.

[14]Basil Chubb, ed., *A Source Book of Irish Government* (Dublin: Institute of Public Administration, 1964), p. 90.

[15]Defence Policy, approved by the Executive Council, 13 November 1925, S.4541, Cabinet Minutes and Papers, SPOD.

[16]Private Secretary, Minister of Defence to Secretary, Executive Council, 14 April 1927, S.3442, Cabinet Minutes and Papers, SPOD.

[17]Conversation with Commandant Peter Young, OIC, Army Archives, 21 August 1986.

[18]The 19 November 1923 scheme included provisions for a military college. The first public announcement that a college would be organized came in 1927 (*The Irish Times*, 18 March 1927), but it was not created until 1930. See *A Call to Arms* (Dublin: Department of Defence, 1945), p. 83.

[19]The 1923 scheme called for (in addition to infantry units) engineer, air service, artillery, medical, police, armored car service, signal, and cavalry units. The plan eventually emerged publicly with some minor changes in July 1924 in the form of a White Paper, "Army Organisation." This was also published under "Army Organisation: Full Text of the White Paper Recently Issued," *An T-Oglach* 2, New Series (2 August 1924): 12-15.

[20]G-2 Report #21854, From M.A. London, 28 April 1928, 2633-18, MID, WDGS, RG165, NA.

[21]Address by the President, Meeting of Heads of Departments, 14 October 1928, P 35/152, Patrick McGilligan Papers, Archives Department, University College, Dublin.

[22]*Dail Debates* 3 (1923), col. 1194. The question of the size and strength of the military forces came up at least every year during the budget debates on the Defence Estimates. Some members of the Dail did not want a strong military for fear that its loyalty would be directed toward the government and not the state. Others feared that it would fall into the hands of a secret society such as the old Irish Republican Army (*The Irish Times*, 10 October 1924).

[23]J. Sheenan, ed., *Defence Forces Handbook* (Dublin: Department of Defence, 1984), p. 8.

[24]Moynihan, *Speeches by de Valera*, p. 193.

[25]G-2 Report #31651 from M.A. London, 21 February 1934, 2633-18, MID, WDGS, RG165, NA.

[26]Longford and O'Neil, *De Valera*, pp. 276-81.

[27]Moynihan, *Speeches by de Valera*, pp. 302-29, 416-22; Paul Montgomery Canning, *Retreat from Empire: British Attitudes and Policy toward Ireland 1921-1941* (Ann Arbor, MI: University Microfilms International, 1982), pp. 363-67, 373-93, 407-9; Malcolm MacDonald, *Titans and Others* (London: Collins, 1972), p. 82.

[28]T. Ryle Dwyer, *Irish Neutrality and the U.S.A., 1939-47* (Dublin: Gill and MacMillan, 1977), pp. 47-65. The official reason for neutrality was partition, but there had to be other reasons, including the total lack of defense capabilities of the army.

[29]Joseph T. Carroll, *Ireland in the War Years* (New York: Crane, Russak and Company, 1975), p. 130; Robert Fisk, *In Time of War: Ireland, Ulster and the Price of Neutrality 1939-1945* (Philadelphia: University of Pennsylvania Press, 1983).

[30]Sheenan, *Handbook*, p. 12. There had been, from the beginning, plans for a reserve force (see "The Army Code," *An T-Oglach* 1 [1 December 1923]: 3), but the various attempts to create an adequate reserve during the 1920s and 1930s clearly did not work.

[31]Raymond James Raymond, "The Marshall Plan and Ireland, 1947-1952," in P. J. Drudy, ed., *The Irish in America: Emigration, Assimilation and Impact* (New York: Cambridge University Press, 1985), pp. 295-328.

[32]Lord Longford and Anne McHardy, *Ulster* (London: Weidenfeld and Nicolson, 1981), pp. 95-96; David Miller, *Queen's Rebels: Ulster Loyalism in Historical Perspective* (New York: Barnes and Noble, 1978), p. 133.

[33]Patrick Buckland, *A History of Northern Ireland* (New York: Holmes and Meier, 1981), pp. 88-89.

[34]Ronan Fanning, "The United States and Irish Participation in NATO: The Debate of 1950," *Irish Studies in International Affairs* 1 (1979): 38-48. Fanning accepts the official view that Ireland could not join an alliance designed to protect democracy when a member of that alliance, Britain, occupied part of Ireland. On the other hand, it has been argued that other factors were involved, including political pressures that caused the Irish to reject the invitation. See Raymond James Raymond, "Ireland's 1949 NATO Decision: A Reassessment," *Eire-Ireland* 20 (Fall 1985): 19-42. The traditional view is held by Sean Cronin, "The Making of NATO and the Partition of Ireland," *Eire-Ireland* 20 (Summer 1985): 6-18.

[35]Carroll, *Ireland in the War Years*, pp. 113-17, 119; Fisk, *In Time of War*, pp. 166, 171, 218, 367. Fisk shows how the British virtually played with the Irish over war materiel. For another account of what Ireland had in terms of military equipment see Bernard Share, *The Emergency: Neutral Ireland 1939-1945* (Dublin: Gill and MacMillan, 1978), pp. 45, 47, 68, and the various photographs showing military forces and equipment.

[36]Memorandum for President, Visit of McBride, 22 March 1951, 740.13/3-2251, and Bruce MacArthur (Paris) to Secretary of State, #1377, 31 August 1951, 740A.5/8-3151, Decimal File, Department of State, Record Group 59, National Archives.

[37]Executive Session of the Senate Foreign Relations Committee (Historical Series), vol. 3, pt. 2, 82d Cong., 1st sess. 1951 (Washington, DC: Government Printing Office, 1951), pp. 560-61.

[38]American Embassy to Department of External Affairs, 10 January 1952; Minister of External Affairs to C. H. Huston, United States Embassy, 29 January 1952, S.14106 I, Cabinet Minutes and Papers, SPOD.

[39]Semi-Monthly Progress Report as of the 30th September 1952, Department of Defence, S.15063, Cabinet Minutes and Papers, SPOD.

[40]Dail Eireann, *Report of the Special Committee on the Defence Bill 1951* (Dublin: Stationery Office, 1952).

[41]Norman MacQueen, "Ireland's Entry into the U.N. 1946-56," in Tom Gallagher and James O'Connell, *Contemporary Irish Studies* (Manchester: Manchester University Press, 1983), pp. 65-80. The Soviets first claimed that they would not permit Ireland to join the United Nations because they did not have bilateral relations with it, but later changed that argument to one where they claimed that Ireland had not joined in the war effort that created the United Nations. Actually one can argue that the Soviets voted against Ireland because they did not want to add a pro-Western state to an organization in which the USSR was already outnumbered. Only after a careful deal was made between the United States and the Soviet Union was Ireland permitted to join. That came when the superpowers agreed to permit sixteen states to enter in 1955: Albania, Austria, Bulgaria, Cambodia, Ceylon, Finland, Hungary, Ireland, Italy, Jordan, Laos, Libya, Nepal, Portugal, Romania, and Spain. For the impact upon the army see Sheenan, *Handbook*, p. 67, and the articles in *An Cosantoir* 45 (July 1985).

[42]Moynihan, *Speeches by de Valera*, pp. 466-69.

[43]Fergal Tobin, *The Best of Decades: Ireland in the Sixties* (Dublin: Gill and MacMillan, 1984), pp. 2, 6-7. The impact of this change is also discussed in William G. Shade, "Strains of Modernization: The Republic of Ireland under LeMass and Lynch," *Eire-Ireland* 10 (Spring 1979): 26-46.

[44]Bell, *The Secret Army*, pp. 289-336; Coogan, *The IRA*, pp. 377-418. Coogan argues that it cost the Dublin government £400,000 for each year the campaign continued, and it lasted from 1956 to 1962. In contrast, the current problems in Northern Ireland, according to one estimate, cost the Republic £1,000,000 per day (*The Irish Press*, 29 April 1986), and the cost to Britain is £1.5 billion per year (*The Irish Times* [14 April 1986]).

[45]Lt. Col. F. Steward, "25th Anniversary--32 INFBN: A Short History," *An Cosantoir* 45 (July 1985): 236.

[46]Comdt. Dorcha Lee, "Twenty-Five Years On," ibid. 45 (July 1985): 242-43.

[47]Ibid. Lee claimed: "In the area of equipment alone it hastened the acquisition of the FN rifle, the MAG, combat uniforms, up-to-date armoured cars, signal equipment and transports."

[48]*The Irish Times*, 28 September 1985.

[49]Longford and McHardy, *Ulster*, pp. 113-21. The crisis in Londonderry occurred in January 1969, but a much more serious clash came in August 1969 as an aftermath of an Apprentice Boys march.

[50]Sean MacStiofain, *Revolutionary in Ireland* (London: G. Cremonesi, 1975), p. 115.

[51]Sheenan, *Handbook*, pp. 80-81.

[52]*The Accession of Ireland to the European Community* (Dublin: Stationery Office, 1973) contains the documents on the accession as they were given to the Oireachtas. See also P. J. Drudy and Dermot McAleese, *Ireland and the European Community* (New York: Cambridge University Press, 1984), p. 3; and David Coombes, *Ireland and the European Communities: Ten Years of Membership* (Dublin: Gill and MacMillan, 1983), pp. 1-5.

[53]Committee on Institutional Affairs, *Selection of Texts Concerning Institutional Matters of the Community from 1950 to 1982* (Luxembourg: European Parliament, 1982), pp. 366-91.

[54]Ad Hoc Committee for Institutional Affairs, "Report to the European Council (March 1985)," in Roland Bieber, Jean-Paul Jacqué, and Joseph H. H. Weiler, *An Ever Closer Union: A Critical Analysis of the Draft Treaty Establishing the European Union* (Luxembourg: Office for Official Publications of the European Communities, 1985), pp. 350-52. In this report Chairman James Dooge, the Irish representative, "did not agree to the inclusion of the section on security and defence." It is clear that he had to disassociate his country from the section of the report, for it referred to the Atlantic Alliance as "the framework for and basis of our security," among other things.

[55]Sheenan, *Handbook*, p. 17.

[56]Patrick Keatinge, *A Place among Nations: Issues of Irish Foreign Policy* (Dublin: Institute of Public Administration, 1978), p. 90.

[57]Colonel Jonathan Alford, "North's Strategic Value Is a Non-Issue," *The Irish Times*, 31 January 1986. Colonel Alford, then deputy director of the International Institute for Strategic Studies, London, argued in this article that strategic considerations had nothing to do with the British government's decision to sign the Hillsborough Agreement of November 1985. In effect he argued that Ireland has no strategic value in the present East-West conflict. In case of a war with the Warsaw Pact, as Colonel Alford argues, troops would be leaving Ireland, not entering it.

[58]William Fitzgerald, *Irish Unification and NATO* (Dublin: Dublin University Press, 1982), p. 37; Patrick Keatinge, *A Singular Stance: Irish Neutrality in the 1980s* (Dublin: Institute of Public Administration, 1984), pp. 66-67. There is some talk about Soviet interest in invading Ireland with a large airborne force; for that reason some have argued that Ireland should concentrate its military expenditures on defense against such an attack. Such speculation, however, overlooks the likely environment of the next war, which would virtually preclude any hope of a Soviet force reaching Ireland in the air. The realization of what will happen in the air has led the U.S. Army to introduce the concept of air-land war as its basic doctrine. In addition, Soviet tactics call for the employment of airborne

forces to support the main attack on the ground. That would be at some distance from Ireland. No one who has studied Soviet tactics could support the argument that airborne forces would be used against Ireland before the total collapse of Western European defenses, and thus there would be no need to use them.

[59]Sir John Hackett, *The Third World War: August 1985* (London: Sidgwick and Jackson, 1978) and *The Third World War: The Untold Story* (London: Sidgwick and Jackson, 1982). For a discussion of his ideas on Ireland see Keatinge, *A Singular Stance*, pp. 60-62.

[60]Such an invasion would have to precede the outbreak of war in Europe, and the pro-Soviet attitude would have to be so blatant as to justify such an invasion. That would contradict de Valera's often-stated guarantee that Ireland would never be used as a platform for an attack upon England. He said so as early as 1920 while in the United States, repeated it during the 1921 treaty negotiations, and said the same thing again during the 1938 negotiations. For the role of the IRA see Kevin Kelly, *Britain's Longest War* (Westgate, CT: Laurence Hill and Co., 1982): pp. 269, 272.

[61]The strength of the IRA has always been a matter of debate. At times active elements have fallen as low as several hundred, and seldom have they amounted to more than a few thousand. Its power rests not so much upon the active elements, but upon the sympathy of large numbers on both sides of the border for its self-imposed mission to drive the British out of Ireland. Kelly, *Britain's Longest War*, p. 267. He gives the results of two polls that reflect IRA support among people in the Republic. The strength of the Catholic Church in Irish life will probably never disappear, at least not in the foreseeable future; the recent vote on the issue of divorce once again proved the power of the institution. *New York Times*, 26 June 1986.

[62]The sideshow effect can be clearly seen in what the American press publishes about events in Ireland. The *Philadelphia Inquirer*, for instance, publishes no more than two full articles per month on the northern crisis, and the bulk of that information is found in the "International News in Brief" columns where very short statements are made. The *New York Times* may average four full-length articles per month, but even in that once-Irish town the bulk of the news from Ireland is found under the "Around the World" heading. That is also true in Pittsburgh and Cleveland where I recently looked for articles. Only in Boston may more detailed coverage be found, but only marginally. In many ways Americans virtually ignore what is happening in Northern Ireland, as do many in the Republic.

[63]The European reaction to the Anglo-Irish Agreement of 15 November 1985 reflects this attitude. See *The Irish Times*, 1, 16, 18 November 1985.

[64]Coogan, *The IRA*, pp. 534-45. This particular problem has grown appreciably since the signing of the 15 November 1985 Hillsborough Agreement. The violent reaction of the majority in the north virtually dominated the Dublin press from the signing into the early summer of 1986, when the referendum on the divorce issue came to dominate the news. On numerous occasions the Reverend Ian Paisley has stated that a civil war in the north could only spill into the south.

[65]Kelly, *Britain's Longest War*, pp. 9-141. The existence of the IRA threat in the south has virtually converted the army, the only real armed force in the country, into a guard and police escort service. In the debates on the Defence Estimates in May 1986, the government reported that "escorts for explosive and blasting operations were provided on about 900 occasions, almost 4,500 escorts for the protection of movement of cash were provided; about 150 requests for bomb disposal teams were handled." *Dail Debates* 366, cols. 2183-84.

[66]Sheenan, *Handbook*, p. 63.

[67]Ibid., p. 65.

[68]*Estimates for Public Services 1986* (Abridged Version) (Dublin: Stationery Office, 1986), pp. 59-60.

[69]Padraig O'Malley, *The Uncivil Wars: Ireland Today* (Boston: Houghton Mifflin, 1983), pp. 388-92. O'Malley discusses the economic problems through 1982; those conditions have remained at best as they were then. It is difficult to get a clear idea of exactly what is happening in the economy, but on the streets of Dublin one does get the idea that conditions are bad and getting worse.

[70]*The Way Forward: National Economic Plan, 1983-1987* (Dublin: Stationery Office, 1982). This was the plan offered by Fianna Fáil, but Charles Haughey and his party lost the election in November 1982, the third general election in less than eighteen months. The new coalition government did not develop its plan, *Building on Reality, 1985-1987* (Dublin: Stationery Office, 1984), until October 1984; the debate on the plan can be found in *Dail Debates* 352 (1984), cols. 249ff.

[71]*The Irish Times*, 28 August 1985; *Dail Debates* 352 (1984), cols. 2403-18, 2497-98.

[72]Sheenan, *Handbook*, p. 16.

[73]Ibid., pp. 18-24. The precise plans for the Emergency years are not available for review, but they may be soon; the recently passed National Archives Bill in theory will open files under a thirty-year rule. The dispositions of the forces during the Emergency, however, are very similar to those of today, with some exceptions to take care of the Northern Ireland crisis.

[74]The question of the exact role of the FCA in today's force structure has been a problem for some time. In 1959 a staff study concluded that the FCA should be integrated into the PDF in much the same way as the various classifications of personnel were used to fill out units during the Emergency. At that time a particular unit would include regulars, reservists, and volunteers. The idea in 1959 was to increase the level of FCA training and proficiency, but the system clearly did not work and in 1979 the FCA and PDF were again separated. The FCA headquarters, now established in each of the four commands, controls and administers all FCA units in that command area. Under this current organization the FCA is essentially used to support the PDF by manning "the various army barracks when the Army were along the Border." See *Dail Debates* 366, Col. 2197.

[75]The question of current force levels is difficult to determine since they are constantly changing. The figures here were taken from the *Revised Estimates for Public Services, 1985* (Dublin: Stationery Office, 1985), p. 175; and Sheenan, *Handbook*, p. 18.

[76]Sheenan, *Handbook*, pp. 18-34; Hughes to O'Grady, 19 June 1985.

[77]*An Cosantair* 45 (March 1985). This issue is devoted to the air corps. Sheenan, *Handbook*, pp. 6-63; Hughes to O'Grady, 19 June 1985; *The Irish Times*, 2 October 1985.

[78]*Revised Estimates, 1985*, p. 175; *The Irish Times*, 2 October 1985. *The Irish Times* claimed that "there is no training in air-to-air firing in the Air Corps. Nor are there home-based radar reporting facilities or reaction mechanisms to counter overflying by unauthorized aircraft. Notification of such incidents takes place, but this is provided by outside traffic agencies. Irish Air Corps fliers tow drogues for target practice for Army and Navy gunners, but their own pilots do not fire on drogues in the air, nor is there any indication that such training is planned for the future."

[79]*Evening Herald* (Dublin), 26 August 1985. See page 11 under the headline "Salmon--95 M that get away." The article included a picture of one of Ireland's patrol ships with the caption, "Too few ships to protect what is ours."

[80]The issue of conscription is a very emotional one in Ireland. Many argue that "the past is the present" in Ireland, and this is one issue that helps prove the point. Both in World War I and World War II (see Joseph L. Rosenberg, "Irish Conscription, 1941," *Eire-Ireland* 10 [Spring 1979], pp. 16-25), the British tried to impose a draft, in the former for the whole island and in the latter only for Northern Ireland. In both cases the uproar forced withdrawal of the plan. There is clearly no chance that conscription will ever reach the level of a political debate, much less a serious effort at implementation.

[81]Fitzgerald, *Irish Unification and NATO*, pp. viii, xi.   The question of finding funds in the United States to pay for the arming of Ireland is now compounded by the drive in America to balance the budget.   Even though the U.S. Supreme Court declared a key section of the Gramm-Rudman-Hollings Budget Law unconstitutional, it does not appear that the drive for a balanced budget will disappear.   What happened to the aid from the United States to support the Hillsborough Agreement may indicate what will happen to aid for rearmament.   One group in the American Congress, the Friends of Ireland, wanted $500 million in one sum, but as of July 1986 only the House of Representatives voted the money, $250 million over five years. See *The Irish Times*, 16 November 1985.

[82]*The Irish Times*, 28 September, 18, 20, 27 October 1986; *Dail Debates* 366 (1986), cols. 2184-86, 3198-99.

[83]Anglo-Irish Agreement 1985, *New York Times*, 16 November 1985; *The Irish Times*, 16 November 1985; *Dail Debates* 352 (1985), col. 73.

[84]*Dail Debates* 354 (1986), cols. 909-13.

[85]Ibid., cols. 1053-84.

[86]*The Irish Times*, 2 October 1985.

[87]*Dail Debates* 366 (1986), cols. 199-200.   Funds for the purchase of defense equipment were reduced by 14 percent in the 1986 Defence Estimate.   The opposition spokesman on defense on 23 May 1986 argued that "this is a very big reduction when one realizes that our equipment is almost obsolete, some of it almost 35 years old and costing more to restore and keep in working order than to replace it with new equipment. . . . We need a great many small arms urgently and a flexible type of adaptable folding stock would be purchased to ensure that we get the maximum use from the equipment."

FINLAND

John Vloyantes

As is true for all countries identified as neutrals, Finland's neutrality has distinctive characteristics.[1] Those characteristics can best be discerned through the examination of certain periods in the history of Finnish foreign policy. The historical perspective should occupy a particularly large place in the study of Soviet-Finnish relations as well as of those between Finland and its Scandinavian neighbors.

HISTORICAL PERSPECTIVE

Pre-Independence[2]

Finland was part of the Russian Empire from 1809 to 1917. For centuries prior to its submission to the tsars, Finland had been a province of the Kingdom of Sweden. Under Swedish rule the Finns enjoyed a considerable degree of autonomy and may be said to have pursued a distinctly independent foreign policy. Finnish interests were often served by trying to influence the policy of Swedish kings and of their governments. In a number of instances the Finns acted independently in relations with foreign powers and, toward the end of the eighteenth century, some Finns even ventured to plan for the establishment of national independence. It is thus not surprising that they nurtured expectations of exceptional treatment under Russian domination.

The waxing power of Russia filled the void left by the gradual waning of Sweden's regional influence. In 1809, Russia incorporated Finland into its empire. Tsar Alexander I, in a gesture to gain the allegiance of the Finns, granted them considerable autonomy by creating the Grand Duchy of Finland. That political unit had its own laws and legislature, civil service and judiciary, currency and customs tariffs, and even its own defense forces. The Finns were regarded as both citizens of Finland and subjects of the tsar. Their leaders were, within limits, able to develop and pursue national interests and to deal with the Russian government as if it were a foreign power. The stage was being set for a nationalist movement.

Finns appreciated their autonomy, and Russian imperial authorities viewed an autonomous Finland as a bulwark against Swedish and Western influences. But in the years preceding World War I, the Russian bureaucracy tried to extend its sway over Finland as part of a general policy to unify the diverse regional institutions of the empire. The Finnish elite regarded that "Russification" policy as a cultural onslaught from an inferior civilization. Political leaders divided into two important groups, one of which favored conciliation and concessions in order to achieve a modus vivendi with the Russians and to preserve the essential elements of the Finnish way of life and its institutions. Those individuals, called the "Old Finns," or "Compliants," refused to participate in the passive resistance advocated by the opposing group. One of the Old Finn leaders was Juho Kusti Paasikivi, who laid the foundations for his country's post-World War II relationship with the Soviet Union.

With the outbreak of war in 1914, Finnish nationalists saw an opportunity to advance their interests by associating with Germany. A Finnish battalion joined the Germans on the Eastern Front in 1916 and participated in action against the Russians. On 4 December 1917, following the Bolshevik Revolution, Finland became an independent state soon recognized by Lenin's government. Bloody civil war between Whites and Reds marked its first months of independence. The conflict ended when the White forces of General K. G. Mannerheim, aided by German troops, emerged victorious in May 1918.

Interwar Years[3]

The study of Eastern Europe after World War I, from Finland to the Mediterranean, offers an interesting illustration of great-state/small-state relations and of small-state efforts to enjoy the fruits of independence. The political climate after the Great War favored the maintenance of independence, the assertion of sovereignty, and the pursuit of national policies, including neutrality. Germany had been defeated and demilitarized. The multinational Austro-Hungarian Empire had collapsed, and its former territories either were made into newly independent states or annexed to neighboring countries. Russia lost a vast amount of borderland, including Finland, to the newly created successor states. Neither the new Bolshevik regime nor Germany would be in a position to assert effective regional power until the 1930s. The smaller East European countries naturally feared the revival of German and Russian military ambitions but hoped that some sort of balance between the two would work to help safeguard their independence.[4] It was desirable for these new countries to avoid being dragged into the net of one or the other of the reawakening great powers in the region. Neutrality, if recognized and respected, could be a means of achieving that objective. The League of Nations, with its vision of collective security, provided another hope for the small countries of the region, but prospects for its success faded in the wake of Japanese, Italian, and German aggression during the 1930s. The tenuousness of the situation became painfully evident after the *Anschluss* in March 1938 and with the dismemberment of Czechoslovakia following the Munich Conference.

Britain and France approached the Soviet Union in the spring of 1939[5] for the purpose of establishing a united front to halt German expansion. During the course of the Anglo-French-Soviet negotiations, the Western powers gradually acceded to Soviet insistence on a clear-cut mutual-assistance commitment, to become active if any of the parties were attacked directly or faced hostilities as the result of assisting another European state that had asked for help. Vyacheslav Molotov pressed the Anglo-French negotiators to recognize the implications for Soviet security if the independent countries on its western border were conquered by or became allied to Nazi Germany. The British government, after some hesitancy, accepted the Soviet position, which Max Jakobson, the distinguished Finnish diplomat and writer, subsequently labeled as the "Soviet Monroe Doctrine."[6]

As the Anglo-French-Soviet negotiators worked to hew out an agreement, the small states were nervously preoccupied with maintaining their territorial integrity and sovereignty. Fearing and distrusting both the Germans and the Soviets, they would not agree beforehand to the transit of Soviet troops over their territory in order to engage the Germans in the event of war. Moscow, in turn, suspected that many leaders in the border states harbored anti-Soviet, if not overtly pro-German, feelings. German influence was particularly evident in Bulgaria, Hungary, and Romania.

In Finland, anti-Soviet sentiment was especially strong. The Finns instinctively distrusted the Soviets and feared that they would seek the return of former tsarist-controlled territories as soon as their strength allowed them to do so. For example, the Finnish government continued to be in dispute with Moscow over the autonomous rights of the Karelian-speaking population of Eastern Karelia. Such rights had been guaranteed by the Treaty of Tartu between the newly independent Republic of Finland and the Soviet Union in October 1920. Finnish elites, believing in the position of their country as an "outpost of the West," persisted in harboring anti-Russian feelings. They also viewed the Soviet Union as a state different from others, because it aimed at domination by means of internal subversion through the manipulation of native Communists. Although the left had been defeated and shattered in the civil war and the political influence of the Communists had been muted, the Social Democratic party had nonetheless revived to become the largest party by 1939. Still, concern over internal subversion inspired by the Soviets remained strong during the inter-war years and resulted in the prohibition of all Finnish Communist party activities in 1930. Thus, the Finns were preoccupied with shutting out the Soviet Union and with purifying their country from within.[7]

Hitler, in the meantime, had realized that if success were not to elude him at this juncture, he would have to modify his tactics and seek an agreement with Stalin, outbidding the British and French. In order to pursue his regional objectives, Hitler also realized that he would have to share hegemony over Eastern Europe, at least temporarily, with the despised Bolsheviks. Accordingly, he resorted to the historic expedient of a spheres- of-influence accommodation with the Soviets. The Nazi-Soviet Pact of 23 August 1939 dealt the final blow to the shaky interwar system in Eastern Europe. Britain and France had been finessed and isolated.[8] German troops marched into Poland on 1 September 1939, followed sixteen days later by Soviet forces. The Soviets now had the opportunity to extend their influence over a large part of the region and in so doing had shifted their strategic position westward. The revival of German power had restored to that country its earlier position of strength.[9]

The Nazi-Soviet Pact replaced the antagonistic relationship between Germany and the Soviet Union with a bilateral agreement.

The Finns, who had a preference for German influence and dreaded Soviet hegemony, learned that Hitler had abandoned them in this deal with their eastern neighbor. Finland had not been consulted in the matter, nor had it been informed of the agreement. By consigning Finland to the Soviet sphere, Berlin had handed Moscow a tangible claim to a Soviet Monroe Doctrine in the Baltic. On 5 October 1939, the Soviets invited the Finnish government to send a delegation to Moscow.

The Anguish of Choice, 1939-1944

Countries that seek neutrality generally do so in order to avoid having to choose between contending great powers and also to avoid having to make concessions to one or another of those powers. They calculate the risks, costs, advantages, and possible consequences of the choice that is thrust upon them as a function of the circumstances. They also assess the motives behind the demands made on them by the contending great powers and attempt to lessen risk through both a clear perception of the relevant facts available and an evaluation of their own perceptions of the situation. In the end, when the time for decision comes, a choice is made; frequently it represents a guess or a gamble.

Soviet-Finnish negotiations before the Winter War have been described in detail elsewhere; suffice it here to provide a brief summary of the events.[10] Stalin himself conducted the negotiations that began on 11 October 1939, arguing that for defensive reasons it was necessary to prepare for the protection of his nation's second most important city, Leningrad. The Soviet-Finnish border would have to be pushed further north to remove that city from the range of modern artillery. Finland, moreover, would have to cede both the islands in the Gulf of Finland and part of nearby Petsamo in the Arctic and to lease the Hangö Peninsula on the southern coast of Finland, west of Helsinki, to the Soviet Union. In exchange, Finland would receive a section of Eastern Karelia, twice as large in area as the territories to be ceded.

Paasikivi headed Finland's negotiating team. A Conservative, he had always been part of a group advocating conciliation with the USSR, recognition of its strategic interests, and avoidance of provocative attitudes that might challenge Soviet prestige. Paasikivi, however, was bound by instructions not to compromise independence or neutrality.

During the meetings, Helsinki altered its instructions in order to yield ground in the Karelian isthmus, but not to the extent that Stalin wanted. A Soviet base so close to the Finnish capital was regarded as an intolerable threat, both to neutrality and to the independence of Finland. The talks broke down, and the Finnish delegates went home on 13 November. Foreign help was not forthcoming; Finland stood alone--and knew it. But no one seriously believed that Stalin would go to war. Rather, observers expected a prolonged period of pressure and tension. The Finnish government had guessed wrong, however, when it rejected Paasikivi's and Mannerheim's advice to make concessions to the Soviets on the assumption that their purpose was essentially defensive. On 30 November, Stalin attacked. After a heroic, now universally acclaimed stand by the outnumbered Finnish units, Helsinki, in the absence of Western aid, was forced to sign a peace treaty.

In the Treaty of Moscow (12 March 1940), Finland ceded the entire province of Viipuri, including the city of the same name, its second most populous; Hangö island, in the Gulf of Finland; and territory in the northeastern part of the country. Finland was required to build a railroad and to lease the Hangö area to the Soviet Union for use as a naval base.

The Finns seem to have had little choice but to accept the reality of enhanced Soviet power and to live with it. However, events in the spring and summer of 1940 appeared to offer another option. The conquest of Norway and Denmark and the stunning defeat of France presented the prospect of invincible German might. The Soviets reacted by annexing the Baltic states of Latvia, Lithuania, and Estonia during the summer. Finnish opinion, unreconciled and embittered by the loss of the Winter War, feared that Finland would share the fate of the hapless Baltic republics. The Finns became increasingly sensitive to what they regarded as intimidation and pressure from the Soviet Union. Nevertheless, their country remained unoccupied and, except for Hangö, unannexed.[11]

For the better part of the year before the 22 June 1941 German attack on the Soviet Union, Finland under President Risto Ryti leaned toward association with Germany, especially after pro-German Field Marshal Rolf Witting took office. This was a period of increased German-Soviet strife and of preparations for the struggle that was to come. Finland chose to cast its lot with Hitler and declared war on the Soviet Union on 26 June.[12] The "Continuation War" was an unfortunate choice.[13] Finland signed an armistice with the victorious Soviet forces on 19 September 1944, but it still found itself engaged in a vicious "Lapland War" to expel Nazi forces that were carrying out a scorched-earth policy of tremendous detriment to the northern third of the country.

NEW REALITIES AND POSTWAR REORIENTATION, 1944-1948

Germany's fall and Finland's defeat resulted in severely crippling but not fatal consequences for the Finnish state. The crucial facts were that no foreign occupation took place, and no social and political revolution occurred to establish a regime abjectly subservient to the Soviet Union. Finland's constitutional system remained intact, as did its political party system, even though a strong Communist party and Communist front organization, the SKDL (Finnish People's Democratic League), came into being. Internal political stability and independence were based upon the collaboration of two of the major political parties, the Social Democrats and the Agrarians, neither of which was under the control of the Soviet Union. The Social Democrats and Agrarians joined in coalition with the SKDL to form a government under the premiership of Paasikivi. Marshal Mannerheim served as caretaker president until 1946, when Paasikivi became head of state.[14]

Finland signed a formal peace treaty at Paris in February 1947. It is one of several treaties that should be regarded as part of the postwar settlement. The Finnish document was based upon the 1940 Treaty of Moscow, which ended the Winter War, and the 1944 Armistice Agreement terminating hostilities between Finland and the Soviet Union. Under its terms, Finland again ceded most of the Karelian isthmus, including the city of Viipuri; Hangö reverted to Finland but Petsamo was ceded to the USSR. The Soviet Union was given a base at Porkkala, twelve miles from Helsinki, leased with access rights for fifty years. Reparations in kind totaling $300 million at 1938 prices had to be paid within six years, and Finland undertook to conduct a trial of "War Responsibles," who included the Social Democratic leader Väimö Tanner and seven other prominent persons who had held office between 1939 and 1944. As in the case of the other defeated allies of Germany, an Anglo-Soviet Allied Control Commission was established for Finland, under the general direction of the Soviet High Command.[15]

The legal settlement had to be supplemented with a changed mode of thinking for the Finns, designed to reflect new realities. Paasikivi emerged as the wise and articulate leader who would guide and implement changes for Finland's postwar foreign policy.[16] For him, the fundamental political fact of life was self-evident: Finland's future independence required simply and unequivocally the correct assessment of the basic geopolitical facts.   The Soviet Union was the immediate neighbor to the east, and nothing could change that.   In any contest for the assertion of influence in the region, the USSR commanded decisive advantages because of the defeat and decline of Germany, the relative weakness of Sweden, and the distance of the United States and Britain.

Paasikivi reasoned that Moscow's interest in Finland was purely strategic.   Finnish policy had to be made credible beyond any doubt to Soviet leaders, and Finnish political parties had to accept in good faith the new Soviet image.   As early as 6 December 1944, in the first postwar independence day observation, he declared that "there are obtainable in the future good and faithful relations with our great neighbor.   Distrust must be thrown out and friendship established."[17]   Finns had to discard old modes of thinking that had dwelled upon irredentist resentments, hatred of the Russians as a "hereditary foe," and contempt of them as cultural inferiors.   The Paasikivi Line would work as a means of assuring Finnish independence, but it could similarly be considered a necessary condition of independence.   Soviet policymakers could and did utilize it to criticize or to put pressure upon governments and politicians when, in their judgment, there were violations of its spirit.

The years from 1944 to 1948 saw the shaping of major changes in the postwar world.   A global settlement of sorts was taking place.   It included the agreements of the victorious Grand Alliance and subsequent treaties with the defeated countries in Europe.   In the wake of its defeat, Finland tried to find a position which would allow it to preserve itself both as a social and governmental entity. Above all, the future relationship with the Soviet Union had to be defined.   Paasikivi had provided a formula for achieving that while simultaneously maintaining national independence.   Neutrality would be difficult to assert as long as the Soviet Union occupied a base on Finnish soil, but if Finnish independence were maintained, it could perhaps in time find its expression in neutrality.

In the summer of 1947, the government practiced what could be considered a sort of neutralism by avoiding policies which conflicted with the interests of the superpowers.   The Finns took such a position, however, only after Moscow had dispatched an official note to Helsinki, stating that Finnish participation in proposed

Marshall Plan aid would be deemed an act hostile to the Soviet Union.

Not long after 1948 began, with its mounting Cold War tensions, Finnish diplomacy achieved its most signal success. Finnish-Soviet dealings were given a basis upon which to form a firmly rooted relationship through the Treaty of Friendship, Cooperation, and Mutual Assistance, signed on 6 April. In the treaty's preamble the Soviet Union acknowledged Finland's aspirations for neutrality. In the substantive part of the document Finland obliged itself to fight to repel an attack on the Soviet Union by Germany or any state allied with the latter--meaning the United States and its allies. Article Two stated that the parties "shall confer with each other if it is established that the threat of an armed attack as described in article one is present."[18] From the beginning the Finns have optimistically interpreted the treaty to mean that there would be no unilateral determination about the existence of such a threat and that there would be consultation on what to do about it.

THE SUN SHINES MORE BRIGHTLY

The cause of Finnish independence, neutrality, and outward orientation surged forward in the period after 1955. Those advances are attributable chiefly to a generally improved international climate and to the growth of stability in the Finno-Soviet relationship.

In the late summer of 1955, the Soviet Union proposed to return to Finland the naval base on the Porkkala peninsula, which it had leased for fifty years. In return, Finland had to agree to extend the validity of the 1948 treaty for twenty years. For Finland, the departure of the Soviets was an event of profound significance. It confirmed the wisdom of the Paasikivi Line and opened the path for the expansion and international recognition of Finnish neutrality. In 1956, Urho Kekkonen succeeded Paasikivi as president and took advantage of the opportunities to steer the ship of state more toward neutrality and toward a more outward orientation for Finland's international activities.[19] The more positive Soviet attitude, illustrated by the withdrawal from Porkkala, opened the way for Finland to become a member of the Nordic Council, which had been formed in 1952 to promote cooperation among Scandinavian governments and parliaments. The Finns had originally declined membership, anticipating a negative Soviet reaction. Now they began to cultivate their Scandinavian relationships. With Finnish membership, the organization's neutral component, represented until then by Sweden alone, would be augmented, and latent Scandinavian neutrality could be enhanced. The identity of Finland as a Scandinavian country, as distinct from a Baltic or East European one, could now be more fully developed.[20]

Combined with the expanding outward orientation of Finland during this period was the explicit recognition of its neutrality by Britain, France, and the United States. Neither of those developments met with opposition from Moscow. Moreover, the Soviet evacuation of Porkkala in 1955 was followed during the 1956 Twentieth Congress of the Soviet Communist Party by an official statement referring to Finland as a neutral country. A year later, in 1957, an authoritative Soviet treatise on international relations stated that the Finnish-Soviet treaty of 1948 was in effect a pact to guarantee Finnish neutrality rather than a treaty of mutual assistance, such as existed between the Soviet Union and the Warsaw Pact. In the event of a clash between East and West, Finland would not abandon its neutrality by joining Western forces, and it would prevent them from passing through its territory on their way to the USSR. In so doing, Finland would be acting in a manner consistent with its neutrality by maintaining its territorial integrity.[21]

In 1956, Finland was invited to become a member of the United Nations, in an East-West package deal by which both superpowers agreed to withhold the veto of several states applying for membership. The Soviet Union had previously vetoed the application. The Finns could now more fully participate in the affairs of the world community.

Between 1958 and 1962, two crises appeared on the horizon and Finnish-Soviet relations entered a period of uncertainty. First, the "Nightfrost" resulted from Soviet displeasure with and pressure upon the Karl Fagerholm government, which was formed after the election of July 1958. It was during the period after Paasikivi had left the presidency and before the position of President Kekkonen had been firmly established. Those months also witnessed the return of Tanner and his anti-Soviet faction to a dominating position in the Social Democratic party, as well as an increased voice for the conservative National Coalition party. Cabinet posts were given to members of the Tanner faction and to the National Coalition. Moscow viewed the composition of the Fagerholm government as an alarming development and instituted a series of moves to indicate its misgivings. With no firm support from the Agrarian party and lukewarm support from Kekkonen, Fagerholm resigned in December 1958.

Second, the "Note Crisis" began in late October 1961 when the Soviet Union unilaterally invoked a provision of the 1948 Treaty of Friendship, Cooperation, and Mutual Assistance calling for military consultation in view of a perceived West German threat. The thought of military consultations stirred apprehensions in Helsinki, for they could burden Finland with commitments which would undermine the cherished neutrality so painstakingly built and only recently recognized. President Kekkonen, a skillful diplomat, played the "Scandinavian card" to defuse the crisis. He argued that if the Soviet Union were to withdraw its proposal, public opinion in the Nordic countries would be reassured and there would be no need for military preparations--not only in Finland and Sweden but also in Denmark and Norway, the two Scandinavian members of NATO. Kekkonen also pointed out that such an action would be convincing evidence that the Soviet Union was sincere in its desire to practice peaceful coexistence, even in times of serious danger.

In the end, Kekkonen preserved Finland's neutral stance from the threat of involvement in the conflicts of the great powers and quieted apprehensions in Scandinavia.[22] The clouds of crisis floated away and a new emphasis was placed upon independence, neutrality, and outward orientation, based upon stability both in Soviet-Finnish relations and in the Scandinavian region.

ACTIVE NEUTRALITY

Finnish neutrality from the end of the war in 1944 until the period after the Note Crisis was of the essentially passive variety, based upon impartiality and restraint. Finland wanted as much as possible to be a traditional neutral like Sweden or Switzerland, as it had tried to be in the interwar era. During the years that Paasikivi dominated policy, until 1956, he emphasized the credibility of the Paasikivi Line and the maintenance of independence. Neutrality was not fully possible with the Soviet occupation of Porkkala; moreover, under the terms of the 1948 treaty, Finland had undertaken a commitment for possible joint military action if the Soviet Union were attacked through Finnish territory. The Soviet withdrawal from Porkkala was indicative of a wider and more dynamic interpretation of Finnish neutrality.[23]

Active neutrality was the brainchild of President Kekkonen and reflected his personality as well as the realities of that period in Finnish and world politics.[24]   Chief among the initiatives espoused by his country as a result of that policy were the Nordic Nuclear Free Zone and the European Security Conference, which resulted in the 1975 Helsinki Accords.[25]   Kekkonen's proposal for the creation of a Nuclear Free Zone for the Nordic area in 1963 was based on a proposal advanced in 1961 by Östen Unden, Sweden's foreign minister.   When Kekkonen offered his proposal, there were no nuclear weapons in any of the Scandinavian countries, nor was there any prospect of their imminent introduction.[26]   Indeed, Norway and Denmark, from the beginning of their NATO membership, had adhered to a "no bases policy" on their territory.   Kekkonen, however, urged his plan with the object of making certain that the region remained nuclear free, and that the status not depend upon the unilateral policies of four countries but upon a common policy affirmed through mutual understanding.[27]   Kekkonen also went on to propose a treaty arrangement with Norway to protect the Finno-Norwegian border area from possible warfare.   The Norwegians rejected Kekkonen's schemes since, they argued, the security of their country depended partly on their option of receiving nuclear weapons.   That option would be denied them if they were to withdraw from NATO or to agree to neutralization of the frontier.[28]

Norway thus has been seen as the main stumbling block to Finnish efforts to advance the idea of a northern nuclear-free zone.   Finnish support of such an idea has frequently been viewed by Western observers as an effort to further Soviet policies in the Nordic region because it would diminish the solidarity and strength of the NATO alliance.

Finland's sponsorship of the Conference on Security and Cooperation in Europe (CSCE) was its boldest move in activist neutrality. The foreign ministers completed the first phase of the conference on 7 July 1973.   The agenda for the second phase comprised four main topics: questions relating to the security of Europe; cooperation in the fields of science, technology, and the environment; cooperation in humanitarian and other fields; and follow-up of the conference.   The second stage of the conference convened in Geneva on 18 September 1973, and talks continued until the summer of 1974.[29]   With the 1975 meeting in Finland's capital, Helsinki could share with Vienna, Geneva, and The Hague the reputation of cities providing the setting for the formation of constructive internationalist policy.

Finnish activist neutrality also used the United Nations for opportunities to further international cooperation.[30]   The Finns, deservedly proud of their role in peace-keeping operations, have assumed the chairmanship of UN committees.   Finland was elected to a term on the Security Council and, in 1971, Max Jakobson, the head of its delegation, was a serious contender for the post of secretary-general.   The Finnish delegation maintains close and regular consultations with other Nordic delegations on all levels and on all issues.   It also maintains a cautious vigil to avoid voting on issues that might be construed as involvement in the conflicts of the superpowers.   In response to the dictates of active neutrality, Finns in the United Nations and in international conferences have on a selective basis moved toward cooperation with the neutral and nonaligned countries and can even be identified as part of a group for common action.

In recent years the Finnish delegation has moved toward closer association with certain Third World countries on the subject of human rights.   In a forthright expression of Finland's growing participation in that domain, reflecting its maturing activist role, Dr. Klaus Törnudd, who as undersecretary of state headed the delegation at the meeting of experts on human rights at the CSCE in Ottawa on 8 May 1985, stated that "threats to peace constitute threats to human rights . . . the danger of war must not be invoked as a pretext for neglecting the realization of human rights."[31] The Finns, along with other neutrals and small states, find that a favorable international climate helps to strengthen their position and, similarly, that active neutrality contributes to bringing about that favorable international climate.

Soviet Union

As noted above, the Finns have endeavored to enhance the neutral provisions of the 1948 treaty with the Soviet Union and to enlarge their capacity for outward orientation.   The Soviet withdrawal from Porkkala, as well as Finnish membership on the Nordic Council and development of a special relationship with both the European Free Trade Association (1969) and the European Economic Community (1973), have all worked to establish Finland more firmly as an independent; that, in turn, has contributed to the international acceptance of its neutrality.   The Soviet Union also has recognized Finnish neutrality, but Moscow is wary of categorically embracing it,[32] preferring to stress that Finland and the USSR are an example of the coexistence of states with different economic systems. It frequently lauds the "good neighborly relations" it has with Finland.[33]

Although desiring to be a neutral, Finland has a relationship with the Soviet Union which, *in certain situations*, makes it a part of the Soviet security system. Based on the terms of the 1948 treaty, Finland is obligated to consult and to cooperate with the Soviets in specified circumstances. That is crucial to the concept of its neutrality, because neutrality by the traditional definition does not permit a state to be a member of an alliance.[34] Finnish neutrality, however, serves Soviet security interests by cancelling out a threat from Finland and should be seen as being coupled with the assurances of the Paasikivi-Kekkonen Line. There has developed a parallel policy of pursuing neutrality and independence on the one hand and recognizing Soviet security and hegemonic interests on the other.

The Soviet Union desires predictable Finnish behavior. It wants to know what to expect. Its leaders do not want Soviet antagonists to be able to speculate that Finland might be inclined to side with them.[35] The Soviets remember Finnish rejection of the proposals of 1939, and the revanchism of the "Continuation War" of 1941-1944. They have been suspicious that important groups have been covertly pro-German or pro-Western and prefer leaders like Paasikivi and Kekkonen, who dispel such anxieties. The Soviets, since 1962, have accepted the Social Democratic party, and current President Mauno Koivisto enjoys their confidence. The present era of good feeling and trust reflects the stability of Finno-Soviet relations, and to all intents and purposes the "needling" or "nagging" of Finland about its reliability has ceased from Soviet sources.[36]

Over the course of time there seems to have developed a realization that, because of the existence of new weaponry capable of delivering missiles at very great distances, the strategic importance of Finland to the Soviet Union is not as relevant today as it was in 1948. The significance of the treaty is now in its political value. It is additionally relevant for both the Soviet Union and Finland as a symbol. For the USSR, it symbolizes the reliability of this former enemy, which can be counted upon to behave in a predictable way. The past is blotted out--the matter is settled; indeed, it is celebrated. For the Finns, the treaty acknowledges independence and neutrality. It imparts firmness and stability to the relationship. And in Finland, too, the treaty is celebrated.[37]

Scandinavian Countries

The behavior of the Soviet Union and Sweden has served to affect Finnish neutrality and independence. If Sweden were to join NATO, that act would be viewed by the Soviets as a destabilizing occurrence, and Moscow would move to draw Finland into its orbit and thus terminate or greatly weaken the latter's independence and neutrality. In turn, if the Soviet Union were to move to absorb Finland into its orbit and to convert it into another Eastern European satellite, the Swedes would be expected to react and probably to take steps to join NATO. One also might expect Norway and Denmark to seek closer ties with the Alliance. Such a move on the part of the Soviets would, consequently, be viewed by Sweden, Norway, and Denmark as a destabilizing initiative.

In short, the extent to which the Soviet Union refrains from acts designed to establish hegemony over Finland is directly linked to the extent to which Sweden will maintain its neutrality. Conversely, the extent to which Sweden maintains its neutrality and steers clear of association with NATO is the extent to which the Soviet Union will maintain its policy of accepting Finnish neutrality and independence. A healthy stability thus devolves to the region if both of Finland's neighbors respect the appropriate perceptions and play the appropriate roles.[38]

The strict, traditional neutrality of Sweden has, therefore, a salutary effect on Finnish neutrality and independence, as do the Norwegian and Danish "low profile" commitments to NATO. Both of the latter countries have refused to have NATO bases and nuclear weapons located on their soil. Moreover, the Norwegians do not station troops permanently in the (Norwegian) Finnmark, which borders on both the Soviet Union and Finland.

It has been observed that efforts to plan for a Northern European Nuclear Free Zone may be somewhat superfluous. "Finland cannot have nuclear weapons in light of stipulations of the 1947 peace treaty, Sweden will not have them, and Norway and Denmark will not have nuclear bases on their soil in peacetime. In effect, the Scandinavian area *is* a nuclear-free zone."[39]

It seems apparent that Finland's orientation, by virtue of its cultural and political affinities, is toward Northern and not Eastern Europe. Its neutrality has institutionalized and deepened those affinities.

EUROPEAN ECONOMIC INTEGRATION AND NEUTRALITY[40]

Finland's leaders viewed efforts to participate in the economic integration of Europe as a means toward developing the economic strength of the country, while concurrently complementing a foreign policy of outward orientation. A prime objective of Finland and other European neutrals--Austria, Sweden, and Switzerland--is to establish a relationship with the dynamically expanding Western European economy. These four nations began negotiations with the European Economic Community (EEC) in November 1971. Kekkonen knew, however, that the route for Finland's association with the Common Market would have to pass through Moscow. The Soviets were suspicious of the possible political undertones of association with the EEC, but the Finns concluded that such misgivings could be reduced by collateral economic agreements with the USSR and COMECON.

Here was an example of "balancing" economic associations with East and West. In a sense, this might differ from a policy of strict neutrality, in that taking sides is not totally avoided, but arrangements were to be made with both blocs. Those associations were limited, however, to nonpolitical areas, because Finland could not become a member of either bloc. The Finnish-Soviet Treaty on the Development of Economic, Technical, and Industrial Cooperation, signed in April 1971, projected long-term cooperation in the areas of trade, economics, and production. Negotiations for an agreement with COMECON came on the heels of the Finnish-Soviet treaty and were concluded in the spring of 1973. Finland became the first non-Socialist nation to have an association with COMECON. In turn, Helsinki affirmed that it was not seeking membership in the EEC but only wanted a trade agreement. Discussions began in December 1971.

A negative attitude in Moscow persisted, and the green light was not given to Kekkonen until after he made an unofficial visit to Moscow in early September 1973. In a commentary to the Finnish cabinet, he affirmed that the EEC agreement was "purely commercial." Kekkonen argued that the treaty was consistent with all of Finland's international obligations and that his government had been able to base its foreign policy on good neighborly relations and on strict observance of the agreements that had been concluded. He emphatically declared that nothing had changed in that respect and that nothing would.[41] The Finnish Parliament approved the trade agreement with the EEC on 16 November 1973.

In all probability, the decisive reason behind Soviet acquiescence to the Finnish agreement with the EEC was the fact that the Finns, especially President Kekkonen, had won the Soviet leaders over to the view that a strictly economic agreement with the EEC was a sine qua non for the future economic life of Finland. If Moscow persisted in opposing Helsinki's agreement with the Common Market, it would have placed the region's strongest power in the position of inflicting serious injury to a small neighboring state by an inflexibly negative attitude for selfish, unilateral ends. A stubborn rejection by the Kremlin also would not have fared well with world opinion at a time when the Conference on European Security and Cooperation was in progress. There was, as well, broad national unity in support of Kekkonen's endeavors, pursued at a time of postcrisis stability in Finno-Soviet relations and enhanced by the benign international climate of détente.

"FINLANDIZATION"

The concept of "Finlandization" has attracted much attention, and Finns are chagrined by the derogatory connotations it carries. Some severe criticisms of the term have been made,[42] but its true sense remains to be stated with precision. George Maude, who has written one of the most perceptive articles on the subject, concludes that it is a concept which cannot be ignored.[43]

The term has a significance beyond a Soviet-Finnish context because it implies that it is not possible for a country to maintain its independence if the Soviet Union is in a position to undermine it. Espousers of the concept claim that Finlandization will spread, and they are sounding an alarm to warn other states of their impending fate, especially the countries of Western Europe. They claim that Finland's subservience has advanced to the point that it has become servile and that the Finns do what they believe the Soviets want them to do on the basis of anticipated response.[44] The expression grew out of the polemics of the Cold War, and it continues as an epithet. Serious efforts to analyze how a border state of a superpower attempts to achieve independence and neutrality have been thus hampered.

At the end of World War II the choice for the Finns seemed clear regardless of past behavior or wishes: the Paasikivi Line. It was the only rational one, given the political and geographical realities of the time. Yet, can what has emerged as the Paasikivi-

Kekkonen-Koivisto Line be equated with the popular notion of Finlandization? Only in a very restricted sense. Finland could not have followed an anti-Soviet policy during the postwar period. It was obliged to come to terms with Soviet supremacy in the region and to acknowledge its security interests. The Paasikivi-Kekkonen-Koivisto Line was the logical means by which that could be achieved. It allowed the Soviet Union to come to terms with Finnish independence and, in time, to accept the country's neutrality. It can be claimed that the extent to which this independence and neutrality have been viable is the extent to which the popular notion of Finlandization is wanting. That has been the view of this writer and others[45] who have studied Finnish-Soviet relations and Finnish neutrality.

DEFENSE POLICY

Finland's defense policy since the end of World War II has been a natural consequence of the postwar peace treaty, its special relationship with the Soviet Union, and its policy of neutrality. The 1947 Paris Peace Treaty restricts the maximum size of the active-duty armed forces to 41,900 (34,400 soldiers, 4,500 sailors, and 3,000 airmen) and their equipment to defensive weaponry. Additionally, the 1948 treaty with the Soviet Union prescribes that the armed forces' mission is to repel aggression against Finland itself or against the Soviet Union through Finnish territory.[46]

Current figures indicate the armed forces to be at a total level of 34,900 (25,000 conscripts). Finland enforces universal conscription, and the terms of active-duty service range from eight months for lower ranking enlisted personnel to eleven months for noncommissioned and reserve officers. The military potential is considerably enhanced by the large reserve force of over 700,000 (about 15 percent of the nation's population), which can be called during a mobilization. Some 44,000 reservists per year conduct refresher training. Finland produces some light equipment but relies on foreign sources for its advanced weaponry. Overwhelmingly and as unsurprisingly, those purchases are from the Soviet Union and from neutral Sweden. Less significant acquisitions come from Western Europe and the United States.[47]

CONCLUSIONS

It may be observed that the study of Finnish neutrality is properly the study of a cluster of inextricably interwoven concepts. The first and most important of them is the political independence of the country and the way it is respected and accepted by the Soviet Union. That is complementary to the Paasikivi-Kekkonen Line, which defines policy and basic attitudes toward the Soviet Union. Neutrality is thus based upon enduring stability and order in Finnish-Soviet relations. Finnish-Soviet stability is in turn strengthened by a general stability in the Baltic-Scandinavian region. And because of regional stability, Finland's independence and neutrality are correlated with and integrated into the political, economic, and cultural unity of the Scandinavian countries and, more broadly, into the Western European economic and cultural life of which it is a part. The extent to which Finland enjoys a favorable international climate is the extent to which that cluster of interdependent concepts retains cohesion and vitality.

NOTES

[1]On the general topic of neutrality see Peter Lyon, *Neutralism* (Leicester: Leicester University Press, 1963); and Cyril E. Black, Richard A. Falk, Klaus Knorr, and Oran R. Young, *Neutralization and World Politics* (Princeton: Princeton University Press, 1968). See also the review article by Klaus Törnudd, "A New Contribution to the Theory of Neutral Foreign Policy," *Cooperation and Conflict* 5, no. 4 (1970): 282-85, a lengthy review of Daniel Frei, *Dimensionen neutraler Politik--Ein Beitrag zur Theorie der Internationalen Beziehungen*, Etudes et travaux de l'Institut universitaire de hautes études internationales de Genève (Geneva: Librairie Droz, 1969).

[2]For historical perspective see Pennti Renuall, "The Foreign Policy Attitudes of the Finns during the Swedish Rule," *Finnish Foreign Policy: Studies in Foreign Politics* (Helsinki: Finnish Political Science Association, 1963), pp. 3-23. In the same volume see also Jaakko Numminen, "Finland's Foreign Policy: An Autonomous Grand Duchy and the Winning of Independence," pp. 23-33. See also Max Jakobson, *Finnish Neutrality: A Study of Finnish Foreign Policy since the Second World War* (London: Hugh Evelyn, 1968), pp. 3-5; and George Maude, *The Finnish Dilemma: Neutrality in the Shadow of Power* (London: Oxford University Press, 1976), pp. 3-7.

[3]On the interwar years for Finland see Jakobson, *Finnish Neutrality*, pp. 3-21; and Roy Allison, *Finland's Relations with the Soviet Union, 1944-84* (New York: St. Martin's Press, 1985), pp. 5-9.

[4]Maude, *The Finnish Dilemma*, p. 7.

[5]On the Anglo-French-Soviet negotiations of 1939 see Lord Strang, *Home and Abroad* (London: André Deutsch, 1956), pp. 156-98. See also Great Britain, Foreign Office, *Documents on British Foreign Policy, 1919-1939*, 3d ser., vols. 5 and 6 (London: H.M. Stationery Office, 1952-53).

[6]Max Jakobson, *The Diplomacy of the Winter War* (Cambridge: Harvard University Press, 1961), pp. 57-96.

[7]Maude, *The Finnish Dilemma*, p. 6; and Jakobson, *Finnish Neutrality*, p. 6.

[8]See James E. McSherry, *Stalin, Hitler and Europe*, Vol. 1, *The Origins of World War II, 1933-1939* (Cleveland: World Publishing Company, 1968). On the Nazi-Soviet Pact see Gerhard L. Weinberg, *Germany and the Soviet Union, 1939-1941* (Leiden: E. J. Brill, 1972); and R. J. Sontag and J. S. Beddie, eds., *Nazi-Soviet Relations, 1939-1941* (Washington, DC: Department of State, 1948).

[9]See A. W. DePorte, *Europe between the Superpowers: The Enduring Balance* (New Haven: Yale University Press, 1979), pp. 30-31; and Hajo Holborn, *The Political Collapse of Europe* (New York: Alfred A. Knopf, 1951), pp. 111-37. On Eastern Europe during the interwar years see Hugh Seton-Watson, *Eastern Europe between the Wars, 1918-1941* (New York: Harper and Row, 1967), pp. 410-12.

[10]See Jakobson, *The Diplomacy of the Winter War*; C. Leonard Lundin, *Finland in the Second World War* (Bloomington: Indiana University Press, 1957); G. A. Gripenberg, *Finland and the Great Powers: Memoirs of a Diplomat*, trans. Albin T. Anderson (Lincoln: University of Nebraska Press, 1965); Kusti Paasikivi, *Toimintani Moskovassa ja Suomenessa 1939-1940*, vols. 1 and 2 (Porvoo: Werner Söderström, 1958); Väimö A. Tanner, *The Winter War* (Stanford: Stanford University Press, 1957); Ministry of Foreign Affairs of Finland, *The Development of Finnish-Soviet Relations during the Autumn of 1939, Including the Official Documents* (London: George G. Harrap and Co., 1940).

[11]See Lundin, *Finland in the Second World War*.

[12]Lundin, ibid.; and Hans Peter Krosby, *Suomen Valinta, 1941* (Helsinki: Kirjayhtym, 1978). The latter reference, published in Helsinki and forthcoming in English by the University of Wisconsin Press, is based largely on German documents and includes a full account of Finnish-German relations in 1940-41.

[13]During the course of the war, Great Britain also declared war on Finland. The United States did not and even maintained a diplomatic representation until summer 1944, thus underscoring the "special case" of Finland as an "Axis" state.

[14]Sigyn Alenius, *Finland between the Armistice and the Peace* (Helsinki: Werner Söderström, 1947); D. W. Kirby, *Finland in the Twentieth Century: A History and Interpretation* (London: C. Hurst and Co., 1979).

[15]For extracts from the treaty of peace with Finland see App. 1 in Allison, *Finland's Relations with the Soviet Union*, pp. 171-73.

[16]The study of the Paasikivi Line, later the Paasikivi-Kekkonen Line, is indispensable to the study of Finnish neutrality. See John H. Hodgson, "The Paasikivi Line," *American Slavic and East European Review* 18, no. 2 (April 1959): 145-73; A. Kuusisto, "The Paasikivi Line in Finland's Foreign Policy," *Western Political Quarterly* 12, no. 1 (March 1959): 37-49; Marvin Rintala, *Four Finns: Political Profiles* (Berkeley: University of California Press, 1969); J. K. Paasikivi, *Paasikiven Linja I, Puheita Vuosilta, 1944-1956* (Porvoo: Werner Söderström, 1962). See also Juhani Suomi, "Up from the Bottom of the Valley," *Yearbook of Finnish Foreign Policy, 1984* (Finnish Institute of International Affairs), pp. 14-18; Osmo Apunen, "Continuity and Change in Finnish Foreign Policy from the Period of Autonomy to the Kekkonen Era," *Yearbook of Finnish Foreign Policy, 1984*, pp. 19-30.

[17]See John P. Vloyantes, *Silk Glove Hegemony: Finnish-Soviet Relations, 1944-1974, A Case Study of the Theory of the Soft Sphere of Influence* (Kent, OH: Kent State University Press, 1975), p. 45.

[18]Allison, *Finland's Relations with the Soviet Union*, App. 2, pp. 174-75.

[19]See Jakobson, *Finnish Neutrality*, pp. 45-47.

[20]On Finnish-Scandinavian relations and their relationship to Finnish neutrality and foreign policy see Klaus Törnudd, *Soviet Attitudes toward Non-Military Regional Cooperation*, Commentationes Humanarum Litterarum 28, no. 1 (Helsingfors: Societas Scientiacum Fennica, 1961), pp. 120-22. See also Vloyantes, *Silk Glove Hegemony*, pp. 158-66.

[21]See S. B. Krylov and V. N. Durdenevski, *Mezhdunarodno-pravovye formy mirnogo sosushchestvovaniya gosudarstvy i natsiy*, cited in *Ulkopoliittisia Lausutoja ja Asiakirjoja, 1963* (Helsinki: Finnish Foreign Ministry, 1964), p. 15. See also Allison, *Finland's Relations with the Soviet Union*, pp. 90-95.

[22]On the "Note Crisis," see Allison, *Finland's Relations with the Soviet Union*, pp. 43-52; Vloyantes, *Silk Glove Hegemony*, pp. 109-25; and Raimo Vayrynen, *Stability and Change in Finnish Foreign Policy*, Research Reports, Department of Political Science, University of Helsinki, Series A, 1982, pp. 43-48.

[23]See "Preamble, The Treaty of Friendship, Cooperation, and Mutual Assistance between the Republic of Finland and the Union of Soviet Socialist Republics," in Allison, *Finland's Relations with the Soviet Union*, App. 2, p. 174.

[24]A rich variety of material exists on President Kekkonen and his conception of neutrality. For speeches by Urho Kekkonen, see Tuomar Vilkuna, ed., *Neutrality: The Finnish Position*, trans. P. Ojansuu and L. E. Keyworth (London: Heinemann, 1970). The *Yearbook of Finnish Foreign Policy, 1981* (Finnish Institute of International Affairs) devoted the following pieces to his departure from the presidency: Kari Möttölä, "The End of an Era--The Continuation of a Policy," pp. 2-3; a speech by Prime Minister Mauno Koivisto, "On the Occasion of President Urho Kekkonen's Announcement on 27th October 1981 that He Will Relinquish His Post," pp. 4-5; Jan-Magnus Jansson, "Urho Kekkonen's Era," pp. 6-7; Juhani Suomi, "Urho Kekkonen and Finland's Relations with the Soviet Union," pp. 8-10; "Portrait of a Man, Urho Kekkonen, a Statesman for Peace," pp. 10-11.

[25]A large number of works can be consulted on Finnish neutrality in general and active neutrality in particular. In addition to works previously cited, the following should be consulted: L. A. Puntila, "Finland's Neutrality," in *Finnish Foreign Policy, Studies in Foreign Politics* (Helsinki: Finnish Political Science Association, 1963), pp. 218-27; Raimo Vayrynen, "Neutrality and Non-Alignment: The Case of Finland," *The Non-Aligned World* 1, no. 3 (July-September 1983): 346-60; Jaako Blomberg, "Finland's Foreign Policy of Neutrality in Times of Detente and Tension," *Yearbook of Finnish Foreign Policy, 1984*, pp. 2-3; Steve Lindberg, "Are We Counting Our Chickens," *Yearbook of Finnish Foreign Policy, 1984*, pp. 4-10.

[26]Vloyantes, *Silk Glove Hegemony*, pp. 160-62.

[27]See K. Möttölä, ed., *Nuclear Weapons and Northern Europe: Problems and Prospects of Arms Control* (Helsinki: Finnish Institute of International Affairs, 1983).

[28]Allison, *Finland's Relations with the Soviet Union*, p. 61.

[29]See Maude, *The Finnish Dilemma*, pp. 83-91.

[30]See Jakobson, *Finnish Neutrality*, pp. 102-8.

[31]Statement by the Head of the Delegation of Finland, Dr. Klaus Törnudd, Under-Secretary of State, at the Meeting of Experts on Human Rights of the CSCE, Ottawa, 8 May 1985. Sent to the writer by Dr. Törnudd.

[32]See P. H. Vigor, *The Soviet View of War, Peace and Neutrality* (London: Routledge and K. Paul, 1975).

[33]Allison, *Finland's Relations with the Soviet Union*, p. 93.

[34]The writer is particularly indebted to Dr. Pauli O. Jarvenpää, researcher in the Finnish Ministry of Defense, for his analysis of this concept.

[35]The writer is indebted to Dr. K. Möttölä, director of the Finnish Institute of International Affairs, for his analysis of this concept.

[36]This is the view of Dr. Pauli O. Jarvenpää, suggested to the writer.

[37]All of the interviewees listed above confirmed the political and symbolic value of the 1948 treaty and were in agreement that its military value had diminished.

[38]See Vloyantes, *Silk Glove Hegemony*, pp. 158-76; Allison, *Finland's Relations with the Soviet Union*, pp. 52-57; Jakobson, *Finnish Neutrality*, pp. 91-101; and A. O. Brundtland, "The Nordic Balance--Past and Present," *Cooperation and Conflict* 2, no. 2 (1966): 30-63.

[39]Maude, *The Finnish Dilemma*, p. 71.

[40]Parts of this section dealing with Finland's European economic integration are based upon the following: Allison, *Finland's Relations with the Soviet Union*, pp. 118-26; Maude, *The Finnish Dilemma*, pp. 95-126; and Vloyantes, *Silk Glove Hegemony*, pp. 141-51. See also Esko Antola, "Finland and the Prospects for Western European Integration in the 1980s," *Yearbook of Finnish Foreign Policy, 1981*, pp. 37-48; and Mauno Koivisto, *Landmarks: Finland in the World* (Helsinki: Kirjayhtymä, 1985), pp. 121-39.

[41]Statements by Kekkonen to Finnish cabinet on 3 October 1973, as quoted in Vloyantes, *Silk Glove Hegemony*, p. 149.

[42]Fred Singleton, "The Myth of 'Finlandization,'" *International Affairs* 57, no. 2 (Spring 1981): 270-85; Erkki Mäentakanen, "The Myth of 'Finlandization,'" *Yearbook of Finnish Foreign Policy, 1974* (Finnish Institute of International Affairs), pp. 34-39; George F. Kennan, "Europe's Problems and Europe's Choices," *Foreign Policy* 14 (Spring 1974): 3-16; George Maude, "The Further Shores of Finlandization," *Cooperation and Conflict* 17, no. 1 (1982): 3-16.

[43]Maude, "The Further Shores of Finlandization."

[44]See N. Ørvik, *Sicherheit auf Finnisch* (Stuttgart: Seewald, 1972). See W. Laqueur, *A Continent Astray 1970-1978* (New York: Oxford University Press, 1979), pp. 222-45. For a less pessimistic view see Adam M. Garfinkle, *"Finlandization": A Map to a Metaphor*, Monograph No. 24, Foreign Policy Research Institute, Philadelphia.

[45]Vloyantes, *Silk Glove Hegemony*, pp. 177-80; Maude, *The Finnish Dilemma*, pp. 45-49; Allison, *Finland's Relations with the Soviet Union*, pp. 1-4, 166-67.

[46]*The Military Balance, 1986-1987* (London: International Institute for Strategic Studies, 1986), p. 80; Trond Gilberg, "Finland," in William J. Taylor, Jr., and Paul M. Cole, eds., *Nordic Defense: Comparative Decision Making* (Lexington, MA: Lexington Books, 1985), p. 38.

[47]*Military Balance, 1986-1987*, pp. 83-84; Gilberg, "Finland," pp. 37-38, 52-57.

AUSTRIA

Joan Johnson-Freese

Neutrality in Austria has no historical roots prior to World War II. To the contrary, a far greater portion of Austrian history is concerned with the country as a great power, shaping world events with France, England, Prussia, and Russia, than with it as a small, neutral country. As a neutral buffer state between the East and West blocs, it is a relatively recent, pragmatic reality. Neutrality is now, however, fully accepted and maximized by both the Austrian people and their governments.

The Austrians draw on their preneutral, traditional role as diplomats and geopolitical intermediaries between East and West to maintain continuity with their past. Some observers contend that Austria is happier now as a neutral state than it was as a great power. Clearly, many Austrians have sincerely welcomed neutrality as a solution because of their geographic situation and their country's military potential, or lack thereof.[1] It also has been suggested, though, that the generally accepted picture of Austrians as a happy, smiling people is only a facade, and that there is actually a hidden tendency, particularly in Vienna, to live in the past. That perspective implies that although their capacity for survival is certainly a source of pride, Austrians still secretly reminisce and long for the glory days of earlier decades; their friendliness is merely a mask, hiding a haunted and somewhat obsessed people. That obsession is with their own deaths (much like the "death" of their country as a great power); consequently, their lives are overshadowed by a subtle fatalism.

That fatalism is important to the extent that it is reflected in Austria's attitude regarding its potential for defending itself militarily: an attempt is made to put on a good show of defense planning, but the people themselves do not really seem to believe that their efforts are effective.   Such an attitude helps explain both their problems with implementation of their defense planning and their reliance on a pragmatic foreign policy of fence-straddling.

The goal of Austrians at the end of World War II was full sovereignty, which they thought would only become a reality with the complete withdrawal of all occupation forces.   The country sought to rejoin the family of nations as a full, though clearly changed, member.   Since that time, Austria has deliberately created a unique place for itself as a neutral buffer between East and West.

The United States believed that former Chancellor Bruno Kreisky, whose first cabinet came into office in 1970, often exploited Austria's neutral position to justify controversial stances on international issues.   Such was the case, for example, when Kreisky met with Libyan leader Muammar al-Qaddafi in 1982, when his government recognized the Palestine Liberation Organization (PLO), and when Vienna concluded several trade deals with Eastern-bloc countries.   Dr. Kreisky justified those actions with the rationale that they were in the best interest of his government's primary foreign policy goals--the maintenance of independence and the promotion of world peace and security in order to secure that independence--and that those actions were logically in line with Austrian neutrality.

Kreisky left office in April 1983 after his Socialist party failed to win a clear majority in Parliament.   While the Socialist-Liberal coalition which succeeded the Kreisky government, with Dr. Fred Sinowatz as chancellor, took a less confrontational and provocative stance on issues of concern to the West, Austria has generally continued its balancing act between East and West, particularly in its economic bridge-building with other countries.   It is generally fair to say, however, that its interpretation of neutrality changed little with the 1983 change in government.   Therefore, seven points concerning neutrality put forth by former Minister of Foreign Affairs Willibald Pahr, in a 1983 lecture at the Royal Institute of International Relations in   Brussels, are still valid and may be used as organizational reference points for discussion on Austria as a neutral between the East and West blocs.   Briefly stated, Pahr's points regarding Austrian neutrality, to be individually examined in more detail, are that: 1) it was not imposed, but freely chosen; 2) it is an active neutrality; 3) Austria has the full and exclusive right and duty to interpret its neutrality; 4) it is not of an ideological nature; 5) it is an armed neutrality; 6) it demands impartiality; and 7) permanent neutrality has become part of Austrian national consciousness, identity, and pride.[2]

Origins

Between 1945 and 1955, Austria was under the control and administration of a quadripartite occupying force consisting of the United States, the Soviet Union, Great Britain, and France. Vienna was divided into four corresponding sectors, plus an international sector. The Vienna Inter-Allied Command (VIAC) was formed to govern the city.

On 26 October 1955 the Austrian Parliament passed the Federal Constitutional Act on Austria's Neutrality. Austria considers itself a full-fledged member of the Western system of political democracy, while voluntarily opting for a policy of neutrality. Overtures made to the East are for pragmatic economic reasons, or as part of the counrty's self-proclaimed role as a bridge-builder, which Austrians see as important to their future survival as any defense plan. Still, these efforts have often been frowned upon by other Western democracies.

Austrians prefer to stress that neutrality was freely chosen and not imposed. It was not until their sovereignty was fully restored by conclusion of the State Treaty on 15 May 1955 and the last occupying soldier had left their soil on 25 October that Parliament passed the Federal Constitutional Act. It was clearly chosen, however, as the only real option, if they were to have any chance of regaining full sovereignty.

Shortly after the end of the war, leading politicians such as Julius Raab and Leopold Figl, who each eventually served as chancellor, began to come out in favor of neutrality. They recognized it as the only pragmatic means of achieving their postwar goal of full sovereignty. Moreover, they seemed to view it as being consistent with the country's traditional role as East-West go-between, a function that had evolved because of its geographic location.

Full sovereignty began to become a serious possibility for Austria when Nikita Khrushchev realized that Western domination of international relations forced the Soviet Union to make itself accepted as a responsible partner. Since Austria would act as a geographical buffer between East and West and would also to some extent divide NATO's northern and southern flanks, the Soviet leadership thought that allowing it to become an independent neutral state was an affordable gesture which would go far in convincing the West that the USSR should be accepted in the international arena.[3]   Moscow repeatedly cited its gesture in later years as proof of the Soviet Union's new, friendly global attitude.

The goal of full freedom at the end of the war required a state treaty between Vienna and the occupying Allied powers. A peace treaty would have been inappropriate, as Austria had ceased to exist as a state between 1938 and 1945. The Soviets would have preferred Austrian neutrality to be part of the State Treaty, but at the final negotiations in Moscow, the Austrian delegation agreed that their country would become permanently neutral only at the moment that the last foreign soldier left its territory.

Active Neutrality

Austrians have stated that both their neutrality and the country itself are best preserved through a foreign policy of active neutrality directed at preserving peace and stability in the community of states. That orientation is to be distinguished, for example, from the Swiss noninvolved/nonparticipatory attitude toward neutrality. Under the Kreisky government, the policy evolved into a *Weltpolitik*, by which Austria actively sought involvement in world affairs where it thought it could play a constructive role. After 1983, however, the government gradually drew back from that stance and arranged for the replacement of Foreign Minister Dr. Irwin Lanc by Dr. Leopold Gratz in 1984. "Dr. Lanc's departure from the Cabinet [was] seen as the final nail in the coffin of Austria's *Weltpolitik*."[4] Austria's involvement in world affairs has been significantly toned down, but it certainly has not withdrawn into a cocoon of noninvolvement.   The government has simply chosen to be less visible and less provocative toward the West on issues deemed not to be of a critical nature.   In an area such as economics, which is considered critical, policies have stayed substantially the same, with some adjustments to appease the West.

Active neutrality has included Austria's participation in the United Nations since December 1955. Although permanent neutrality may seem inconsistent with belonging to an organization which supports a system of collective security, such has been held not to be the case. The flexibility of the UN system allows the membership of neutral states.[5]   This participation has extended to supplying troops for UN peace-keeping missions in the Congo, Cyprus, and the Middle East, particularly on the Golan Heights between Israel and Syria.

Active neutrality also is consistent with Austria's self-perception as a key player in the balance between East and West. That is evidenced in efforts to have Vienna become the third seat of the United Nations, after New York and Geneva. The development, at its own expense, of the "UN City" in Vienna was accomplished with that aim. The United Nations rents the facility for one schilling per year (about U.S. $0.07) to house, among other agencies, the International Atomic Energy Agency (IAEA), the UN Industrial Development Organization (UNIDO), the UN Relief and Works Agency for Palestine Refugees, and most UN offices dealing with drug traffic and abuse.

Vienna also has been the location for many important international meetings since World War II. Khrushchev and President John F. Kennedy, for example, met there in 1961, and the SALT I Treaty negotiations were carried out in Vienna and Helsinki from 1970 to 1972. President Jimmy Carter and Soviet President Leonid Brezhnev signed the ill-fated SALT II Treaty in the city in 1979. Although they have been able to claim little success, NATO and the Warsaw Pact nations have conducted Mutual and Balanced Force Reductions (MBFR) talks in Vienna since 1973. More recently, Soviet leader Mikhail Gorbachev made proposals in April 1986 at the East German Communist party congress which, he said, were designed to "cut the knot" in the Vienna negotiations. *The Economist* disagreed, however, by stating: "They will complicate the negotiations immensely. This could keep the Great Vienna Hot Air Factory in business for another 13 years."[6] Since then, both sides seem to agree that a broader approach to conventional arms and forces reduction is preferable; the exact nature of that forum is still evolving.

Right of Interpretation

The Austrians had very definite and pragmatic reasons for insisting upon an autonomous, independent declaration of neutrality: they thought that such a strategy granted them the exclusive right and duty to interpret their neutrality. Indeed, Pahr stresses that they never sought or accepted any international guarantee of their neutrality for the very purpose of excluding any outside influence or interference in their interpretation of it. Had the provisions of neutrality been determined in the State Treaty, then the parties to the treaty would have shared the right to cointerpret Austria's neutral policy.[7]

That autonomy and its perception in the international community remains a very sensitive issue for the Austrian government is evidenced by the attention to detail presented in a 14 October 1983 letter to the editor of the *New York Times* from Peter Marboe, director of the Austrian Press and Information Service in New York. In it he states:

> In her otherwise excellent column of Oct. 11, Flora Lewis refers to "the Soviet Union as a guaranteeing power" of Austria's neutrality. Austria's neutrality, introduced by constitutional law on Oct. 26, 1955 (a few months after the State Treaty), was deliberately and unequivocally instituted according to the example of Switzerland. There are no "guaranteeing powers."[8]

Although in that respect Austria modeled its neutrality after that of Switzerland, the similarity between the two countries for the most part ends there. Whereas the Swiss essentially refuse to take positions on most international issues, Austria's active neutrality carries an obligation only to refrain from direct interference in the internal politics of other nations.[9] Commitment to that obligation has, however, been questioned after actions such as the aforementioned recognition of the PLO.

Economically, the emphasis on freedom of action has allowed Austrians to interpret their neutrality as meaning "treating all countries correctly and without favouritism," according to Norbert Steger, former vice-chancellor responsible for foreign trade.[10] Clearly, that attitude has worked to Austria's advantage.

A remarkable spirit of cooperation and consensus through unanimous votes in Parliament, often evidenced before the change of government in 1983, has, to a large extent, continued. The lessons of the pre-World War II civil strife and the subsequent *Anschluss* were well learned by most Austrians, leaving them convinced that "a small country can only survive by sinking its own internal differences, including internal strife."[11]

Although the picture one gets of Austria as a country which enjoys a degree of social accord not found in many other Western European nations is largely true, it has been hard gained and not infallible. Thus, in March 1986 domestic harmony was severely shaken by revelations in the Vienna weekly, *Profil*, and in the *New*

York Times that Kurt Waldheim, diplomat and UN secretary-general from 1972 to 1982, and then candidate for the presidency, had served in the German army in the Balkans from 1942 to 1944. He was accused of involvement in the deportation of Jews from Greece to Nazi extermination camps and in the massacre of civilians with remote links to Yugoslav resistance organizations. Those revelations about his past were contrary to the story that Austria and the world had been told by Waldheim about his years as a German conscript. Reaction was mixed. The slogan of the presidential campaign became "We Austrians will elect the one we want," with the second "we" in bold letters. The nationalistic message was clear: outside meddling was unwanted and resented. Inside the country, Austrian Jews felt a sense of betrayal and fear with the occurrence of random anti-Semitic incidents.

Waldheim was elected to the mostly ceremonial post of president in June 1986. It will take time for the wounds to heal. Some foreign diplomats chose not to attend his inauguration. Within Austria, Chancellor Sinowitz resigned in protest, and Franz Vranitsky succeeded him. The people themselves are uncomfortable with this uncharacteristic upheaval.[12]

In 1960, Vienna joined the European Free Trade Association (EFTA). Much more important and problematic has been Austria's association with the European Community (EC), because of the latter's stated goal of political unity. The customs and trade benefits available through increased links with the EC made association an objective worth fighting for. The Soviets strongly objected to the possibility of Austria's full membership in the EC but were willing to accept a limited Austrian association excluding any political role. After five years of difficult negotiations, an agreement was reached in 1973 between the EC and Vienna which provided for the almost complete dismantling of customs and trade restrictions on industrial and agricultural goods.

As exports account for one-third of Austria's gross national product (GNP) and as the largest share of trade is with EC countries, which buy one-half of its exports and supply two-thirds of its imports, the importance of the agreement is clear. Although more than 80 percent of total foreign trade is conducted with EC/EFTA countries, Austria has not shied away from pursuing a completely independent policy in creating trade links with other countries. That policy has at times drawn strong protest from the West, but the Austrians say that it is completely in keeping with both their neutrality and their historical tradition.

Their economic system is basically a market economy, although the state may intervene in the interests of the economically under-privileged (for example, by means of price controls). Until 1982, there was relatively low unemployment (1.3 percent to 2.4 percent during the period 1974-1981), low inflation, and few labor strikes. Within a year after the 1983 change in government, however, infla-tion doubled to reach almost 5.8 percent, unemployment reached 3.7 percent in 1982 and 4.5 percent in 1983, and the threat of a general civil service strike over pension cuts was very real. The rise in unemployment has in part been due to a rapid influx of Polish immigrants. High civil service salaries and benefits, as well as social welfare costs, also contribute to Austrian economic difficulties. Those problems have accentuated the need for the state to expand its trade activities. In some cases that has meant increasing trade with the Eastern-bloc countries at the very time when the West is encouraging just the opposite.

An important feature in the world of international trade has been Austria's role as business mediator between East and West. Vienna, in particular, has served as both a literal and figurative switchyard in that the roads and railways that once linked main centers of the Habsburg Empire (for example, those connecting Vienna, Prague, and Cracow) still remain. The existence of such a transportation network, observers have commented, makes Austria more "flexibly disposed" to trade with the Eastern European states than with other countries. An example of that attitude is found in the conclusion of a bilateral agreement between Austria and Hungary that abolished visa requirements in 1979 and established a special relationship between the two countries.

In 1982, under the Kreisky government, American-Austrian relations were severely strained when the United States threatened "to impose trade sanctions against Austria if it did not stop the transfer of militarily sensitive products and technology to the Soviet bloc."[13] The United States was particularly upset about the transfer of metals technology, including the production of advanced alloys used in the manufacture of weapons. Although Austria later agreed to tighten its scrutiny of sensitive technology to prevent its illegal transfer to the Eastern-bloc countries,[14] it retains its right to establish and maintain a large and highly variegated trade network.

Its closest economic ties, however, are with West Germany in particular and with Western Europe in general. Such a pattern is logical as Austria is committed and tied to the West in many ways, not the least of which is ideological. Only 20 percent of its trade is outside Europe. Further, although Vienna maintains trade ties with the East, "Austria's foreign trade with COMECON for 1983 was only 12% of the total norm of the 1970's."[15] But with an economic system heavily dependent on trade and with a strong desire to avoid the divisiveness evident in many other European economic systems, Austrians also want to keep their options open and to diversify their trading partners.

One area of diversification of particular interest is the Third World. The potential for controversial trade relations is in some areas as high there as it is with the Eastern bloc. The Austrian engineering and armaments firm of Steyr-Daimler-Puch, for example, has faced exporting difficulties for many years that have not necessarily come from the government. In 1980 a contract for Steyr to sell to Chile 100 Kürassier light tanks and 300 machine guns, a deal worth $16 million, was canceled at governmental insistence after protests expressing opposition to the Chilean dictatorship poured in from Socialist, Church, and youth organizations. The protests culminated in a threatened strike by the railroad workers' union to block the export. After that incident, a new law was introduced requiring that all future arms sales be approved by the interior, foreign, and defense ministers, in consultation with the chancellor. The armaments sale issue illustrates several dilemmas facing Austria: its awkward position as a neutral country in selling arms; the need, but internal inability, to support a domestic arms industry for exclusively national defense purposes; and the important internal economic implications of foreign trade, which have become especially acute since 1983.

Ideology

Although Austria has interpreted its choice of neutrality as requiring it to remain militarily neutral, it definitely does not see itself bound to a stance of ideological neutrality. Such an interpretation is not necessarily unique. Many authorities have held that "permanent neutrality entails an obligation to practice a policy of neutrality" (clearly a normative judgment on their part), but that "states which have opted for this [neutral] status are not required to remain ideologically neutral."[16]

Under the Kreisky government, Austria found itself the target of criticism from the United States and of the vehement public scorn of Israel, and particularly of Menachem Begin, because Kreisky openly supported the idea of the Palestinian right to a homeland. Kreisky personally met with PLO leader Yassir Arafat, and the PLO maintained a permanent representative in Vienna. Kreisky did not allow his Jewish identity to prevent him from expressing sympathy for the Palestinians and a willingness to sell arms to moderate Arabs. Those actions, however, brought questions from the United States and Israel about Austria's role as a neutral and provoked domestic opposition. Kreisky responded to such internal opposition by holding out the promise of increased trade opportunities with the Arab countries, a consideration which has only increased in importance over time. Foreign criticism was answered with renewed pledges of Vienna's commitment to the principles and beliefs of the Western democracies, along with a reiteration of the need for bridge-building.

Another area of controversy has been human rights. The Kreisky government stated its policy as one that focused on individuals, refusing to use it as a political expedient. In other words, it refused generally to condemn other governments for human rights violations but chose to work on behalf of specific individuals. It also was said that Vienna chose to work for the advancement of human rights through a policy of quiet diplomacy. Such a narrow approach also allowed Austria to avoid making unpleasant judgments about actual or potential trade partners. For example, its criticism of the martial law regime in Poland was noticeably low-keyed.

Since 1983, Austria has been more aligned with other Western nations on human rights issues. In fact, in 1985 the government announced sanctions against South Africa, including the halting of investments by state-owned firms, suspending sports contacts, and banning imports of gold coins. Austria had been a main center for Krugerrand sales.

A somewhat embarrassing and domestically disruptive flaw in the carefully cultivated picture of the country as a neutral haven for political refugees of any ideology is its current situation with Polish immigrants. It too has an economic component. In 1981, 34,457 East Europeans, 29,059 of them Poles, applied for political asylum in Austria--more than three times the number of applications made in 1980.[17] Unlike previous years, their numbers were too large to be absorbed by countries such as Australia, the United States, or Canada. Therefore, it appears that they intend to stay on a permanent basis. This large influx of homeless and jobless people already has had a negative effect on labor-management relations and on the sociopolitical harmony which the Austrians enjoy and expect. Consequently, the situation has caused an unprecedented amount of animosity toward Poles and detracts from the public image that Austria wishes to project.

Armed Neutrality

Austrian neutrality is based on the "entrance and occupation price" idea of deterrence. U.S. Army Major John Clarke, in an article suggesting that Vienna's approach to force structure and tactical doctrine might offer ideas for consideration by a resource-constrained NATO,[18] explains this premise succinctly:

> While the Austrians do not feel, in the context of an East-West conflict, the occupation of Austrian territory would be decisive to one side or the other, they are concerned that hostile forces may transit Austrian territory. A neutral state is obligated to prevent the use of its territory as a base of attack by one belligerent upon another. Austria is thus required to maintain forces to insure that the price paid by a transgressor more than offsets the advantage gained by violating Austrian territory. This is the basis of the so-called "entrance price" theory.[19]

The idea that states subject to the status of permanent neutrality must provide for their own armed defense is a well-accepted one.

The minimum level of armed defense that neutrals are expected to maintain is determined by the international standard, based upon the average of defensive efforts undertaken by comparable countries.[20] In practical terms, the proportion of GNP spent on defense is the statistic most often used to make comparisons, although this method does have some shortcomings.

Austria's armed forces in 1986 consisted of 54,700 regular army personnel (air services form a part of the army) and 186,000 reservists. Defense expenditures were approximately $864 million.[21] That is far less than Switzerland's effort. Nevertheless, Vienna's comprehensive national defense plan looks quite impressive on paper, especially for a country hampered by a lack of defensive maneuver space and inhabited by only 7.5 million people. It begins to lose credibility, however, when one examines the resources behind it. Austria spent about $780 million on defense in 1983; nearly three times that amount was spent on the federal railway system during the same period. The fact that the government spends more on supporting the State Opera than on defense may also cause one to question the commitment to national defense. What the figures clearly reflect is the need for an area defense and its subsequent focus on economy-of-force operations.[22]

Austrians are well aware that there are Soviet tanks less than 50 kilometers from Vienna. Therefore, at least in the military, there has been the rational realization that defense plans must be made. Austrian military planners see three scenarios as possible where the use of their armed forces might be appropriate: 1) a situation of external crisis, where the borders would have to be reinforced with additional troops; 2) a violation of neutrality by forces which occupy or exercise influence over a portion of Austria's territory or which violate its airspace; and 3) an invasion of its territory.[23] The basic security fear for Vienna today is that Soviet forces could attempt a Danube crossing into Austria rather than into West Germany, where they would face far more concentrated opposition.[24]

The military defense doctrine, known as *Raumverteidigung*, is based on an area, or zone, defense which relies upon large, light-infantry forces being available upon mobilization. It is also intended that prior knowledge and preparation of the terrain would give those forces a significant home advantage. It must be recognized, however, that this military doctrine is part of a much larger, four-dimensional concept of security. Austrians believe that there are interlocking military, psychological, civil, and economic aspects to their security, that begin with the population's being convinced of a real threat to which it must be prepared to respond. Further, internal political and economic stability are important factors in the willingness of the people to respond. *Raumverteidigung* is only one part of that entire picture.

This defense doctrine was first put forth under the Kreisky government in the mid-1970s. It is based on the premise that certain areas of Austria would be highly valuable to an aggressor either as an invasion route or as a base of operations. Those key areas, designated *Schlusselzonen*, are where defenses would be concentrated. The objective of the Austrian forces in the key zones is to make the price that an aggressor would have to pay too high to justify an attempted advance through or occupation of them. In areas not considered key, but rather simply "area security zones," or *Raumsicherungszonen*, Austrian troops would also engage the aggressor so as not to allow uncontested passage.[25]

Obviously, to a large extent the possibility of success for the plan can be judged by the equipment of the armed forces which would be charged with carrying it out. The Austrian armed forces, or *Bundeswehr*, are composed of about 10-percent long-serving professional soldiers, and 90-percent reservists. Males are subject to universal conscription, meaning that all must serve eight-months active duty and retain a more limited military obligation throughout their adult lives. In 1978 an army reform was adopted to establish a militia of 180,000 by 1986 and of 300,000 by the mid-1990s. In 1985 total mobilization strength of the *Bundeswehr* was estimated at 186,000.[26]

During peacetime, organization of the military is centered around nine commands, one in each of the Austrian federal states. Each of those commands supports at least one reserve training regiment. The training itself is carried out by the full-time professional troops assigned to each command.

The army is structurally divided into three segments: the alert troops, the stationary reserves, and the mobile reserves. The alert troops are the actual active-duty component of the armed forces, organized as a 15,000-man mechanized infantry division of three brigades. The air force, as noted above, is also part of the army and consists of about 4,700 active-duty personnel. The Austrian military establishment is completed by the *Landeswehr*, or reserve components, organized during peacetime into twenty-eight training regiments. The stationary reserves make up the largest element; they are considered stationary in that they are trained to defend a defined geographical area. Their ability and availability to move outside that area are limited. Thus, organization is on a regimental basis with each regiment responsible for the defense of a key zone or security area, with concentrations of forces being clearly in the former. The mobile reserves are much smaller, with more vehicular mobility. They are assigned as the primary combat force in the key zones, while also serving as a backup to alert troops in some instances.

Austria produces about 60 percent of its own requirements for weapons and equipment.[27] However, low investment levels and small production runs keep unit costs high and prevent the acquisition of the number of weapons really necessary for the defense plan. Further, much of the *Bundeswehr* equipment is a generation or more behind that of NATO or Warsaw Pact forces. That is particularly true of their antiarmor and air defense systems. In those areas, the State Treaty has heretofore been interpreted as prohibiting self-propelled missiles. It additionally proscribes nuclear weapons, long-range artillery, chemical and biological weapons, submarines, assault craft, manned torpedoes, and sea mines. The Socialist-Liberal coalition maintains that the treaty could be interpreted as allowing air-to-air missiles.[28]   Insufficient funding has caused difficulties in every area of weapons procurement, though, and particularly in aircraft.

Military planners have been relying on thirty-two 20-year-old SAAB 105 fighter-bombers for air defense. After the Soviet Union reportedly warned Austria not to buy U.S. F-16 jets for replacement, as the Austrian military had wanted, Vienna announced in 1981 that it would buy twenty-four French *Mirage* jets. Allocation of funds was, however, delayed indefinitely. Then, in December 1983, Defense Minister Friedhelm Frischenschlager announced that the government would modernize the air force in 1984 with either Anglo-French *Jaguars*, or (as some clearly preferred) interceptors from neutral Sweden.[29]   In 1985, Austria finally agreed to purchase twenty-four refurbished *Draken* interceptors from Sweden, with the first to be delivered in 1987. Prior to that, it had been stated that "the entire plausibility of Austria's defence is considerably dented by the absence of suitable interceptors to patrol air-space."[30]   The impact of the newly refurbished aircraft on tightening defense has been questioned, though, as the Austrian press has reported that the jets have only 900 flying hours left in them; yet, they are expected to police domestic airspace for the next ten years.[31]

Although Austria's federal budget grew by 8.5 percent in 1983, the defense allocation increased only by 3.4 percent, without reflecting inflation.[32]   Such lack of funding makes upgrading of either weaponry or personnel virtually impossible. It is estimated that perhaps twice as many troops (300,000 or more) are necessary to make the defense plan credible, especially in the absence of sophisticated weaponry. While that strength level is programmed for the mid-1990s, soaring personnel costs, accounting for approximately 55 percent of all defense expenditures, make its achievement problematic. The reason for this monetary drain is that professional soldiers are paid like civil servants; consequently, they are entitled to overtime pay for work in excess of forty hours per week. These payments can total over $30 million annually and wreak havoc on maneuver scheduling. Further, because of such exorbitant personnel costs, investment in new equipment has amounted to only about 12 percent of the defense budget.[33]

Beyond problems of finance, some observers believe that there are also some less tangible but still very real problems with Austrian defense, specifically a "less than committed" attitude. For example, in October 1983 an elaborate early warning system in the Carinthian Alps broke down and remained inoperative for forty-eight hours because the breakdown occurred on a weekend and no one who could authorize repairs could be reached. Although military strategists say psychological commitment is a key aspect of their defense philosophy, such events seem to indicate otherwise. Moreover, these attitudes are not exclusively restricted to the military. Shortly after taking office in May 1983, Liberal Defense Minister Dr. Frischenschlager granted the army a day off to attend peace demonstrations in Vienna.[34] Similarly, the decision to purchase the Swedish *Drakens* was met with a demonstration by 9,000 protestors in Styria, where the jets were to be based. Instances such as these are of concern to Western military observers, who are concerned about Austria's deterrent capacity.

Although it might be argued that such attitudes are consistent with Kreisky's view that neutrality was best defended by basing international organizations in Vienna and by vociferously promoting international peace efforts, his successors seem to have favored more conventional methods of securing Austria's position, at least rhetorically. The purchase of the new aircraft appears to be indicative of this new, more conventional attitude.

Impartiality

Austrians have claimed that as neutrals they have an obligation to hear both sides of any issue. The economic side of that outlook, as already stated, is their professed obligation to treat all countries "without favoritism." Their interpretation of impartiality has been controversial in the West.

Tension was obvious between Vienna and Washington for some time in the early 1980s. Washington, as already noted, complained that Austria was selling sensitive technologies to the Soviet bloc. Chancellor Kreisky supported détente and was annoyed when the United States decided in 1982 to cut financing for the International Institute for Applied Systems Analysis, an East-West research center in Austria that was a child of détente. Kreisky also attacked American policy toward Poland's martial law regime. Americans, in turn, were annoyed at the chancellor's Middle East policies, and they were particularly piqued by his recognition of the PLO and his reception of Libyan leader Qaddafi during a four-day visit to Vienna in February 1982.[35]   To Washington, Austrian actions seemed anything but impartial; rather, they appeared to continue a policy of selective impartiality designed to reap political or economical benefits, accompanied by a clearly lax attitude toward defense.

As a neutral, especially one which openly supported many Arab issues, Austria hoped to avoid being targeted by terrorist attacks, which were reaching an uncomfortable level in Europe by the early 1980s. The government's policy clearly did not provide immunity. The Christmas 1985 attack at the Vienna airport left four dead and many more injured.

That was not the first time Austria had experienced the wrath of Arab terrorists. As a matter of fact, it is thought that at least part of the reason for the targeting of Vienna in 1985 was that two members of the Abu Nidal group, believed responsible for the airport attack, were held in an Austrian prison for the bombing of a synagogue in 1981. The Christmas bombing was seen to be a reminder that the group will continue to push for their comrades' release.   Beyond that motivation, the U.S. State Department is believed to have strong evidence that airports in Paris, Madrid, and Frankfurt were also very thoroughly evaluated by the terrorists in terms of accessibility and effect. Because of airport configuration, security systems, and size of the support organization available in Austria, Vienna was selected as the preferred target.   Further, the terrorists seem to have had relatively easier access to Austria itself than to some of the other countries considered because of a unique immigration arrangement Vienna has with Tunisia, by which Tunisians, unlike other North Africans, are not required to have visas to enter Austria. The terrorists captured after the attack at the airport were carrying stolen Tunisian passports, taken when fifty workers from that country were ousted from Libya in 1984.   This incident vividly pointed out to the Austrians that, even if the Palestinian homeland question were resolved, the terrorist problem would still exist because of splinter groups, and that they are not immune from attack.

National Consciousness

Pahr states that permanent neutrality has become a part of the Austrian identity and a source of national pride.[36]   Much of that national consciousness has very real implications for the country's future, as is evidenced by the incorporation of threat perception into the defense plan. Clearly, without a strategic balance and stability between East and West, there may be no Austria, and the Austrians are acutely aware of that. Yet equally, if not more important, is the fatalistic attitude referred to earlier. When that attitude is considered, along with the demoralizingly close threat of Soviet tanks less than 50 kilometers from the capital and with the Austrian economic situation, one begins to comprehend the true national consciousness and how it relates to defense. Richard Bassett sums up the situation by stating:

> Again and again the argument of neutrality is employed to obstruct attempts to modernize or improve the country's defences. The argument runs: We are neutral--Why spend money on things we shall never use? What this means in fact--and some Austrians admit it-- is: Our situation is hopeless, why try to change it?[37]

With such a notion as a frame of reference, ambiguities in Austrian attitudes toward defense, political, and trade issues become more understandable.

CONCLUSIONS

Militarily, it is evident that Austria does not possess either the manpower or the materiel to make its strategy of area defense operative or credible. Because of budgetary constraints, it is highly unlikely that that situation will evolve positively in the near future. Indeed, budget realities and the desire to increase exports may create new awkward situations for the country, specifically in the areas of arms export and of increased trade with both the Soviet bloc and the Third World.

Probably more than any other neutral nation in Europe, Austria's geographic position compels it to strive for stability and, consequently, for peace. That is the rationale for its policy of active neutrality. Although not a position always favorably looked upon in the West, with whom the Austrians clearly identify emotionally and philosophically, it is considered to be a calculated risk, justified by the country's long-term interests.

In the event of a general war in Europe, geography would probably determine Austria's fate once again. As an obstacle between NATO's northern and southern flanks and a buffer between East and West, it is highly unlikely that Austria could escape invasion by foreign troops. It is this sense of inevitability and fate that makes the Austrians reluctant to commit additional funds to their defense.

NOTES

[1]Fritz Bock, "Austrian Neutrality," in Robert Bauer, ed., *The Austrian Solution: International Conflict and Cooperation* (Charlottesville: University Press of Virginia, 1982), pp. 154-60.

[2]Willibald Pahr, Lecture by the Austrian Minister of Foreign Affairs at the Royal Institute of International Relations, Brussels, 17 February 1983, published in "Austria between the Block Systems," *Studia Diplomatica* 36, nos. 4-5 (1983): 327-36.

[3]Soviet motivations were certainly far more complex than indicated here and included the desire to tempt West Germany into becoming a neutral state and striking a blow at the 1954 Paris Agreements, which were intended to bolster the defense of Western Europe against the Soviet bloc. See William A. Stearman, *The Soviet Union and the Occupation of Austria* (Vienna: Siegler & Co., 1962).

[4]Richard Bassett, "Surprise in Vienna Cabinet Reshuffle," *Times* (London), 13 September 1984.

[5]Hanspeter Neuhold, "Permanent Neutrality and Nonalignment: Similarities and Differences," in Robert Bauer, ed., *The Austrian Solution*, p. 165. See also A. Vedross, "Austrian Permanent Neutrality and the U.N. Organization," *American Journal of International Law* 50 (1956): 61-68; K. Zemanek, "Neutral Austria in the United Nations," *International Organization* 15 (1961): 408-22.

[6]*The Economist*, 26 April 1986.

[7]Bock, "Austrian Neutrality," p. 155.

[8]Peter Marboe, Letter to the Editor, *New York Times*, 22 April 1981.

[9]Bock, "Austrian Neutrality," pp. 157-58.

[10]Richard Bassett, "Exploiting a Chink in the Curtain," Part 1 of a two-part series on Neutral Austria, *Times* (London), 16 February 1984.

[11]Richard Bassett, "Austrians Persuaded to Tighten Their Belts," *Times* (London), 25 April 1984.

[12]See "A Man the World Trusted--But It Didn't Know Everything," *The Economist*, 12 April 1986; "For You to Decide," ibid., 26 April 1986; "Waldheim Comes Home to Roost," ibid., 14 June 1986.

[13]"US Says Austria Let Soviets Have Sensitive Goods," *New York Times*, 14 December 1982.

[14]"Strains are Eased in Austria-US Ties," *New York Times*, 4 February 1983.

[15]Bassett, "Exploiting a Chink in the Curtain."

[16]Neuhold, "Permanent Neutrality and Nonalignment," pp. 166-67.

[17]"Austria Finds Polish Inflow a Burden," *New York Times*, 10 January 1982.

[18]Much of the information on Austria's military doctrine and capabilities is based on Major John L. Clarke's article, "Austria's Raumverteidigung: Central Front Solution?" *Armed Forces Journal International* (September 1985): 46-54.

[19]Clarke, "Austria's Raumverteidigung," pp. 46-47.

[20]Relevant statistics are contained in *The Military Balance*, published annually by the International Institute for Strategic Studies, London.   See Neuhold, "Permanent Neutrality and Nonalignment," p. 164; and K. Zemanek, "Gutachten zu den von dem Volksbegehren zur Abschaffund des Bundesheeres (Bundesheervolksbegehren) aufgeworfen neutralität sprechlichen und neutralitätpolitischen Fragen," *Österreichische Zeitschriften für Aussenpolitik* (Vienna) 10 (1970): 128.

[21]*The Military Balance, 1986-87* (London: International Institute for Strategic Studies, 1986), pp. 81-82.

[22]Clarke, "Austria's Raumverteidigung," p. 54.

[23]Ibid., p. 47.

[24]Ibid., pp. 46-47.

[25]Ibid., p. 47.

[26]Ibid., pp. 47, 50.

[27]The primary companies involved are Steyr (small arms and military vehicles), Swarovski (optical products), and Voest Alpin (steel products).

[28]Richard Bassett, "Air Defences Limited by Lack of Funds," Part 2 of two-part series on Neutral Austria, *Times* (London), 17 February 1984.

[29]*Times* (London), 8 December 1983.

[30]Bassett, "Air Defences Limited by Lack of Funds."

[31]Richard Bassett, "The Holes in Austria's 'Swiss' Defence," *Times* (London), 7 May 1985.

[32]Clarke, "Austria's Raumverteidigung."

[33]Ibid., p. 54.

[34]Bassett, "Air Defences Limited by Lack of Funds."

[35]"US Says Austria Let Soviets Have Sensitive Goods"; John Tagliabue, "With Relations Sour, Kreisky Is Braving a US Trip," *New York Times*, 20 January 1983.

[36]Pahr, "Austria between the Block Systems," p. 330.

[37]Bassett, "The Holes in Austria's 'Swiss' Defence."

YUGOSLAVIA

S. Victor Papacosma

"Violence was, indeed, all I knew of the Balkans: all I knew of the South Slavs."[1] This admission by Rebecca West in the prologue of *Black Lamb and Grey Falcon*, her monumental commentary on the peoples inhabiting Yugoslavia, accurately summed up the knowledge of most Europeans and Americans about the southeastern corner of Europe in the years prior to the outbreak of World War II. Books with catchy titles such as *Through Savage Europe* and *The Incredible Balkans* appeared to perpetuate this turbulent, yet slanted, image of the region. One volume by Professor William M. Sloane of Columbia University did, however, have a most apt title, *The Balkans: A Laboratory of History*. Sloane's preface, written less than four months before the assassination at Sarajevo, states: "In prophecy it [his book] does not indulge because the experiments making in the historical laboratory are absolutely without previous indication or trial, and the elements entering in are difficult beyond measure to test and define."[2] This allusion to a historical or, if one prefers, to a political laboratory is certainly appropriate for much of modern Balkan history and particularly for the post-1945 experiences of Yugoslavia.

YUGOSLAVIA'S FIRST TWENTY-FIVE YEARS

Indeed, one should go back to Professor Sloane's era to discern the origins of some current issues. Yugoslavia, or more accurately, the Kingdom of the Serbs, Croats, and Slovenes--its official name until 1929--emerged as a newly established independent state from the wreckage of World War I. A multinational South Slavic state, its newly acquired lands from the defunct multinational Habsburg

Empire and a mini-Montenegro coalesced around an already independent Serbia that had surfaced earlier from the tottering Ottoman
Empire. The ideal, experimental at best, of a South Slavic union in
an area that also included non-Slavic minorities proved hard to
implement. The numerous nationalities, several languages, two
alphabets, and three major religions worked against a spirit of
unity. A centralized government dominated by Serbs in Belgrade
chafed at the federalist inclinations of the Croatians and Slovenians.
King Alexander used the ensuing turmoil as justification to establish
a royal dictatorship in 1929.

During the 1930s the already strained domestic scene experienced further problems because of economic depression and foreign
pressures. To resist potential threats from defeated or dissatisfied
countries in the region, Yugoslavia had formed the Little Entente
with Romania and Czechoslovakia in 1920-21 and established alliance
ties with France in 1927. These agreements and the subsequent
Balkan Entente with Romania, Greece, and Turkey, signed in 1934,
provided scant security against the revisionist incursions of Italy,
Bulgaria, and Hungary. Nazi Germany's advances eastward provided
the death knell to a joint response. Alliance partners individually
feared being drawn into a conflict which did not affect them directly or was in a distant section of the Balkan peninsula. Ultimately,
such reservations broke down the solidity of the Balkan alliance
system and allowed the Germans and Italians to increase their
influence in southeastern Europe. Collective security pacts gave
way to bilateral agreements and then to fragile unilateral proclamations of neutrality after war broke out in September 1939. Yugoslavia and Greece, in particular, would suffer the tragic consequences of going it alone.

A region that had witnessed the conflicting rivalries of empires
and peoples for more than three millennia, the Balkans certainly
had no tradition of neutrality. It was too much of a strategic
crossroads for it to escape the inroads of stronger powers. Italy
occupied Albania in April 1939. Hitler, playing on Bucharest's fears
of the Soviet Union, which until the Nazi-Soviet Treaty of
Non-Aggression (23 August 1939) had absented itself from Balkan
entanglements, bullied Romania into falling under his "protection."
Bulgaria's inherently revisionist orientation, stemming from its
defeat in World War I and long-standing territorial ambitions in
Yugoslav and Greek Macedonia, drew it into the German camp.
Despite a series of Italian provocations during the summer of 1940,
Greece attempted to adhere to a policy of proper neutrality. Mus-

solini then invaded Greece on 28 October 1940. The heroic resistance of the Greeks pushed the Italians back into Albania. The Yugoslav government attempted to maintain its neutrality and to resist overtures to join the Axis but finally succumbed to Berlin's pressures on 25 March 1941 by signing the Tripartite Pact. Army and air officers, opposed to this move, executed a coup d'état, overthrowing the government. Hitler had already planned to invade Greece to secure the Balkans prior to the Axis invasion of the Soviet Union. The new Yugoslav government's protestations of neutrality notwithstanding, Hitler's generals launched a simultaneous invasion of Greece and Yugoslavia on 6 April 1941.[3]

Hardly prepared for the massive invasion that confronted it, Yugoslavia fell quickly. Although it took a little longer, the same fate confronted Greece, too. The forces of Germany, Italy, Bulgaria, Hungary and Italian-ruled Albania proceeded to partition Yugoslavia into occupation zones under German direction. Whenever it could, Berlin exploited as much as possible the legacy of interwar animosities among the Yugoslav nationalities. Thus, a puppet fascist state under Ante Pavelic was set up in Croatia. The deep-seated nationalist and religious hatreds led to Yugoslavs killing many of each other.

Concurrently, however, resistance organizations emerged to deal with the occupiers. The Chetniks, led by Serbian Colonel Draza Mihailovic, represented the interests of the Yugoslav government-in-exile. Mihailovic's bands, composed mostly of Serbians with a strongly anti-Croatian and anti-Communist orientation, had limited success against the occupiers. Josip Broz Tito, the general secretary of the Yugoslav Communist party, proved more adept in organizing an effective fighting force against the Axis. The Partisans underplayed their Communist objectives and instead stressed the policy of popular front in a war of national liberation. Utilizing the slogan "brotherhood and unity," they also preached national toleration and self-determination for all nationalities. Tito never lost sight of the other basic mission of the Partisans: the implementation of a social and political revolution. The Partisans would succeed in this objective because of superior organization, discipline, and the mastery of guerrilla warfare tactics. Questioning the motives and activities of the Chetniks, whose units were relatively quiescent and suspected of occasional collaboration with the Germans, the British stopped assistance to Mihailovic early in 1944 and concentrated on aiding Tito's Partisans. By the late summer of 1944, when the German forces started retreating, the Partisans were spreading their control over even larger sections of the country. Soviet units would help liberate Belgrade in October but then moved on into Central Europe. Tito had arrived at a prior agreement with Stalin that the liberated areas would fall under Yugoslav administration and that the Red Army would withdraw upon completion of military operations.[4]

YUGOSLAV COMMUNISM: CONSOLIDATION AND CHALLENGES

It had been a costly war, resulting in an economically devastated country and in an estimated 1,700,000 lives lost, more than 10 percent of the population. Yugoslavs themselves stood responsible for much of the bloodshed, first because of their traditional national and religious rivalries and then because of the newer struggle between Communists and anti-Communists. By war's end Tito's People's Liberation Army (renamed the Yugoslav Army in March 1945) had become a regular fighting force, with 800,000 men, comprising 62 divisions, 25 independent Partisan brigades, 6 air squadrons, and 85 small vessels. With this strong armed support, Tito was able to consolidate Communist control by ruthlessly eliminating widespread domestic opposition (Chetniks, Axis collaborators, Croatian rightists) and by making impossible the return of the monarchy. Unlike in other regions of Eastern Europe, the conversion to Communist rule came with minimal Soviet help. More important for this process was the role of the armed forces. A virtually symbiotic relationship between the Yugoslav Communist party and the army had developed during the Partisan struggle and would continue into the postwar era.[5]

Tito set about establishing a regime patterned after the Soviet prototype. The Yugoslav Army at its inception was modeled on the Soviet Red Army and had numerous Soviet military advisers. Several hundred officers and noncommissioned officers completed their basic or higher military education in the Soviet Union.[6] Domestic practices paralleled those instituted by Stalin in Russia. Foreign policy positions were decidedly anti-Western: shooting down American airplanes, claiming Trieste, supporting the Greek Communists in their civil war against the government in Athens, and applauding Soviet efforts to frighten Turkey into a change of policy on the Straits. But because Tito's Communists came to power essentially on their own and because Tito viewed himself as a major Communist leader, Moscow's attempts to control Yugoslav affairs, as it was manipulating regimes more directly under its influence in Eastern Europe, confronted resistance.

Tito's independent ventures irritated Stalin. Yugoslav claims to Austria's southern Carinthia and to Italy's Istrian peninsula and support of the Greek Communists threatened to provoke the West into action and to divert the Soviets from their primary goal of consolidating control over Eastern Europe. Stalin also opposed Tito's initiatives during 1946 and 1947 in the direction of establishing a Balkan federation including Bulgaria and Albania. Tito, in turn, became critical of Soviet attempts to control Yugoslav affairs through secret agents and propaganda and to exploit the economy. These and other disagreements, growing in intensity since the end of the war, resulted in Yugoslav-Soviet relations following "a zigzag pattern until the time when the Soviet designs for economic and political domination became overt."[7] The Belgrade leadership continued to defend itself against a series of accusations that it was pursuing independent actions, and the crisis deepened during the spring of 1948. Stalin resolved to use the forum of the Cominform to issue a resolution on 28 June 1948 expelling Yugoslavia and to list a series of accusations against Tito and his followers. The resolution called on "the healthy elements" of the Yugoslav Communist party to replace the anti-Cominform faction "and to advance a new international leadership of the party."[8]

Belgrade first responded in a spirit of reconciliation. Moscow countered with numerous verbal attacks and measures aimed at breaking the will of the Yugoslav leadership. Already bad relations worsened the following year. By the summer of 1949 a full-fledged economic boycott by the Soviet Union and its allies was in effect. Moscow also renounced the Soviet-Yugoslav Friendship Treaty, organized military maneuvers in satellite countries bordering Yugoslavia, and staged a series of border incidents. According to Yugoslav accounts, more than one thousand skirmishes occurred on the Hungarian and Bulgarian frontiers in the two-year period following the Cominform ouster, and the number of incidents remained very high until 1952.[9]

The determination of Tito and his followers to withstand these pressures stimulated an extensive reorientation of policies at several levels within Yugoslavia, the effects of which would ultimately be felt elsewhere. At the ideological level, Belgrade affirmed its commitment to Marxist principles, condemning the Soviet Union's "state capitalism" and "bureaucratism." By late 1949, Yugoslav theoreticians began emphasizing the need for mass participation in the socialist state and for the general decentralization of economic power.[10] The following spring Belgrade authorized workers' self-management on a nationwide basis, and the practice was institutionalized in 1953 with a law amending the 1946 constitution.   The Yugoslav leadership stressed that there were "independent roads to socialism" and that it was wrong of the Stalinists to superimpose their methods on other nations whose conditions did not parallel the Soviet Union's.   A notion of Yugoslav nationalism was replacing inter-nationalism in the association with communism.

A major question, however, was how long Yugoslavia could withstand the pressures from the East without substantial economic and military aid. Diplomatic isolation and the economic embargo by nations with which Yugoslavia had been closely linked necessitated shifts at the international level.   The West had reaped unsolicited and quick benefits from Yugoslavia's plight: the thirty-three divisions of the Yugoslav army were neutralized and no longer associated with the Soviet bloc.   And when the Greek Communists sided with Stalin in the rift with Tito, Yugoslavia closed its frontier to them in July 1949. (This action contributed significantly to the end of the Greek civil war in October.)   Belgrade also worked to improve relations with Austria and Italy by toning down its claims to their territories.

Further, the United States and its allies increasingly saw the advantages of supporting a Communist state in its troubles with the Soviet Union.   Yugoslavia requested a loan from the American Export-Import Bank and received $20 million in September 1949. The following year formal aid materialized, and the American government officially declared itself in favor of supporting Tito's regime.   In a letter to Congress on 29 November 1950, President Harry Truman stated that the continued independence of Yugoslavia was of great importance to the security of the United States.   He continued: "We can help preserve the independence of a nation which is defying the savage threats of the Soviet imperialists, and keeping Soviet power out of one of Europe's most strategic areas. This is clearly in our national interest."[11]

Western European nations such as Britain and France, but primarily the United States, sent large amounts of aid to Yugoslavia during the 1950s to help it cope with its many economic problems. Exact figures are hard to determine but estimates indicate that from $2 to $2.5 billion of total aid in one form or another reached Belgrade.[12]   This support, much of it military, contributed mightily to the country's ability to stimulate economic development and to protect itself. Backing from the West also served to discourage Soviet designs on Yugoslavia. According to historian Bela Kiraly, then a major general in the Hungarian army, the Soviets had plans to invade. "What saved Tito against the military invasion was the Korean War. America stood up. Consequently, they [the Soviets] assumed that if they invaded Yugoslavia, America would stand up again."[13]

Defense issues held paramount importance for the Yugoslav government. The army had been almost totally dependent on the Soviet Union for its supply of heavy and advanced arms and equipment. Now threatened by invasion from that quarter, Yugoslavia had to enlarge its armed forces and to redeploy. Belgrade began a domestic arms industry producing light weaponry in the country's interior. The massive buildup would peak in 1952 when nearly one-quarter of the nation's income was devoted to defense (the highest percentage in the world that year) and to the maintenance of armed forces totaling 500,000 men. A very heavy drain of resources on an already economically strapped nation, this defense effort found some relief and qualitative buttressing when America began a formal military assistance program in 1951; by 1958 about $750 million of grant aid reached Yugoslavia. Ground forces received, for example, several hundred U.S. M-4 *Sherman* and M-47 *Patton* medium tanks and armored personnel carriers, the air force acquired 210 F-84G *Thunderjet* and 250 F-86 D/E *Sabre* jet fighter-bombers, and the navy obtained one corvette and eight minesweepers. Britain also provided two destroyers and some aircraft. In doctrinal and organizational terms, these preparations stressed conventional defense rather than the Partisan operations of World War II. But in a return to the spirit of that period, the Yugoslav Army changed its name in December 1951 to Yugoslav People's Army (YPA) in order to emphasize the "people's" character of the country's armed forces.[14]

Tito also set about improving relations with non-Soviet bloc neighbors. Enough progress had been made on this front so that on 28 February 1953, Yugoslavia signed a Treaty of Friendship and Mutual Aid with Greece and Turkey. This pact was followed by a military alliance signed on 9 August 1954. The contracting parties agreed that "any armed aggression against one, or several of them, at any part of their territories, shall be considered as an aggression against all the contracting parties" and would lead to joint military action.[15] Aligned with the two newest members of NATO, Yugoslavia became a de facto member of this organization via a back door. Through the intercession of the United States and Britain, renewed attempts were made to settle the delicate Trieste question between the Yugoslavs and Italians. After some very sensitive interludes, compromise was reached in October 1954. The city of Trieste and the immediately adjacent region were granted to Italy, while the bulk of the Istrian peninsula fell under Yugoslav control.[16]

These developments, hardly predictable just a few years before, seemed to reinforce the new orientation of Yugoslavia toward the West. The practical demands of national security had necessitated such an abrupt shift from the country's ideological confreres. In return, however, the Communist leadership was unwilling for ideological reasons to join formally the Western camp. As a universal rule, it was argued, aid might be accepted if it did not impair the sovereignty and independence of the country and if it did not in any way restrict the free and completely unhampered pursuit of domestic and foreign policies. Yugoslavia's communism was, therefore, not tainted by the receipt of aid from the West, since there were no strings attached.

In the attempt to follow a course independent of both Cold War blocs--uncommitted to the West and separated from Moscow--Yugoslavia came to associate itself with developments in other world regions. Like-minded tendencies were finding expression in Asia and Africa among newly independent states that had rid themselves of colonial rule and were now experiencing social revolutions. Tito's contacts with leaders from these areas led to the eventual emergence of the nonaligned movement. As president, he visited Prime Minister Jawaharlal Nehru of India to exchange views, and on 22 December 1954 they issued a joint statement. One of the more significant articles proclaimed that "the policy of nonalignment adopted and pursued by their respective countries is not 'neutrality' or 'neutralism' and therefore passivity as sometimes alleged, but is an active, positive and constructive policy seeking to lead to a collective peace on which alone collective security can really rest."[17] The two leaders also affirmed their support for peaceful coexistence. Tito's links with other statesmen, such as Gamal Abdel Nasser of Egypt and Sukarno of Indonesia, contributed to the advancement of this foreign policy approach which gained increasing momentum during the latter part of the decade.

YUGOSLAV NONALIGNMENT

The crucial determinant in general foreign policymaking in Yugoslavia since 1948 has tended to be a specific reaction to the prevailing status of Belgrade's relations with Moscow. Confronted with a series of unusual challenges since the invasion and occupation of their country in 1941, Yugoslav Communists had responded with a succession of innovative responses. By the mid-1950s it appeared that nonalignment would be the foundation stone of their diplomacy, and such was indeed the case. Within the context of nonalignment there have been periodic shifts of emphasis. While relations with nations outside the Warsaw Pact have proceeded on a fairly even plane, those with the Soviet Union have followed a more erratic course.

Following Stalin's death, the new leadership in Moscow embarked on a policy of rapprochement with Belgrade. The summer of 1953 saw the Soviets proposing a reappointment of ambassadors, an offer accepted by the Yugoslavs who had expressed interest in normalizing relations. The two nations signed a trade agreement the following year. Concurrently, as noted above, Tito was diplomatically active on other fronts, signing the Balkan military pact, mending fences with the Italians, and developing his nonaligned policy with other states. The Soviet Union, in turn, might have been reacting to Tito's seeming successes. Nikita Khrushchev, on arriving in Belgrade on 26 May 1955, apologized to Tito for the Cominform break and, before leaving on 2 June, he acknowledged Tito's insistence on independent roads to socialism. The following June, Tito made a triumphal three-week tour of the Soviet Union.

The impact of de-Stalinization and of Tito's accomplishments on other states in the Warsaw Pact, most notably Poland and Hungary, threatened Soviet dominance and shifted the moderating trend in Moscow. In the aftermath of the 1956 Hungarian Revolution, the Soviet Union commenced a campaign against revisionism and reformism and for a reassertion of its supremacy in state and party matters throughout the Warsaw Pact. The former concession of independent paths to socialism was altered; stress was now placed on certain common principles of socialist revolution that had to be applied in all countries. Moscow's determination to reinforce Communist unity manifested itself in the declaration drawn up in 1957 for the fortieth anniversary of the Bolshevik Revolution. Yugoslavia refused to sign the document. To have done so would have meant an ideological and political retreat and a sacrifice of all that had been gained for Yugoslavia's independent policy since 1948. After warming up, Soviet-Yugoslav relations again chilled but would not reach the low readings of several years before, probably because of the incipient Sino-Soviet feud.   Verbal attacks from Communist centers against Belgrade occurred regularly, as, for example, when Khrushchev in June 1958 denounced Yugoslav revisionism as "the Trojan horse of imperialism."[18]

Tito's attempts to develop a multilateral, nonaligned approach to foreign policy became readily apparent during these middle years of the 1950s.   Tito essentially did not want his ties with the West to compromise the improvement of relations with Moscow nor did he want to abandon the security against potential Soviet threats or aggression provided by the very same West.   This tightrope-walk approach to diplomacy experienced some precarious moments.

Already the Balkan Pact had become a virtual dead letter, largely due to the animosities between Greece and Turkey that had flared up in 1955 over Cyprus.   After Tito's tour of the Soviet Union, the U.S. Congress in July 1956 reacted critically by voting to terminate aid under the Mutual Security Act except if the president determined that it was in America's interest to continue support.   Three months later President Dwight Eisenhower stated that limited aid was appropriate, but the implication was that it would probably end in 1957.   In response to increasing Yugoslav criticism of American foreign policy during 1957, Washington informed Belgrade that its aid program was under review.   Rather than submit to the humiliation of constant review, Belgrade declared in late 1957 that it was preferable to end American military aid.   However, poor relations with the Soviet Union in 1958, Moscow's retraction of a sizeable aid package, and a poor harvest influenced Belgrade to look westward in the summer of 1958, and several nations, including the United States, responded with economic aid and agricultural surpluses.[19]

Tito tried to clarify his nation's stands in a *Foreign Affairs* article in October 1957 by stating: "We have never given anybody reason to hope that we should join the Western bloc, or any other bloc for that matter.   To do so would be contrary to the principles [that is, peaceful coexistence] on which our foreign policy rests."[20] In a later discussion with the journalist C. L. Sulzberger on   28 February 1958, the Yugoslav leader excluded the possibility of neutrality, declaring that it was impossible for any country, including a Communist one, to be neutral.   He reasoned: "It is not possible for any country to be indifferent to the world situation.   There can be

no neutral countries today.   But a communist country does not have
to be a member of a bloc.   It can cooperate with anyone--even
though abstract neutrality is impossible."[21]

To renew his drive for a leading position in the burgeoning
nonaligned movement, Tito undertook a three-month tour in the
winter of 1958-59 of Asian and African states, including India,
Indonesia, Burma, Ceylon, Egypt, Ethiopia, and the Sudan.   In early
September 1961, the First Conference of Nonaligned States convened
in Belgrade.   Twenty-five countries participated, five observed, and
thirty-five national liberation movements, parties, and organizations
sent representatives.   Tito and others pushed for an extended program to advance peaceful coexistence, the involvement of nonaligned
states at summit conferences run by the superpowers, and the
strengthening of the United Nations.   On these points and the
censure of colonialism there was general agreement.   Tito, however,
tended to assume a pro-Soviet position on a number of sensitive
issues.   To the West's dismay, Tito agreed with Khrushchev's definition of disarmament, did not criticize Moscow strongly for the
resumption of nuclear testing, and blamed the German crisis on the
capitalist bloc.[22]

Despite the renewed poor state of Yugoslav-Soviet relations,
Tito looked for an improvement as long as it would not involve a
limitation of Yugoslav independence.   In turn, the Soviets by 1962
expressed interest in an accommodation.   Orthodox Communist rule
and Soviet influence had solidified in Eastern Europe, and Tito's
Yugoslavia no longer loomed as a dangerous threat with its brand
of national communism.   Closer relations between the Soviet and
Yugoslav Communist parties also might increase Soviet influence
among national liberation movements in the Third World.   However,
rapprochement this time resulted largely because of the worsening
Sino-Soviet feud.   The Yugoslav Communists could serve as a special
ally in Soviet attempts to isolate the Chinese Communist party
within the international Communist movement.[23]

The pro-Soviet tilt of the Yugoslav regime manifested itself in
several ways.   Economic relations increased as Yugoslavia entered
into a loose relationship with COMECON in 1964.   Perhaps more
significantly, the Soviet Union became the chief supplier of advanced
weaponry for Yugoslavia, although the armaments were accepted on
terms compatible with the latter's independence.   Beginning in 1962
with the first shipment of sophisticated weapons to the YPA, the
Soviet Union in turn supplied the air force with modern jet
fighter-interceptors (MiG-21 *Fishbed*), helicopters, surface-to-air

missiles, air search radar and communication equipment. Ground forces were extensively modernized after 1964 with the acquisition of Soviet T-54/55 tanks, antitank guns and missiles, and other equipment. The navy received missile and torpedo boats. By the mid-1960s the Soviet Union and its two allies, Poland and Czechoslovakia, became Yugoslavia's main suppliers of advanced arms and equipment. After 1964 an annual average of ten to fifteen officers from the three services attended Soviet military academies to complete their higher professional training. Military ties with Western countries lapsed during these years. However, Yugoslavia still purchased avionics, electronic equipment, and spare parts for arms supplied during the 1950s on a commercial basis from Western countries.[24]

The close associations with Moscow would peak during 1967. Tito's colleague in the nonaligned movement, Egypt's Nasser, fell victim to the Israeli armed forces during the Six-Day War that June. To demonstrate its support for the Arab cause, Yugoslavia worked closely with the Soviets in assisting Egypt during the war. Subsequently, Belgrade launched a vocal "anti-imperialist" campaign against the United States and allowed Soviet planes to fly through Yugoslav airspace for the transfer of military supplies to the Middle East. Such gestures did not, however, imply obeisance to Moscow's policies. Despite Yugoslav participation in multilateral Communist meetings for the first time since 1948, Belgrade opposed convening an all-European Communist parley on restrictive Soviet terms. Moreover, distinctive Yugoslav positions on foreign and domestic affairs prevailed, reflecting broad ideological differences with the Soviet system. The extensive domestic reforms introduced in 1965 for a greater degree of economic decentralization and a withdrawal of Belgrade from economic decision making highlighted that tendency.[25]

TOTAL NATIONAL DEFENSE

The emphases of Yugoslav foreign policy had fluctuated in the post-1948 period. The constants were a commitment to communism and a growing association with the nonaligned movement. It was this former allegiance that drew Yugoslavia to the Soviet orbit, as long as national independence was not compromised. Indeed, the state of relations with Moscow had the capacity to influence many levels of policymaking. This reality registered itself again when the Soviet Union invaded Czechoslovakia on 20-21 August 1968.

Most Yugoslavs had observed with pleasure the developments in Czechoslovakia with its Prague Spring during 1968. Contacts with the new Alexander Dubcek leadership in Prague and also with the independent-minded Nicolae Ceausescu regime in Romania increased during the spring and early summer. The Soviet invasion caught Belgrade, among many others, off guard. The participation by Poland, East Germany, Bulgaria, and Hungary, but not Romania, accentuated Yugoslav fears that their country might be next. The YPA was placed in a state of increased combat readiness, and many reservists were called into active service. Army units were redeployed from border posts facing Greece, Austria, and Italy to new positions on Yugoslavia's eastern and northern frontiers.[26]

Returning from a quick border meeting with Ceausescu on 24 August, Tito proclaimed that, if Yugoslavia's own independence should be threatened, "we shall know how to defend and protect it with all means against whatever side that threat comes from."[27] Tito also drew a parallel between the Soviet invasion of Czechoslovakia to stop a "progressive evolution" and to prevent its spread to other socialist states and Stalin's campaign against Yugoslavia twenty years earlier. He declared: "The glorious proletarian red flag was dirtied once already in 1948, but we have done much to clean the mud from it. Now it has fallen again. Whether we shall succeed in cleaning it as quickly now--that is a question."[28] Tito and Ceausescu met again on 4 September, declaring their determination to resist any aggression.

The articulation of the Brezhnev Doctrine--when socialism was threatened in any country, it was not only a problem for the people of the country concerned, but a common problem and concern for all socialist countries--heightened the fears of Yugoslavs. Belgrade now instinctively looked westward. After some delay the Johnson administration in mid-October announced that America had a "clear and continuing interest in Yugoslavia's independence, sovereignty, and economic development." A destroyer from the U.S. Sixth Fleet put in at Dubrovnik as a symbolic display of support. The NATO Council in its November meeting gave warning signals to the Soviet Union that it should not act against Yugoslavia, and American Secretary of State Dean Rusk referred to a "grey zone," including Yugoslavia, that was to be shielded by NATO.[29]

Having received necessary assurances, Tito, nonetheless, sensed that the Soviet threat was receding and that too close associations with the West might be counterproductive. In late November he noted publicly that he believed the Soviet Union had no reason to attack Yugoslavia and that his country would not call on anybody for help, and specifically would not ask help from America.[30] He also criticized the "grey zone" concept by stating: "We have not recognized any spheres of interest since 1943. The spheres of interest stop at our borders. What sort of zone they have and whether it is grey, I do not know. Here in Yugoslavia it is a bright zone, and we have nothing to fear."[31]

At another level, however, Yugoslavia demonstrated concern for the latest Soviet initiative in Eastern Europe and its apprehensions for future action. Belgrade well recognized that its defense capabilities were inadequate to resist a large, modern, and highly mechanized invasion force. Having to share its 1,700 miles of land borders with seven nations (two of whom, Bulgaria and Hungary, had joined the Soviets in the invasion of Czechoslovakia), Yugoslavia provided several good invasion routes for a modern army. The Hungarian border with its lowlands, in particular, offered an excellent entry for tank formations. Moreover, with the Soviet buildup of its Mediterranean naval forces, Yugoslavia, with its several fine harbors on the Adriatic, loomed even more importantly in Moscow's strategic planning. The Yugoslav response to these challenges would embody both innovative characteristics and old models.

After its intensive and extensive military preparations of the early 1950s, Belgrade slackened its efforts after 1955 upon the normalization of relations with the Soviet bloc. From previous high levels, the defense budget slipped down to 6 percent of national income in 1968, while the YPA numbered only 200,000 men. The country's leadership well recognized the impossibility of substantially increasing defense allocations. The economy could not withstand the strain, and it was politically undesirable to seek foreign assistance. Additionally, the constituent republics, which had benefited from the decentralization process that had developed in the latter part of the 1960s, would resist the excessive concentration of power that would come with the revival of a large-scale standing army.[32]

Since a massive conventional buildup was neither practical nor possible, Yugoslav military planners promoted a defense doctrine referred to as "Total National Defense," or "All-People's Defense." This policy called for the formation in peacetime of a large-scale territorial defense force (TDF) that would consist of territorial armies of citizen-soldiers organized by the political authorities in the six constituent republics and two autonomous provinces. The

National Defense Act of 11 February 1969 incorporated the principle that the country's armed forces consisted of the YPA and TDF. Legally and doctrinally, the TDF was to be co-equal with and not subordinated to the YPA.[33]

Total national defense was based on the premise that if small and medium states wish to remain independent, they must be able to defend themselves rather than to rely on the help of other countries.   With national determination and the mechanisms for mobilizing the entire population in resistance, such states can withstand attack.[34]   The 1963 constitution already forbade military capitulation or surrender of territory under any circumstances. That principle was restated in the 1969 defense law, which added that it was the right and duty of every citizen to participate in national defense and the right and duty of the local political authorities to organize total national defense and to command the battle directly.[35]

The general mission of the YPA is to resist a limited incursion by an invader or to delay sufficiently a massive attack so that the country can carry out its mobilization.   In the latter instance, the YPA will conduct active defense in depth throughout the country. It will transform itself into smaller units waging partisan-style warfare with the TDF only if large unit tactics fail to discourage the enemy from attempting to occupy whole sections of the country. The command-and-control mechanism has been conceived and organized to ensure that large-scale military resistance will continue even if the upper levels of the command structure are destroyed. Yugoslav writers have argued that in using such a strategy an aggressor would require 8.5 soldiers per square kilometer, or 2 million men, to subjugate Yugoslavia completely.[36]   Moreover, it has been concluded that the number of civilians killed in modern warfare tends to exceed the number of casualties suffered by operational units.   "If this is the case, then why not civilian population which will not only strengthen the resistance capability of a country but also, by being trained and equipped, reduce the number of casualties among its own ranks?"[37]   Consequently, the deterrence value of total national defense was to raise significantly the cost of an enemy occupation.[38]

Total national defense as implemented in Yugoslavia was not instantaneously conceived in the immediate aftermath of the Soviet invasion of Czechoslovakia.   Discussion of its basic principles had been conducted for a number of years.   Tito stated in a November 1969 speech that its conception "took shape and developed during the people's liberation war when we called upon the people to defend their independence and liberty."[39]   Since the end of World War II, Yugoslav defense plans had taken into consideration some reliance on guerrilla warfare.   Proponents of conventional defense based on a professional army tended to prevail in decision making in the years immediately following the war, although partisan units were organized during the tense period following the Cominform expulsion.   After this crisis passed, there continued to be some emphasis placed on the mission of partisan warfare in defense, but it was generally a modest role.[40]

Serious discussions for more extensive change began in the mid-1960s, for a number of the reasons already mentioned above. That decision making had advanced significantly was reflected in an interview with Colonel-General Nikola Ljubicic, the new secretary of national defense, published in the Communist party's newspaper, Borba, on 3 December 1967. He referred to the outline of a new national defense law proposal and stated: "The present law does not fully reflect our concept of national defence, the concept of conducting a 'general-popular' defence war, which requires the organization and preparation, not only of the military but also of all the civil organs and organizations as well as the citizens, for the defence of the country."[41]

Established in 1969 and modified substantially in the 1974 National Defense Law for the development of a clearer and more centralized command system, territorial defense consists of a complex mix of staffs, units, and institutions.   Precise figures on the numbers of Yugoslav citizens actually trained, equipped, and organized for combat are hard to come by.   Estimates on the size of territorial defense units during the mid-1970s ranged from 600,000 to over one million.   Together, the YPA and these territorial defense units accounted for about 9 percent of Yugoslavia's total population.   However, this figure does not include other individuals who have received some training for combat or various support roles.   Basic to total national defense is the principle that all of society's resources are mobilized. The 1974 law established an extensive system of defense education, basic and supplementary training to be applied to the population at large (including schoolchildren), and not just to members of the YPA or TDF units.   President Tito in his March 1978 visit to Washington declared: "If necessary, Yugoslavia can deploy on the battlefield about eight million people." That figure was doubtlessly inflated and probably included the more than one million people trained for civilian defense purposes.[42]

Total national defense has been an attempt to apply principles of "people's war" to a "consolidated, semi-industrialized state faced with the possibility of external aggression by a much stronger enemy, taking into account domestic and international political and economic realities and the state of contemporary military technology."[43] Yugoslav theorists have also proffered an appropriate Marxist rationale for total national defense. They have stated that Yugoslavia is implementing the "withering away of the state" and that the resulting progressive socialization of government functions must in time include the armed forces as well. As long as international tensions persist, a standing army of some kind will be required, but some of its functions can be taken over by the "armed people." Additionally, such strategy, it is maintained, is the only defense policy compatible with a peaceful foreign policy.[44]

The application of the total national defense concept has expectedly run into various difficulties. Since territorial defense is financed locally out of the funds of republics, communes, and enterprises, among other administrative units, there have been inevitable economic problems and an uneven distribution of resources. Involving large percentages of the population in diverse training against invisible enemies has naturally created problems in morale, sustained enthusiasm, and efficiency. Although there have been several attempts to clarify the relationship between the YPA and the territorial forces and their missions, a number of difficulties apparently remain to impede smooth operation.[45]

NONALIGNMENT TILTS

Having extensively reinforced Yugoslavia's defensive capabilities in the aftermath of the Soviet invasion of Czechoslovakia, Tito also stressed his commitment to the nonaligned movement and set about reestablishing more cordial ties with Western Europe and the United States. For the first time since the 1950s, Tito visited major Western capitals such as Bonn, Paris, and Brussels, and, in turn, eminent Western European figures, including West Germany's Willy Brandt and Britain's Queen Elizabeth, traveled to Belgrade. Economic relations with the Common Market also increased, with Yugoslavia becoming the first Communist state to enter into a formal agreement with the European Economic Community (EEC) in 1970. The United States reaffirmed its intention to back "the continued independence, integrity and economic growth of Yugoslavia." Richard M. Nixon became the first American president to visit Yugoslavia in September 1970, and Tito reciprocated with a visit to Washington the following year. The two nations also exchanged military delegations for the first time in almost a decade.[46]

Tito, moreover, courted other Communist regimes experiencing difficulties with the Soviet Union. The Tito-Ceausescu relationship moved closer with a succession of meetings and proclamations of joint Yugoslav-Romanian support for the principle of "non-interference in the internal affairs" of Communist countries. By 1970 relations between Yugoslavia and the People's Republic of China had improved after many years of bitter condemnations. Even Albania, Beijing's protégé in Europe and long-time nemesis of Yugoslavia, saw fit to normalize bilateral ties with Belgrade.[47]

Soviet-Yugoslav relations, which had warmed remarkably in the mid-1960s, deteriorated in the wake of the invasion of Czechoslovakia. Dealings remained respectable but cool. They would improve slowly, partly due to the Soviet desire to check the growing influence of China in the Balkans and to divert the Yugoslavs from working too closely with the Romanians, but also to further the campaign for the proposed European Security Conference. Leonid Brezhnev's visit to Yugoslavia in September 1971 highlighted this trend. On that occasion the Soviet leader disowned the Brezhnev Doctrine, labeling it a "Western fabrication." He also reaffirmed the earlier principles of noninterference and mutual respect contained in the 1955 Belgrade and other declarations. Similar statements were exchanged on Tito's visit to Moscow in June 1972.[48]

A drift toward a more balanced nonalignment on the part of Yugoslavia seemed to be developing as a result of the foreign policy decisions taken after August 1968. Concurrently, in the early 1970s, American-Soviet relations seemed to be improving. Although Belgrade viewed this trend of détente favorably, it also expressed concern that the bilateralism of the two superpowers might lead to the imposition of their "condominium" on third countries. The Czech invasion suggested that a small nation belonging to an alliance is at the mercy of the superpower in that alliance. Additionally, stabilization of the Central European front could divert expansionist tendencies and increase instability on the flanks, most notably in southeastern Europe.[49]

Foreign policy issues alone did not influence the mission and composition of the Yugoslav security forces. Domestic issues also became involved to the extent that in 1971, at the height of a movement for greater national affirmation in Croatia, an opinion poll indicated that 54 percent of the officers and noncommissioned officers singled out "nationalism and chauvinism" as the main dangers to the country.[50]   The federal approach, implemented by Tito after World War II with the establishment of six federal republics and two autonomous provinces and the subsequent decentralization, had neither appeased all parties nor their inclination to assert local interests.   Just one indicator of that phenomenon was that only a tiny minority of the total population chose to be defined as Yugoslavs, while the large majority of citizens identified with one or other of the specific national groups.[51]   The grim reality was that domestic forces working against Yugoslav unity always presented lucrative opportunities for foreign enemies to exploit for their own purposes.

Tito reacted sharply to the national crisis in Croatia.   Supported by the army and party loyalists, he oversaw the purging in late 1971 and 1972 of "nationalistic" and "liberal" Communist leaders in Croatia, Serbia, Slovenia, and Macedonia.   In the campaign to reverse earlier policies of decentralization, the Yugoslav army assumed a helpmate role in strengthening federal authority from Belgrade.   It was appropriate for this function, if only because it was the only Yugoslav institution not affected by self-management policies.   Furthermore, the YPA and the party had similar institutional roots: they had grown together out of the Partisan struggle and from that period were highly integrated ideologically and organizationally.[52]   The YPA's political role, which had become relatively passive by the mid-1960s, would be changed by Tito in light of 1971 events, and in December 1971 he affirmed that the YPA played an internal political role as well as an external security role for the country.   The army would be used to defend socialism "when we see it in danger or when there are no other means to defend it."[53]   The 1974 constitution institutionalized that political role of the armed forces.   Consequently, "in no other European Communist state does the military play as integral a part in political affairs."[54]

PRELUDE TO "YUGOSLAVIA AFTER TITO"

Tito reached his eightieth birthday in May 1972. Domestic and foreign issues had regularly challenged his rule for more than twenty-five years, and world observers deliberated whether his successors could ward off threats to Yugoslav independence, unity, and Communist rule as successfully as he had.   Speculation on "Yugoslavia after Tito" had become commonplace.

The tenacious leader had already tried to assure a smooth succession upon his passing with the establishment of a collective presidency formula in 1971 that was subsequently revised in the 1974 constitution.   The state presidency would consist of nine members: one from each of the six republics and two autonomous provinces, with the head of the Communist party as the ninth and ex officio member.   The party presidency included twenty-three members representing constituent party organizations of the republics, provinces, and armed forces.   After Tito's death the leadership posts were to rotate annually among the members of the two presidencies.[55]

Tito held on to power until his death on 4 May 1980.   The years after 1972, therefore, witnessed a continuation of many established policies.   Thus nonalignment, which had served Yugoslav interests rather well since Tito embraced it as a national policy in the 1950s, remained basic to Yugoslavia's dealings with other countries.   Apart from the fact that both Tito's stature and that of Yugoslavia had risen in world circles, nonalignment also offered an ideology for export to counter the policies of the superpower blocs. Yet to the concern of the Yugoslavs, the original spirit of nonalignment experienced some transformation by the 1970s. Anticolonialism and opposition to the Cold War blocs and the arms race no longer united all the nonaligned countries.   Newly independent states feuded with each other, and the Arab world reflected sharp divisions.   Some states cultivated extremely close ties with one or the other of the superpower blocs. Tito expended considerable energies prior to and during the Sixth Conference of Nonaligned States in Havana during September 1979 to curb the attempts of Cuba's Fidel Castro, the meeting's host, to pass a resolution that the Soviet bloc constituted a "natural ally" of the nonaligned states.[56]

Despite some ups and downs, a relatively balanced nonalignment characterized Yugoslav foreign policy for the remainder of the 1970s.   American-Yugoslav relations became temporarily   strained because of Belgrade's staunch support of the Arab cause in the 1973 Yom Kippur War and its vocal criticism of Washington's policy. The following spring Tito sharply questioned the objectives of NATO maneuvers in the northern Adriatic at a time when the Trieste dispute with Italy had flared up again.   A final settlement on the boundary question came in 1975, when Italy withdrew all its claims. That same year President Gerald Ford stopped off in Yugoslavia after his participation in the Helsinki Conference.

The newspaper release of information on the so-called Sonnenfeldt Doctrine in the early spring of 1976 aroused considerable apprehension in Belgrade. In a private briefing to American ambassadors in Europe, Helmut Sonnenfeldt, a high-level U.S. State Department official, reportedly implied that Washington's policy should resist opposing Soviet objectives in Eastern Europe and passively allow Moscow to consolidate its hold on the region. Both Yugoslavia and Romania, fearing a Soviet-American deal to create zones of influence, sensed relief when President Ford disassociated himself from any doctrine of that type.[57]

Presidential candidate Jimmy Carter then stated in October that American security interests would not be directly threatened if the Soviet Union went into Yugoslavia. That blunder temporarily fueled controversy in NATO circles as well as in both countries. Shortly following Carter's electoral victory, the State Department issued a statement to clarify America's position: "The U.S. has a fundamental interest in the continued independence, unity and territorial integrity of Yugoslavia. This is the policy which all administrations since Truman have pursued and which this administration will continue to pursue."[58] During Tito's visit to Washington in 1978, Carter proclaimed that Yugoslavia's independence was a "basic foundation of world peace."[59] After the Soviet invasion of Afghanistan, the American president in February 1980 stated in a message well received in Belgrade:

> If we are called upon to give any kind of aid to the Yugoslav people in the future, we would seriously consider it and do what, in our opinion, would be best for them and for us. I've had frequent conversations with other major European leaders about the need to strengthen our ties with Yugoslavia and to protect them as a nonaligned country without being dominated or threatened successfully by the Soviet Union. We'll take whatever action is necessary to carry out these goals--but commensurate with actual need and commensurate with specific requests from Yugoslavia itself.[60]

Belgrade's relations with Moscow did not resume the cordiality characteristic of the years immediately preceding August 1968. Tito warily viewed Soviet attempts to influence the nonaligned movement. He did allow the Soviets to fly through Yugoslav airspace to supply the Arabs against Israel in 1973--out of his total commitment to the Arab cause and not from pro-USSR sentiments. Having steadily increased their naval presence in the Mediterranean, the Soviets actively sought increased access to Yugoslavia's Adriatic ports, but Belgrade regularly turned down such requests. To regulate the visits of naval ships, the Yugoslavs passed a law in April 1974 stipulating that there could be no more than three combat vessels and two auxiliary naval vessels of any foreign country in its territorial waters at any time. Other measures restricted the extent and nature of repair work in Yugoslav shipyards and served to ensure that those naval support facilities would not be transformed into foreign bases. During his November 1976 visit, Brezhnev reportedly requested closer Yugoslav cooperation with the Warsaw Pact, more liberal overflight rights, and greater access to Yugoslav facilities--all of which were firmly refused by Tito. Belgrade also has expressed concern about Moscow's tacit backing for Bulgarian claims to Macedonia and voiced strong criticism both of the USSR's invasion of Afghanistan and the Soviet-backed Vietnamese invasion of Cambodia.[61]

Despite the continued development of a domestic arms industry, Moscow remained Yugoslavia's most important arms supplier, a position it had held since the early 1960s. Purchases were essentially in heavy weapons such as surface-to-air missiles and also MiG fighter-bombers. In an apparent effort not to provoke Moscow, Belgrade did not vigorously pursue military purchases with Western Europe or the United States. During the mid-1970s, when an attempt was made to buy equipment from Washington, Tito drew back after it became a subject of discussion in the American press. Additionally, it seems that Yugoslavia was not able to afford the expensive systems and to accept U.S. foreign military sales credits, regarded by the Yugoslavs as possibly compromising their nonaligned status. The Americans, in turn, expressed concern about their technology possibly finding its way to the Soviets. Sales did increase, but they remained at quite low levels in the late 1970s.[62]

YUGOSLAVIA AFTER TITO

Post-Tito Yugoslavia has not changed much. The country survived the transition without an internal power struggle over succession, did not experience a nationalities crisis strong enough to tear asunder the federal structure, and did not tempt a foreign power to invade or intervene actively in its domestic affairs. Yugoslavia is, however, suffering through very serious economic problems, which would have been evident with or without Tito, and it has had to cope with a very nasty situation in the Kosovo region, where the Albanian minority has tried to expand its local autonomy. To date, relative continuity seems to describe the general guidelines of Yugoslav domestic and foreign policies. That continuity is based, however, on more than three decades of frequent adjustments in response to numerous internal and external challenges.

Perhaps Yugoslavia's most serious problem is the economy. It owes $20 billion to Western countries, suffers from an inflation rate of around 80 percent (in 1986), and claims an unemployment rate of around 15 percent, but which approaches 30 percent in some regions. Part of the complex problem lies in the lack of a unified domestic market and in the high level of decentralization in economic decision making that evolved under Tito's guidance.[63] The recent world economic crisis and stringency measures on the part of Belgrade to curb the unwieldy debt problems had as a major consequence a decline in trade with the EEC and with the West, in general. Due to the drying up of petroleum imports from Iraq, a result of the war with Iran, the Yugoslavs have had to rely increasingly on the Soviet Union as a source of supply, because only the Soviets were willing to sell oil without requiring payment in hard currency. Additionally, although Yugoslav products are not generally up to the standards of quality found in the European Community states and find shrinking markets there, they are usually of superior quality and design compared with those generally produced within COMECON. Consequently, the volume of trade with the COMECON states and, particularly, with the Soviet Union has expanded noticeably and approached nearly 50 percent of all commercial exchange in the early 1980s. Obviously aware of the consequences of such trends leading to growing dependency, the Yugoslavs reportedly informed Soviet Premier N. A. Tikhonov, during his March 1983 visit, that Soviet-Yugoslav trade could not enjoy such dynamic growth in the 1985-1990 period as it had in the recent past. Seeking to shore up its ongoing ties with the West, Yugoslavia signed a new agreement for trade with the EEC for the five-year period from 1986 to 1990.[64]

One of the constant high costs of Yugoslavia's nonaligned policy has been defense, and this pattern has carried through into the post-Tito era. Despite the budgetary constraints imposed during economically difficult times, defense expenditures for 1986 were scheduled to eat up more than 50 percent of the federal budget and

5.2 percent of national income.[65] Belgrade has continued the long-standing policy of maintaining a large active-duty military. Currently, the armed forces number about 210,000, with 161,500 (110,500 conscripts) in the army, 36,000 (7,000 conscripts) in the air force, and 12,500 (5,500 conscripts) in the navy. Conscription is universal for all males, beginning at the age of eighteen. A conscript serves fifteen months of active duty, after which he becomes a reservist in the regular army, whose ranks total about 500,000, or in the territorial force of his republic. The large majority joins the latter.[66]

Since the early 1960s, the Soviet Union has been Yugoslavia's prime foreign source of heavy military equipment. Thus, Belgrade has supplied its armed forces with Soviet T-54/55 and PT-76 tanks and is producing the Soviet T-72 tank under license. Other purchases have included MiG fighter-bombers and surface-to-air missiles (SA-2, SA-3, SA-4, SA-6, SA-7 systems). Although purchases from the West have been limited in comparison, military support equipment and a number of weapons have been or are being produced in Yugoslavia under license from Western manufacturers. A few examples are the 20-mm antiaircraft cannon built under license from Hispano-Suiza (Swiss-based), the Aérospatiale-Westland *Gazelle* helicopter (France), and the TAM 4500, 5000, 5500, and 6500 truck series from Magirus-Deutz (West Germany).[67] "In general, licensing is seen as an economical method of obtaining weapons, components, and technological know-how, although the technology is not state-of-the-art."[68]

An important legacy of the Tito-Stalin split was the expansion of the arms industry from small-scale to rather ambitious proportions. Inspired by the Yugoslav need to become increasingly self-sufficient in arms production, the industry has become rather diversified and ranges from the manufacture of rifles to that of naval ships and aircraft. In the latter category, Yugoslavia has entered into a joint venture with Romania for the production of the *Orao*, a light attack jet and trainer, which has demonstrated excellent performance characteristics. Yugoslavia is also one of the few nations to have developed advanced production of midget or pocket submarines. Deemed necessary for the effective defense of its islands and indented coastline, those small submarines have also been bought by Sweden.[69]

Beyond serving Yugoslavia's needs, military weapons production has now become increasingly geared toward export, particularly to Third World markets. Belgrade can argue that its weapons are appropriate for other nonaligned states, not only because of their suitability to harsh conditions of use in many Third World states but also because their purchase can substitute for a possible arms dependency on the United States or Soviet Union. It has been logically determined that weapons exports can provide necessary funds to cover debt servicing and imports. Statistics indicate that from 1976 to 1980, Yugoslavia ranked tenth among world arms exporters and that in 1980 it was the eighth leading exporter. For the period from 1981 to 1985, the value of exports in arms, military equipment, and military engineering services increased at an average annual rate of 17 percent, and the Yugoslav leadership plans to achieve an annual export growth of 15 percent for the 1986-1990 period. Emphasis is to be placed on technical modernization to permit military units a great degree of maneuverability and mobility and to make possible strong antitank and air defense and powerful fire support for combat units.[70]

CONCLUSIONS

Tito's personal aspirations for a world role, commitment to communism (or rather to his variant brand), and determination to guarantee Yugoslavia's independence have irritated singly, but not collectively, one or the other of the two superpowers on various occasions. Those patterns combined to forge Yugoslavia's nonalignment, a policy that Tito's successors have continued. But the more recent splintered state of the nonaligned movement, the country's pressing economic problems, and the lack of a leader with the prestige and stature of Tito have defined a lower profile for Yugoslavia in its diplomacy. The diminished role of Belgrade was quite evident in the Eighth Conference of Nonaligned States which met in September 1986 in Zimbabwe.

The independent and multidimensional facets of Yugoslav nonalignment cannot wholly satisfy either the United States or the Soviet Union. Although some American conservatives have criticized the ongoing toleration of Yugoslavia's Communist regime and its frequent anti-American statements on world issues,[71] Washington's policy toward Belgrade has shifted negligibly. President Ronald Reagan's first visit by a leader of a European communist state was from Yugoslavian President Mika Spiljak in early February 1984. During their meeting Reagan reaffirmed America's continued support of Yugoslavia's independence from the Soviet bloc and promised help in Belgrade's attempts to solve its economic problems.[72]

Yet if Yugoslavia cannot belong either to NATO or to the Warsaw Pact, its continued nonalignment is for the time being an acceptable option for both blocs. An attempt to force the country out of its nonaligned role would be too disruptive to the status quo in this highly sensitive region of Europe. Bearing in mind the prevailing patterns of American and Soviet policy, one would more than likely come to the aid of Belgrade in case the other sought to assert its interests in Yugoslavia. One Yugoslav foreign minister candidly summed up this situation when he stated: "As Yugoslavs, we need the Americans to protect us from the Russians. As communists, we need the Russians to protect us from the Americans."[73]

It is a dangerous game, in which the Yugoslavs have had some success playing off one side against the other. The inevitability of changing world conditions demands that Yugoslav leaders, who might not be blessed with some of the innate skills and luck of Tito, give constant attention to their national security policy and to the nuances of NATO and Warsaw Pact policymaking. The rhetoric of striving for world peace and disarmament and of abolishing the superpower blocs aside, Yugoslavs have to concede that East-West rivalry benefits the continued independence of their country. Smaller nations in this region have suffered from great-power consensus on spheres of influence. The Churchill-Stalin "percentages agreement" in October 1944 established a dangerous and haunting modern precedent, and Belgrade has been quite sensitive to it.

Hegemony in the Balkans has been the goal of great powers ever since it became apparent that the Ottoman Empire was "the sick man of Europe." Although it seemed in the immediate aftermath of World War II that the Soviet Union had achieved that objective, it did not come to pass. Yugoslavia asserted its independence, then Greece warded off the attempt of Greek Communists to attain power, Albania proclaimed its independence by shifting its allegiance to the People's Republic of China, and Romania periodically expressed an independent foreign policy. Only Bulgaria remained faithful to Moscow's direction and policies. That such patterns developed is partly attributable to Yugoslavia's regional actions. To protect and to justify their national independence, Tito and his followers formulated their own brand of Marxist-Leninist communism, espoused and gave direction to nonalignment, and conceived a realistic national security policy finely tuned to the capabilities of the nation to defend itself against superior forces. Those initiatives have been both bold and innovative. Life in the Yugoslav political laboratory has indeed been daring.

NOTES

[1]Rebecca West, *Black Lamb and Grey Falcon* (New York: Viking Press, 1943), p. 21.

[2]William M. Sloane, *The Balkans: A Laboratory of History* (New York: Eaton and Mains, 1914), p. viii.

[3]For details on the coup d'état, see D. N. Ristic, *Yugoslavia's Revolution of 1941* (University Park: Pennsylvania State University Press, 1966).

[4]Among the many works dealing with the occupation and resistance that can be consulted are Milovan Djilas, *Wartime*, trans. Michael B. Petrovich (New York: Harcourt Brace Jovanovich, 1977); Mateo J. Milazzo, *The Chetnik Movement and the Yugoslav Resistance* (Baltimore: Johns Hopkins University Press, 1975); Walter R. Roberts, *Tito, Mihailovic and the Allies, 1941-1945* (New Brunswick, NJ: Rutgers University Press, 1973); Phyllis Auty and Richard Clogg, eds., *British Policy towards Wartime Resistance in Yugoslavia and Greece* (New York: Barnes and Noble, 1975).

[5]Milan N. Vego, "Yugoslav Armed Forces since 1968," *RUSI and Brassey's Yearbook* (1983): 138; Robin Alison Remington, "Armed Forces and Society in Yugoslavia," in Catherine McArdle Kelleher, ed., *Political Military Systems: Comparative Perspectives* (Beverly Hills, CA: Sage Publications, 1974), p. 167.

[6]Vego, "Yugoslav Armed Forces," p. 139.

[7]Milovan Djilas, *Tito: The Story from Inside* (New York: Harcourt Brace Jovanovich, 1980), p. 35.

[8]R. Barry Farrell, *Jugoslavia and the Soviet Union, 1948-1956* (Hamden, CT: Shoe String Press, 1956), p. 81. For a brief summation of the Tito-Stalin break see Stephen Clissold, "Yugoslavia and the Soviet Union," *Conflict Studies*, no. 57 (April 1975): 5-6.

[9]Nora Beloff, *Tito's Flawed Legacy: Yugoslavia and the West since 1939* (Boulder, CO: Westview Press, 1985), p. 148; David L. Larson, *United States Policy towards Yugoslavia, 1943-1963* (Washington, DC: University Press of America, 1979), p. 217.

[10]F. Stephen Larrabee, "Yugoslavia at the Crossroads," *Orbis* 16, no. 2 (Summer 1972): 381.

[11]As quoted in George W. Hoffman and Fred W. Neal, *Yugoslavia and the New Communism* (New York: Twentieth Century Fund, 1962), p. 148.

[12]Stevan K. Pavlowitch, *Yugoslavia* (New York: Praeger, 1971), p. 224.

[13]Kiraly made this statement for an oral history project sponsored by the BBC and edited for publication by Michael Charlton in *The Eagle and the Small Birds--Crisis in the Soviet Empire: From Yalta to Solidarity* (Chicago: University of Chicago Press, 1984), p. 78.

[14]Vego, "Yugoslav Armed Forces," pp. 139-40; A. Ross Johnson, "The Role of the Military in Yugoslavia: An Historical Perspective," in Roman Kolkowicz and Andrzej Korbonski, eds., *Soldiers, Peasants, and Bureaucrats: Civil-Military Relations in Communist and Modernizing Societies* (London: George Allen and Unwin, 1982), p. 183; Adam Roberts, *Nations in Arms: The Theory and Practice of Territorial Defense* (New York: Praeger, 1976), pp. 147-50.

[15]Farrell, *Jugoslavia and the Soviet Union*, p. 143. For details on this Balkan alliance consult John Iatrides, *Balkan Triangle: Birth and Decline of an Alliance across Ideological Boundaries* (The Hague: Mouton, 1968).

[16]For details on the complex Trieste problem see Bogdan Novak, *Trieste, 1941-1954--The Ethnic, Political and Ideological Struggle* (Chicago: University of Chicago Press, 1970).

[17]"Joint Declaration: Tito-Nehru," *Review of International Affairs* 5 (1 January 1955): 7.

[18]Pavlowitch, *Yugoslavia*, pp. 256-63.

[19]Ibid., pp. 264-66; Larson, *United States Foreign Policy towards Yugoslavia*, pp. 282-86; Pierre Maurer, "United States-Yugoslav Relations: A Marriage of Convenience," *Studia Diplomatica* 38, no. 4 (1985): 440.

[20]Josip Broz Tito, "On Certain Current International Questions," *Foreign Affairs* 36, no. 1 (October 1957): 77.

[21]C. L. Sulzberger, *The Last of the Giants* (New York: Macmillan, 1970), p. 452.

[22]Josip Broz Tito, *The Belgrade Conference* (Belgrade, 1961), pp. 3-49; Pavlowitch, *Yugoslavia*, pp. 267, 291-93.

[23]A. Ross Johnson, *The Sino-Soviet Relationship and Yugoslavia* (Santa Monica, CA: Rand Corporation, P-4591, April 1971), pp. 4-5.

[24]Vego, "Yugoslav Armed Forces," pp. 140-41; A. Ross Johnson, *The Role of the Military in Communist Yugoslavia: An Historical Sketch* (Santa Monica, CA: Rand Corporation, P-6070, January 1978), pp. 6-7.

[25]A. Ross Johnson, *The Washington Papers: Yugoslavia in the Twilight of Tito 16* (Beverly Hills, CA: Sage Publications, 1974), pp. 31-32; Pavlowitch, *Yugoslavia*, pp. 323-31.

[26]Vego, "Yugoslav Armed Forces," p. 141.

[27]As quoted in Dennison I. Rusinow, "Yugoslavia and Stalin's Successors, 1968-69: How Belgrade Reacted to the Invasion of Czechoslovakia," *American Universities Field Staff: Southeast Europe Series* 16, no. 7 (August

1969), p. 4.

[28]As quoted in Rusinow, "Yugoslavia and Stalin's Successors," p. 4.

[29]Pavlowitch, *Yugoslavia*, p. 333.

[30]Rusinow, "Yugoslavia and Stalin's Successors," pp. 8-9; Pavlowitch, *Yugoslavia*, pp. 334-35.

[31]As quoted in Roberts, *Nations in Arms*, p. 127.

[32]Robin Alison Remington, "Yugoslavia and European Security," *Orbis* 17, no. 1 (Spring 1973): 209; A. Ross Johnson, *Total National Defense in Yugoslavia* (Santa Monica, CA: Rand Corporation, P-4746, December 1971), pp. 2-3.

[33]Johnson, *Total National Defense in Yugoslavia*, pp. 2-6; Johnson, "Role of the Military in Yugoslavia: An Historical Perspective," pp. 185-86.

[34]Remington, "Armed Forces and Society in Yugoslavia," p. 173.

[35]A. Ross Johnson, "Yugoslav Total National Defense," *Survival* 15, no. 2 (March-April 1973): 55; D. S. Gedza, "Yugoslavia and Nuclear Weapons," *Survival* 18, no. 3 (May-June 1976): 116-17.

[36]Johnson, *Total National Defense in Yugoslavia*, pp. 5-7.

[37]Gedza, "Yugoslavia and Nuclear Weapons," p. 117.

[38]Remington, "Armed Forces and Society in Yugoslavia," pp. 172-73.

[39]As quoted in Roberts, *Nations in Arms*, p. 137.

[40]Roberts, *Nations in Arms*, pp. 142, 150-51. For an early argument based on the partisan experience consult Lieutenant General Dushan Kveder, "Territorial War: The Concept of Resistance," *Foreign Affairs* 32, no. 1 (October 1953): 91-108.

[41]Colonel-General Nikola Ljubicic, "Yugoslavian National Defense," *Survival* 10, no. 2 (February 1968): 49.

[42]Adam Roberts, "The Yugoslav Experiment in All-People's Defence," *RUSI and Brassey's Defence Yearbook* (1978-79): 112-15.

[43]Johnson, *Total National Defense in Yugoslavia*, p. 9.

[44]Horst Menderhausen, *Territorial Defense in NATO and Non-NATO Europe* (Santa Monica, CA: Rand Corporation, R-1184-ISA, February 1973), p. 86; John D. Windhausen, "Yugoslavia," in Richard A. Gabriel, *Fighting Armies: Nonaligned, Third World, and Other Ground Armies, A Combat Assessment* (Westport, CT: Greenwood Press, 1983), p. 248. For a selected compilation of Tito's public statements on Total National Defense see Milan Andric, "President Tito on Total National Defense," *Yugoslav Survey* 18, no. 4 (November 1977): 3-24.

[45]Roberts, "Yugoslav Experiment in All-People's Defence," pp. 114-17; Vego, "Yugoslav Armed Forces," p. 160.

[46]Pavlowitch, *Yugoslavia*, p. 364; Johnson, *Yugoslavia in the Twilight of Tito*, pp. 34-35; Maurer, "United States-Yugoslav Relations," pp. 443-44; Aurel Braun, *Small-State Security in the Balkans* (Totowa, NJ: Barnes and

Noble, 1983), p. 171.

[47]Johnson, *Sino-Soviet Relationship and Yugoslavia*, pp. 9-12.

[48]Stephen Clissold, ed., *Yugoslavia and the Soviet Union* (London: Oxford University Press, 1975), pp. 83-89; Remington, "Yugoslavia and European Security," pp. 207-8.

[49]Lilita Dzirkals and A. Ross Johnson, eds., *Soviet and East European Forecasts of European Security: Papers from the 1972 Varna Conference* (Santa Monica, CA: Rand Corporation, R-1272-PR, June 1973), pp. 42-51.

[50]Johnson, "Role of the Military in Yugoslavia: An Historical Perspective," p. 188; Robert Dean, "The Yugoslav Army," in Jonathan R. Adelman, ed., *Communist Armies in Politics* (Boulder, CO: Westview Press, 1982), p. 89.

[51]In 1971, 1.3 percent of the population declared itself Yugoslav; the percentage increased to 5.4 in the 1981 census. Rade Milovanovic, "The National Composition of the Population," *Yugoslav Survey* 24, no. 3 (August 1983): 22. For an overview of the nationalities problems see George Schöpflin, "Nationality in the Fabric of Yugoslav Politics," *Survey* 25, no. 3 (Summer 1980): 1-19.

[52]Vego, "Yugoslav Armed Forces," pp. 142-43; Larrabee, "Yugoslavia at the Crossroads," pp. 391-92.

[53]As quoted in Larrabee, "Yugoslavia at the Crossroads," p. 392.

[54]Dean, "The Yugoslav Army," p. 83.

[55]Stevan K. Pavlowitch, "Yugoslavia after Tito: The Grey Zone on NATO's Balkan Flank," *Survey* 25, no. 3 (Summer 1980): 20-21; Adam Roberts, "Yugoslavia: The Constitution and the Succession," *The World Today* 34, no. 4 (April 1978): 142-43.

[56]Alvin Z. Rubinstein, "Does Nonalignment Have a Future?" *The Nonaligned World* 2, no. 3 (July-September 1984): 388-93; Michael M. Milenkovich, "Yugoslavia and the Third World," in Michael Radu, ed., *Eastern Europe and the Third World* (New York: Praeger, 1981), p. 290. For details on this conference see Dietrich Schlegel, "Die Blockfreien in und nach Havana," *Aussenpolitik* 28, no. 4 (1977): 450-58; Irena Reuter-Hendrichs, "Jugoslawiens Ringen um die Blockfreiheit," *Aussenpolitik* 31, no. 1 (1980): 70-83.

[57]Dusko Doder, *The Yugoslavs* (New York: Vintage, 1978), p. 154; Aurel Braun, "Soviet Naval Policy in the Mediterranean: Yugoslavia and the Sonnenfeldt Doctrine," *Orbis* 22, no. 1 (Spring 1978): 124-26.

[58]As quoted in Maurer, "United States-Yugoslav Relations," p. 449.

[59]Ibid., p. 444.

[60]As quoted in David Andelman, "Yugoslavia: The Delicate Balance," *Foreign Affairs* 58, no. 4 (Spring 1980): 848.

[61]Pedro Ramet, "Soviet-Yugoslav Relations since 1976," *Survey* 26, no. 2 (Spring 1982): 68-69; Braun, "Soviet Naval Policy," pp. 115-16, 123; Pavlowitch, "Yugoslavia after Tito," p. 29; Richard B. Remnek, "The Politics of Soviet Access to Naval Support Facilities in the Mediterranean," in Bradford Dismukes and James M. McConnell, eds., *Soviet Naval Diplomacy* (New York: Pergamon Press, 1979), pp. 382-86.

[62]Ramet, "Soviet-Yugoslav Relations," pp. 70-71; Nils H. Wessell, "Yugoslavia: Ground Rules for Restraining Soviet and American Competition," *Journal of International Affairs* 34, no. 2 (Fall-Winter 1980-81): 319; Vego, "Yugoslav Armed Forces," pp. 150-52; Pavlowitch, "Yugoslavia after Tito," p. 22; Maurer, "United States-Yugoslav Relations," p. 444; Andelman, "Yugoslavia: The Delicate Balance," p. 845.

[63]Roger Thurow, "Tito's Legacy," *Wall Street Journal*, 8 May 1986.

[64]*Quarterly Economic Review of Yugoslavia*, no. 4 (1985): 11-12; O. N. Haberl, "Yugoslavia and the USSR in the Post-Tito Era," in Pedro Ramet, ed., *Yugoslavia in the 1980s* (Boulder, CO: Westview Press, 1985), pp. 288-91; Ljubomir Baban, "Yugoslavia and the EEC: Trade and Financial Relations," *Review of International Affairs*, no. 863 (20 March 1986): 4-7.

[65]*Jane's Defence Weekly* 4, no. 24 (14 December 1985): 1283.

[66]John D. Windhausen, "Yugoslavia," in Richard A. Gabriel, ed., *Fighting Armies: Nonaligned, Third World and Other Ground Armies--A Combat Assessment* (Westport, CT: Greenwood Press, 1983), pp. 254-55; International Institute for Strategic Studies, *The Military Balance, 1986-1987* (London: IISS, 1986), pp. 87-88.

[67]Ramet, "Soviet-Yugoslav Relations," p. 71; *The Military Balance, 1985-1986*, pp. 87-88; James P. Nichol, "Yugoslavia," in James Everett Katz, ed., *Arms Production in Developing Countries* (Lexington, MA: D. C. Heath, 1984), pp. 344-50.

[68]Nichol, "Yugoslavia," p. 345.

[69]Ibid., pp. 345-47; *Jane's Defence Weekly* 5, no. 15 (19 April 1986): 681; *International Defense Review* 18, no. 3 (March 1985): 298.

[70]Nichols, "Yugoslavia," pp. 339-43; *Jane's Defence Weekly* 5, no. 13 (5 April 1986): 606.

[71]A biting analysis of American policy toward Yugoslavia is found in the article by the former U.S. ambassador to Belgrade, Laurence Silberman, "Yugoslavia's 'Old' Communism: Europe's Fiddler on the Roof," *Foreign Policy*, no. 26 (Spring 1977): 3-27.

[72]*Washington Post*, 2 February 1984.

[73]As quoted in Pierre Hassner, "Western European Perceptions of the USSR," *Daedalus* 108 (Winter 1979): 137.

ALBANIA

Boleslaw A. Boczek

Among the European nations remaining outside the military alliance systems, Albania occupies a unique position. Not only does it enjoy the reputation of the most tightly controlled Stalinist type of police state, compared with which the Soviet Union appears to be a liberal democracy, but also externally its policy is unique in the world. This small Balkan country,[1] lost, as it were, in the time warp of the 1950s, strikes the observer by its rigid and self-reliant parochialism which borders on xenophobia. Yet, unlike some ancient "ethnocentric 'nationalisms,'"[2] this narrow attitude is combined with an extraordinary revolutionary fervor to spread what it claims to be the only true Socialist ideology, namely Marxism-Leninism in its Albanian edition.

Albania's ideology and its domestic and foreign policies are intrinsically linked with the name of Enver Hoxha, the late first secretary of the Party of Labor, who ruled over the "Land of the Eagles" (Shqiperia) for more than forty years. Hoxha left his successor, Ramiz Alia, a heritage of foreign relations that is unparalleled in the whole international system. This former ally of Yugoslavia, then Soviet satellite and member of the Warsaw Pact, and finally outpost of China in Europe, is now pursuing a policy of virtual isolation. Concurrently, Albania defies the two greatest "bandits," American "imperialism" and Soviet "social imperialism," and places China in almost the same category of powers. Moreover, it refuses membership in the nonaligned movement, that "amorphous and heterogeneous group of states,"[3] which it regards as another imperialist plot to subjugate the oppressed and poor peoples of the world. Even the New International Economic Order is, in the Albanian view, "another attempt to perpetuate the enslavement and exploitation of the peoples."[4] No other country could afford being

213

so truculently defiant toward its external environment and especially toward the superpowers and the Third World.

The change in Albania's leadership after Hoxha's "heart ceased to beat" in April 1985[5] has rekindled interest in this otherwise rather forgotten little Balkan nation. Speculation had arisen even prior to Hoxha's death about the future course of foreign policy under Alia. It is often overlooked, however, that Hoxha, already before the open break with China, had cautiously and selectively begun moves that can be interpreted as a gradual opening up to the outside world.[6]

The future course of Albania's foreign policy is of great concern to both NATO and the Warsaw Pact. The two alliances appreciate the country's strategic location on the southern flank of NATO at a sensitive Mediterranean point, with its narrow entrance to the Adriatic and proximity to Italy and Greece. Geographical position alone warrants an inquiry into the national security policy of this unusual extra-bloc European nation.

The customary handicaps encountered by analysts of foreign and security policies of Communist countries are compounded in the case of Albania, which is the world's most hermetically closed and unpenetrated society. No official Albanian documents or other, including secondary, sources directly relating to the security policy of that country are available, and it is impossible to subscribe to Albanian armed forces journals. The analysis of security policy must necessarily be based on inferences from the otherwise abundant writings of Hoxha[7] and other Albanian publications, including the daily press (Zëri i popullit), and intelligence information from Western sources, available in international affairs, strategic, and military publications.[8]   The linguistic problem has been resolved by the Albanians themselves, since all the major works and statements of the leadership and many other texts have been translated into French, English, and other major languages.[9]   Eyewitness accounts of those few individuals allowed to penetrate the otherwise impenetrable fortress can also be of interest.[10]

HISTORICAL ROOTS OF ISOLATION POLICY PRIOR TO WORLD WAR II

As a sovereign state, Albania dates back only to 1913. Prior to that date, its people had been subjected to more than four centuries of Ottoman Turkish domination. The London Conference of Ambassadors of Austria-Hungary, France, Germany, Great Britain,

Italy, and Russia recognized by treaty the proclamation of independence by Albanian nationalists in Vlorë in 1912.[11] It is interesting to note that the treaty made provisions for the neutralization of the newly created Balkan state and for the designation of the great powers as guarantors. That act points to the sensitive position occupied by Albania in the Balkan and overall European balance of power. However, as a result of the fundamental changes in conditions produced by World War I, the neutralization was allowed to lapse.[12]

The Neutralization Act of 1913 remains only a curious historical footnote accompanying the birth of Albania. The real roots of its current isolation policy can be discerned, apart from the orthodox ideology of the Communist leadership, in its geographical location at the crossroads of other ethnic groups and empires, its rugged and rather inaccessible terrain, and its history, which has left an indelible imprint upon the Albanian national character. Unlike the Serbs or Bulgarians, the Albanians, an ethnic group of Indo-European, but otherwise of uncertain origin,[13] had never established a state of their own. Divided into tribes and clans, they were for centuries an object of foreign invasions and oppression.[14] That historical experience reinforced feelings of xenophobia and, eventually, in the age of European nationalism, generated toward the end of the nineteenth century a nationalist movement that ultimately led to the creation of an independent Albanian state.[15]

An almost paranoid concern about preserving national identity and independence has been a consistent theme of Albanian leaders from the very beginning of the Communist regime. In public appearances they have frequently referred to the long period of foreign domination, and they regularly commemorate as national heroes Skanderbeg, the fifteenth-century rebel against the Turks, and the leaders of the Albanian nationalist movement prior to independence.[16] One can claim without exaggeration that Communist Albania is the most nationalist state in this age of nationalism. Its history also is used by the leadership to rationalize the country's policy of semi-isolationist self-reliance. It is argued that since in their past struggles the Albanians were on many occasions abandoned and betrayed by foreign powers, their security can be safeguarded by the Albanians alone, especially in the prevailing conditions of imperialist and social-imperialist encirclement.

The Hoxha-Alia policy of self-reliance is in stark contrast to the policy during the short period of independence prior to the Communist rule. Before World War II, when Albania was for most of the time under the rule of the corrupt King Zog, it was subjected to constant, mostly Yugoslav and Italian, interference in its affairs. In the 1930s it became a virtual colony of Italy and, in April 1939, Mussolini's troops occupied the country.   During World War II Albania, a rather secondary theater of war, served as a bridgehead for Italy's disastrous Greek campaign.   Following Italy's capitulation in 1943, German troops occupied Albania for a year, but even before the collapse of Nazi Germany the Communist partisans, led by Hoxha and helped by Tito and British intelligence operatives, took over power in Tirana.   Significantly, no Soviet troops were present at the birth of this Stalinist state in southeastern Europe.[17]

FROM THREE CONSECUTIVE ALIGNMENTS TO SEMI-ISOLATION, 1944-1978

The prewar security policy pattern of relying upon a foreign protector repeated itself after 1944 when Hoxha's Albania first became a satellite of its larger Yugoslav Communist neighbor (1944-1948), then an ally of the Soviet Union (1948-1961) and a member of the Warsaw Pact, and finally a European outpost and client state of Communist China (1961-1978).   Each of these three one-time patrons of Albania extended political support and economic and military aid to its protégé.   As an ally of Yugoslavia and subsequently of the Soviet Union, Albania relied on their military protection.   The Chinese connection was not a military alliance, however, although some contacts between the military of the two states were maintained.

During the Yugoslav period of Albania's alignment policy,[18] Tito developed plans for a Balkan federation that would include a merger of Albania with the heavily Albanian-populated province of Kosovo in Yugoslavia.   This scheme aroused fears in Albania, since such a plan amounted to the end of its independence as understood by the nationalists, including Hoxha.   Yugoslavia's break with the Cominform in 1948 was therefore a welcome development for Albania.   It provided a chance for Tirana to free itself from impending Yugoslav domination and to gain a more distant, hence safer, protector.[19]

The alliance with the Soviet Union provided Albania with needed economic and military assistance, protection against Yugoslavia, and political support, as, for example, in its admission to the United Nations.   As long as hostility characterized Soviet-Yugoslav relations, Albania remained a loyal satellite of the USSR. But Nikita Khrushchev's rapprochement with Tito during the mid-1950s, a decline in Moscow's commitment to provide economic aid, and especially Soviet hints at support for Greek irredentist claims in Albania,[20] prompted Hoxha (otherwise worried about the threat of de-Stalinization and liberalization which might jeopardize his position) to side with China in the emerging Sino-Soviet dispute. Hoxha marked this turnabout first by serving as an oblique mouthpiece for Chinese interests, and then, beginning in 1961, by openly identifying his country as Beijing's ally and Moscow's sworn enemy.[21]

Albania's membership in the Warsaw Pact remained only nominal until 1968. Following the Soviet invasion of Czechoslovakia in August 1968, the Albanian Parliament officially declared the country's withdrawal from this "instrument of enslaving peoples."[22] Diplomatic and other relations with the USSR had been severed in 1961;[23] all the Soviet experts had to leave Albania, and a flotilla of eight Soviet submarines was ordered to vacate the naval base at Vlorë.[24] This was the same base that Marshal Malinovskiy, during a visit in 1959, found to be an ideal haven for Soviet submarines to launch an attack on Greece and to assert control of the Mediterranean.[25]

Apart from China's economic and political support and the reinforced unity in Albania's purged party, Hoxha's defiant anti-Soviet posture became possible primarily because of his country's geographical distance from the Soviet Union and Yugoslavia's non-alignment. Thus, Albania shifted into its third alignment in its post-world War II history. China served as its protector and virtually only supplier of vitally needed credits, industrial machinery, technical assistance, and military hardware and spare parts.[26] However, during the early 1970s, following China's rapprochement with the United States, the first signs of disagreement between Tirana and Beijing became visible.[27] In the orthodox view of Hoxha,[28] favoring one superpower over the other betrayed revolutionary Marxism-Leninism. Moreover, the Chinese "three worlds" theory--which divided the world without any ideological criteria into the superpowers, the other developed countries, and the developing world--came under attack by the Albanians, because it ignored the class nature of the struggle between socialism and capitalism.[29] Relations grew steadily worse. After Mao's death in 1976, the polemics between the two countries degenerated from muted criticism into open verbal abuse. For Albania, China became another "warmongering social-imperialist" country[30] bent on neocolonial domination of the Third World[31] and embarked on the road to capitalism through its "four modernizations" program.[32]

The year 1978 marked the climax of Sino-Albanian links, with an exchange of diplomatic notes formally ending their association.[33] Economic and cultural relations were terminated, but it is significant that, unlike in the case of the Soviet Union, diplomatic relations have continued at the chargé d'affaires level in Beijing and ambassadorial level in Tirana. In Hoxha's assessment, with China "there exist only purely formal diplomatic relations, and no concrete relationship."[34] Thus, in 1978, for the first time in its modern history, Albania stood alone, a "granite island in a hostile sea," its foreign and defense policy entirely free from any external attachment.

Yet, as discussed below, Hoxha was not only a rigid ideologue but also a pragmatist. Already in the 1970s, while increasingly stressing the need for self-reliance, he allowed a slight but steady opening up to the West in Albania's trade relations as if anticipating that after the break with China Albania could not, in the long run, survive economically in absolute isolation. This policy has been continued by his successor, Ramiz Alia.

PHILOSOPHICAL AND CONCEPTUAL ASSUMPTIONS OF SECURITY POLICY: THEORY AND PRACTICE

The philosophical and conceptual assumptions of Albania's security policy are intrinsically related to that country's semi-isolationist foreign policy orientation[35] which, in turn, has been determined by its geography, the historical experience of its people, and the orthodox ideology of its leadership. The geographical location was the major factor that allowed Albania to cut its ties from Moscow and the Warsaw Pact. Historical experience produced, in reaction to foreign penetration, a feeling of extreme nationalism[36] and an almost paranoid concern about Albania's sovereignty and independence. "The foreign policy of new Albania is a policy of complete independence and national sovereignty . . . the voice of Albania is solely the voice of its people and no other people," proclaimed Alia in 1984.[37] Ideology excluded association not only with capitalist states but also with any Communist state that departed from pure Marxist-Leninist thought as interpreted by Hoxha and now Alia, a long-time chief ideologue of the Albanian Communist party. Consequently, total mobilization of the nation's resources, consolidation of national unity under a monolithic party rule, and strict discipline became axioms of domestic policy. In foreign affairs this approach involved a strategy of autarky and isolation from the outer world. Such an orientation prevented foreign penetration, considered dangerous to the social and political values of the regime, and, by implication, a threat to Albania's security and independence.[38]

The policy of self-reliance and isolation was firmly established by the mid-1960s when the break with Moscow had become an accomplished fact. The impressive gains achieved by Albania, with China's aid, in industry, transport, and other branches of the economy, even including a surplus in food production,[39] allowed Albania to secure a modicum of economic independence in the late 1970s and "to stand on its own two feet"[40] when the final break with China occurred in 1978.

The Tirana leadership rationalized its policy of isolation with four arguments.[41]   First, as a people who lived through centuries of foreign domination and suffering, the Albanians are duty bound to show solidarity with the peoples under imperialist and social-imperialist oppression.   In Albania's view all the governments of the world, except its own, are oppressive.   Hence, contacts with the governments of the ruling classes must be limited to a minimum or--in the case of the two major imperialist powers, the United States and the Soviet Union--completely banned.   Second, the encirclement and blockade of Albania by imperialists, social-imperialists, and world reaction requires, in the interests of the only true Socialist state, that contacts with other states be considered always in terms of class struggle.   Third, history has taught Albania that its people cannot rely on foreign powers for their survival and independent existence.   Fourth, and very nationalistically,   there are innumerable dangers to which the national culture of a small nation can be exposed by contacts with the denationalizing international cultures of American imperialism and Soviet social imperialism.   To reconcile that situation with Marxist internationalist ideology, the Albanian Marxists point out that proletarian internationalism does not entail what they call "national nihilism."[42]   Such organizations as the European Economic Community, the Council of Mutual Economic Assistance, and the two military alliances ultimately serve the objective of denationalizing the cultures of small nations.[43]

In terms of Albanian law, the main principles of foreign policy are anchored in the country's constitution of 1976.[44]   Apart from ideological and revolutionary rhetoric, of interest are the provisions that ban the establishment of foreign bases and the stationing of foreign troops in Albania, as well as the procurement of credits from abroad or the granting of concessions to foreign companies.[45]

In this study the foreign policy orientation of Albania is labeled as "semi-isolation" because, while it is true that the country has a low level of involvement in the international system and is certainly a most impenetrable society,[46] it is not entirely isolated from international politics. On the one hand, Albania rejects all international arms control agreements, boycotts the Conference on European Security and Cooperation meetings (the "Helsinki process"), does not participate in such nonpolitical cooperative ventures as the Mediterranean Action Plan of the United Nations to clean its own sea,[47] and, in general, is not a party to any regional organization. On the other hand, it is a member of a number of global organizations and maintains diplomatic relations with more than one hundred countries.[48]   Specifically, since 1955, Albania has been a member of the United Nations, which offers it an excellent forum for spreading its ideology (as can be seen from the addresses of its delegates at General Assembly sessions), and nine UN system agencies (UNCTAD, UNIDO, FAO, ICAO, ITU, UNESCO, UPU, WHO, and WMO).[49] It also participated in the Third UN Conference on the Law of the Sea (1973-1982).

Albania has diplomatic relations with all the Communist countries except the Soviet Union; many countries of Africa, Asia, and Latin America; Australia, Canada, Turkey, and Japan; and all the Western European countries except the Federal Republic of Germany, Ireland, and the United Kingdom.   Such an impressive number is rather misleading, since most of these relations are purely formal without an actual exchange of diplomatic missions.   Still, at least sixteen foreign diplomatic representations are present in Tirana.[50]

In the Albanians' rather ethnocentric frame of reference, all governments, except their own, are more or less evil.   The United States and the Soviet Union are the greatest and equal evils, the "greatest robbers of countries and peoples,"[51] with whom absolutely no relations of whatever kind can be maintained.   In relations with the Communist countries, other than the Soviet Union, Albania makes a distinction between the ideological and state levels.   Although China has been condemned as revisionist and even social-imperialist, diplomatic relations have continued and, significantly, attacks on China have become milder in the past three or four years.   In 1984, Alia did not include China among the great "enemies of the freedom of the peoples."[52]   Also, as part of Albania's strategy of opening up to the outside world, trade relations with China have been resumed following a visit to Albania by a Chinese trade delegation in 1983.[53]

Although the Soviet satellite regimes are branded as revisionist, diplomatic relations are maintained with them at the chargé d'affaires level (except Romania with which ambassadors are exchanged). Trade relations with these countries, strictly on a barter basis, have been quite considerable in relative terms.[54] Especially friendly relations exist with North Korea, and good relations have been established with Vietnam, Laos, and Kampuchea, whose pro-Vietnamese government was recognized by Albania in 1983.[55]

Yugoslavia is a crucial country in Albania's foreign relations.[56] Diplomatic and trade relations are maintained, but tension continues for at least two reasons. First, the relatively liberal regime of Yugoslavia is perceived by Albanian Communists as a threat to their rule. Second, there is the issue of the Albanian national irredenta in Kosovo. A large number of Albanians (about 1.5 million, or about four-fifths of the region's population) live in this Yugoslav autonomous province. Supported by Tirana, these people demand separation of the province from Serbia and its establishment as the seventh Yugoslav republic.[57]

There are two more reasons why Albania's foreign policy orientation can be categorized as only *semi*-isolation. First, quite unlike such past models of isolation as Japan and the United States and, more recently Burma--all of which had no interest in changing the external environment--Albania vociferously supports all kinds of violent revolutionary struggle, including the Iranian Islamic revolution.[58] For that purpose Tirana maintains a well-developed international propaganda machine in the form of publications and a radio station broadcasting eighty hours daily in eleven languages.[59] Second, the past decade has witnessed a slow but steady trend away from the extreme end of the isolation-involvement spectrum. Diplomatic, trade, and cultural relations have expanded with other countries, especially with Italy and Greece, but also with Yugoslavia, Turkey, France, and Japan, for example.[60] This pattern is likely to move toward a normalization of relations with the United Kingdom[61] and, very importantly for Albania's economic plans, with the Federal Republic of Germany.[62]

The various symptoms of opening up to the outer world do not, however, imply any change in the fundamental philosophical assumptions of Albania's foreign and defense policy. They are only pragmatically motivated attempts of the leadership to reduce the backwardness of the country's economy and technological know-how.

Otherwise, there exists at this time no compelling reason for Albania to abandon its policy of not aligning itself with any bloc of nations, let alone with a military alliance.

STRATEGIC AND TACTICAL MILITARY DOCTRINE

Although it is virtually impossible to obtain concrete information from Albanian sources about strategic and military doctrine, its major features can nonetheless be inferred from the philosophical assumptions underlying the country's security policy. Albania's fanatic nationalism and extreme Marxist-Leninist ideology require that it follow the doctrine of the total defense of every square inch by all citizens able to bear arms for the protection of the fatherland.

In the early 1970s the strategic doctrine must have been a subject of debate within the leadership, but Hoxha's principles of self-reliance and total defense of Albanian territory prevailed. During the process, in 1974, the longtime defense minister and politburo member Beqir Balluku was purged from office and subsequently executed on charges of high treason, along with Petrit Dume, the chief of the general staff, and other high officials of his ministry. Their crime was to recommend a defense strategy in case of invasion that involved giving up the coastal areas and retreating into the mountains, from where guerrilla warfare could be continued against the invaders. It was then that Hoxha ordered the construction of thousands of concrete blockhouses and pillboxes which now dot the Albanian landscape on beaches, foothills, and fields, along roadways, and in villages and towns.[63] Most of these structures are small, sunken sentry boxes for one or two soldiers and would be no match for a modern army of the 1980s. Still, these rather obsolete defense measures point to the military tactic that Albania would adopt in case of a foreign invasion. They are symbolic of its determination to mobilize every possible resource in the implementation of total defense by a nation in arms, ready to be called up at any moment to repulse the aggressor. Visitors from abroad are assured that every Albanian knows which pillbox he or she is to occupy in an emergency.[64]

Apart from any deterrence value that these primitive defense measures may have,[65] their primary function is likely to be to sustain and constantly to whip up the beleaguered fortress mentality in an effort to rationalize the ruthless totalitarian measures applied by the Communist regime against its own people. In fact, it is a constant propaganda theme of Albania's rulers, inculcated into the citizenry from childhood, that their country is a little "granite island in a hostile sea." Its position in the capitalist and revisionist blockade calls for continual vigilance and readiness to build socialism "with a pick in one hand and a rifle in the other," a slogan to be seen on many banners and posters all over Albania.[66]

Despite a primitive military infrastructure, Albania's defense expenditures are estimated to be relatively high in terms of percentage of gross national product, amounting to 5.5 percent in 1984, compared to Yugoslavia's 4.6 percent (of gross material product). In terms of percentage of government spending, only Switzerland and Yugoslavia, among the extra-bloc European countries, spend more than Albania, with percentages for 1981, 1983, and 1984 amounting to 21.4, 21.3, and 21.3 for Switzerland, 14.9, 18.0, and 19.1 for Yugoslavia, and 11.5, 10.4, and 11.0 for Albania. However, per capita defense expenditures of Albania are estimated to be among the lowest of the European countries remaining outside NATO and the Warsaw Pact, with only Cyprus and Malta spending less.[67]

Albania naturally claims that its strategy of people's defense is to be implemented with total reliance upon its own resources. Following the successive breaks with Yugoslavia (1948), the Soviet Union (1961), and finally China (1978), Tirana has indeed had no ally to count on in its strategic calculations. As noted above, the constitution itself precludes the establishment of foreign bases and stationing of foreign troops in Albania. It is interesting to note that in response to China's suggestion in the early 1970s that Albania join a military alliance with Yugoslavia and Romania, Hoxha ordered new and bigger pillboxes, thus asserting the strategy of self-reliance also present in national defense policy. Nonetheless, despite such gestures in peacetime, it is doubtful whether, in case of an emergency, Tirana would decline foreign military assistance. The leadership would certainly dialectically rationalize such aid from whatever source it might originate.

NATIONAL SERVICE POLICY

In no other country can a visitor see so many uniforms as in Albania. From their early childhood, the young Shqipetars, both boys and girls, are brought up in martial spirit by war games, songs and poems.[68]   The regime's defense strategy is favored by demography. The population, estimated at 3 million in 1985,[69] is the youngest in Europe, with an average age of 25.[70]   Abortions are banned, and the national increase rate per 1,000 population in 1984 was 20, three points higher than the world rate and four times higher than the European average.   Demographic projections point to an increase in population to 3.4 million in 1990 and 4 million by the year 2000.[71]

Military training starts during school-age years with young "sons and daughters of Eagles" receiving one month of basic training per year.   Women are not subject to obligatory military service, but until age 35 they are required to do one week of training every year.[72]

Albania maintains some 54,000 troops under arms, including 42,000 regular armed forces and 12,000 paramilitary forces, consisting of a 5,000-member internal security force and 7,000 frontier guards.[73]   Unknown thousands of plainclothes secret police agents are not counted in these estimates.   Slightly more than half (22,400) of the regular armed forces of 42,000 consists of conscripts whose terms of compulsory duty vary according to the type of service: two years for the army, and three years for the other services.[74] One legacy of the Chinese presence is the absence of rank designation on military uniforms.[75]

The army makes up about 75 percent of the armed forces, with 31,500 men (20,000 conscripts).   The navy has a force of 3,300 (1,000 conscripts), and the air force 7,200 (1,400 conscripts).   Following their military service, all able-bodied men until age 56 are called up as reserves for special three-week refresher courses and exercises.   The total number of reservists is estimated at 155,000, out of whom 150,000 are in the army and 5,000 in the navy and air force.[76]   Ethnically, the armed forces constitute a homogeneous group in which 93.1 percent are Albanians by origin.[77]   There appears to be no reason to doubt the loyalty of these forces in an emergency, considering the spirit of extreme nationalism pervading the population and the political indoctrination along party lines, adopted by Albania from the Soviet mode.[78]

Even so, the waves of purges in the Ministry of Defense and the higher echelons of the officer corps in 1974-75 prompted speculation on the opposition in the armed forces to Hoxha's policy of self-reliance and on the existence of a faction favoring an improvement of relations with Moscow.[79]   Continued efforts by Hoxha to maintain the military firmly under party control[80] resulted in a new purge in 1981 in which Prokop Murra, an economist and candidate member of the politburo, succeeded the purged Kadri Hazbiu, brother-in-law of the liquidated Mehmet Shehu, as minister of defense. In 1985, just before Hoxha's death, Alia reemphasized the leading role of the party in the armed forces, declaring that they "are loyal weapons of the Party and people."[81] Having succeeded Hoxha, Alia is certain to strengthen further the party's control over them. However, if there is to be any radical change in Albania's regime, it will have to attract the support of the armed forces, which, in the final analysis, hold the crucial position in a power struggle within a totalitarian society.

WEAPONS ACQUISITION POLICY

The weapons and equipment of the armed forces are antiquated and range, in terms of technology, from World War II to the 1960s, at best. As long as Albania was a loyal ally of the Soviet Union, it was supplied by that country. Following the break with Moscow, China became the source, but again with the cooling of the Sino-Albanian friendship, aid was progressively reduced. Since 1978, Albania has had to rely upon its own industrial base to meet its defense needs, receiving no military aid from any foreign source.[82] There are no hard data available, but it appears that Albania must have some munitions industry, developed with Chinese aid in the 1960s and 1970s, and that it can produce some light weapons and equipment. However, there is an acute shortage of spare parts, so some military equipment may not be serviceable.[83]

According to the latest estimates, the Albanian army (one tank brigade, four infantry brigades, three artillery regiments, and six light coastal artillery battalions) is armed with 190 tanks of the old T-34 and T-54 types. It has some 13 reconnaissance armed fighting vehicles and some 80 armored personnel carriers. Its artillery consists of M-1942 and SU-76 self-propelled 76-mm guns; D-44, Type-56 85-mm guns; M-1931/37, 122-mm guns; and Type-59-1 130-mm guns; M-1938, Type-60 122-mm and M-1937, Type-66 152-mm gun/howitzers; D-1 152-mm howitzers; Type-63 107-mm multiple rocket launchers; and 120-mm and 160-mm mortars. Antitank weapons include T-21 82-mm recoilless launchers; and M-1942 45-mm, M-1943 57-mm, and D-44, Type-56 85-mm guns. Air defense includes 50 guns of the types M-1939 37-mm and ZU-23 twin 23-mm.[84]

The navy, which has its bases at Durres, Vlorë (Valona), Sazan Island, and Pasha Liman, possesses three Soviet *Whiskey* class submarines (one of which is a training submarine), two Soviet *Kronshtadt* large patrol craft, six Chinese *Shanghai II* and twelve Chinese P-4 attack craft, thirty-two Chinese hydrofoils of *Huchwan* class, and about a dozen small mine countermeasures vessels. In addition, one submarine, two patrol craft, and two minesweepers are in reserve.[85]

The Albanian air force has some 100 combat aircraft: six squadrons with 20 MiG-15/F-2, 20 MiG-17, 40 MiG-19/D-6, and 20 Chinese Shenyang J-7. It also has one squadron of transport aircraft consisting of 3 Ilyushin Il-14m and 10 Antonov An-2; two squadrons of helicopters (30 Mi-4); one training squadron with MiG-15 UTI; and some five SA-2 sites of surface-to-air missiles.[86]

CONCLUSIONS

Most analysts concur[87] that at least in the foreseeable future there is little likelihood of change in the basic premises of Albania's security policy. As before, it will continue to be predicated on a strategy of self-reliance and on a policy of semi-isolation, although the latter will likely continue to be gradually tempered. Any speculation to the contrary has so far been discouraged by Alia who, in his statements since Hoxha's death, has stressed loyalty to his mentor's teachings and continuity in domestic and foreign policy. In his major foreign policy address in August 1985, widely distributed by Albanian diplomatic missions, Alia emphasized that "those who dream of and expect changes in our line, who interpret the usual normal political and diplomatic acts of our independent and sovereign state as 'opening up' of Albania or 'tendencies' to get closer to one side or another, are wasting time."[88] He also paid tribute to Hoxha's ideology and policy at the Party Congress in November 1986.[89] By those "usual normal political and diplomatic acts," Alia must have meant the expanding contacts with some Western nations, a process already initiated by Hoxha and continued by his successor. These developments are not likely, however, to alter the main line of Albania's foreign and defense policy.

As a matter of fact, keeping away from alliances has served Tirana's security policy better than earlier ties to allies who tried to use the alliance with Albania for the pursuit of their respective interests. The strategy of self-reliance without foreign tutelage has proved adequate to preserve that country's independence in tense situations of the post-World War II era, and the new leadership has no objective incentive to depart from it. It will, however, try to combine this strategy with a policy of expanding nonpolitical contacts with countries that can help Albania narrow the gap separating it from modern societies. Neither superpower will be among those countries, however. Tirana's policy is not only realistic from the Albanian point of view, but it also makes a contribution to international security by easing bipolar confrontation in a strategically important region of Europe.

There is no doubt that, in the hypothetical case of a general war between NATO and the Warsaw Pact, Albania at all costs would try to avoid being drawn into the conflict between the evil forces of imperialism and social imperialism. However, the chances are that, in view of its geostrategic position in the Mediterranean, it would become an early target for either of the belligerents.

What the reaction of NATO would be to any Soviet Afghanistan-style intervention in Albania in peacetime, either in the form of "fraternal aid" to a pro-Soviet faction or otherwise, must remain in the realm of pure speculation.[90] Whether the Western Alliance has a contingency plan to deal effectively with this kind of crisis cannot be answered here. The fact remains that, like the European neutral and nonaligned nations outside the legal limits of NATO, Albania represents a grey area on the map of Europe whose position is all the more sensitive as it is located in a strategically vital region of the Alliance's southern flank.

NOTES

[1]The area of Albania is 11,100 square miles (28,748 sq km). *Britannica Book of the Year 1986* (Chicago: Encyclopaedia Britannica, 1986), p. 619.

[2]"Ethnocentric 'nationalism'" is the concept applied by some sociologists and political scientists to the feeling of exclusiveness in ancient times of such ethnic groups as Jews or Greeks. See Anthony Smith, *Theories of Nationalism* (New York: Harper, 1971), pp. 154-60.

[3]Piro Vito, "The Theory of 'Non-Aligned Countries' Serves the Superpowers, the Bourgeoisie and the Reaction," *Rruga e partisë*, no. 1 (1979): 58 [in Albanian], quoted in Bernard Tönnes, "Grundlagen der albanischen Isolationspolitik," *Südost-Europa* 31 (1982): 443.

[4]Priamo Bollano and Lulzim Hanna, "The 'New Economic Order'--A New Attempt to Perpetuate the Enslavement and Exploitation of the Peoples," *Rruga ë partisë*, no. 12 (1978): 46-54 [in Albanian], quoted in Tönnes, "Grundlagen der albanischen Isolationspolitik," p. 550.

[5]Eric Bourne, "With New Leadership Albania May Become More Modern Society," *Christian Science Monitor*, 12 April 1985.

[6]See F. B. Singleton, "Albania and Her Neighbors: The End of Isolation," *The World Today* 31, no. 9 (September 1975): 383-90; Charles Meynell, "Albania's Tortuous Opening-Up," *The World Today* 40, no. 11 (November 1984): 449-51.

[7]A selected bibliography of Albanian political literature in French translation is included in Gabriel Jandot, "La stratégie albanaise dans l'évolution mondiale," *Stratégie* 107, no. 2 (1985): 129-34.   Among the many works by Enver Hoxha of interest here are: *Réflexions sur la Chine (Extrait du Journal politique)*, 2 vols. (Tirana: Nëntori, 1979); *L'impérialisme et la révolution* (Tirana: Nëntori, 1979); *Les Khrouchtcheviens (Souvenirs)* (Tirana: Nëntori, 1980); and Hoxha's report at the Eighth Party Congress, 1981: *Rapport présenté au VIIIe Congrès du P.T.A.* (Tirana: Nëntori, 1981).

[8]See, for example, data on Albanian military power in International Institute for Strategic Studies, *The Military Balance, 1986-1987* (London: IISS, 1985), p. 81.

[9]There is an excellent and relatively up-to-date bibliography listing, in 653 pages, Albanian and foreign books, articles, and other materials on Albania: in general, its history, politics (including foreign relations and national defense), law, and economy.   See Armin Hetzer and Viorel S. Roman, *Albanien: Ein bibliographischer Forschungsbericht--Albania: A Bibliographic Research Survey* (Munich: K. G. Saur, 1983).   However, even this otherwise thorough research aid has very little to offer in the area of security policy.

[10]Of particular interest is Paul Lendvai, *Das einsame Albanien: Reportage aus dem Land der Skipetaren* (Zurich: Edition Interfrom, 1985).   See also Paul Lendvai, "Albania: An Impenetrable Fortress," *Christian Science Monitor*, 3 April 1985.

[11]In Albanian literature this early period of the country's history is discussed in Arben Puto, *L'indépendance albanaise et la diplomatie des grandes puissances* (Tirana: Nëntori, 1982).

[12]Cyril E. Black, Richard A. Falk, Klaus Knorr, and Oran R. Young, *Neutralization and World Politics* (Princeton: Princeton University Press, 1968), pp. 31-32.

[13]Searching in a typically nationalistic fashion for the roots of their national identity, the Albanians claim to be descendants of the ancient Illyrians.   See *Les Illyriens et la genèse des Albanais* (Tirana: University

of Tirana, 1971).

[14]See, in general, Kristo Frasheri, *The History of Albania: A Brief Survey* (Tirana: University of Tirana, 1964).

[15]The Albanian nationalist movement is examined in Stavro Skendi, *The Albanian National Awakening 1878-1912* (Princeton: Princeton University Press, 1967).

[16]See, for example, Ramiz Alia's address commemorating the 100th anniversary of the foundation of the League of Prizren, in *Rruga ë partisë*, no. 6 (1978): 9-27, cited in Tönnes, "Grundlagen der albanischen Isolationspolitik," p. 446.

[17]Lendvai, *Das einsame Albanien*, p. 26.

[18]On this Yugoslav period in Albania's post-World War II history see briefly V. R., "Albania: A Balkan Bridgehead," *The World Today* 6 (January 1950): 73-83.

[19]Additionally, it made it easier for Hoxha to liquidate his main rival, the pro-Yugoslav chief of secret police, Koçi Xoxe. V. R., "Albania: A Balkan Bridgehead," pp. 76-77.

[20]For the nature of these claims see "Greek Claims in Southern Albania," *The World Today* 2, no. 10 (October 1946): 488-94.

[21]A standard work examining this period of Albanian history is W. E. Griffith, *Albania and the Sino-Soviet Rift* (Cambridge, MA: MIT Press, 1963). See also Anton Logoreci, "Albania: A Chinese Satellite in the Making?" *The World Today* 17, no. 5 (May 1961): 197-205; Stavro Skendi, "Albania and the Sino-Soviet Conflict," *Foreign Affairs* 40 (April 1961): 471-78; and Wayne S. Vucinich, "The Albanian-Soviet Rift," *Current History* 44, no. 261 (May 1963): 299.

[22]See "The Warsaw Pact Is an Instrument of Enslaving Peoples," *Zëri i popullit*, 13 September 1968. Parliament declared withdrawal of Albania from the Warsaw Pact on 13 September 1968. Lendvai, *Das einsame Albanien*, p. 96.

[23]Mile Veljovic, "Albania after Enver Hoxha," *Review of International Affairs* 36 (5 May 1985): 29.

[24]Lendvai, *Das einsame Albanien*, p. 103. Two Soviet submarines were held back by force by the Albanians on this occasion.

[25]Malinovskiy made this remark, overheard by Hoxha, in a conversation with Khrushchev. See Hoxha, *Les Khrouchtcheviens* (p. 376 in the English edition of *The Khrushchevites*).

[26]Chinese aid to Albania is estimated to have amounted to $5 billion, but it must be borne in mind that Albania supplied China with oil, chromite (of which it is the world's third largest producer), and other minerals. Lendvai, *Das einsame Albanien*, p. 70.

[27]See, for example, M. Deloince, "Situation et perspectives de la politique étrangère de l'Albanie," *Défense nationale* 30, no. 3 (1974): 81; D. G. Fontana, "Recent Sino-Soviet Relations," *Survey* 21 (1975): 121-44; Dietrich Schlegel, "Spannungen zwischen China und Albanien," *Aussenpolitik* 23 (June 1972): 365-77.

[28]Hoxha's views on China are presented in his *Réflexions sur la Chine*.

[29]See Hoxha, *Réflexions sur la Chine*; and Enver Hoxha, *Problèmes de l'évolution mondiale actuelle* (Tirana, 1980), pp. 41, 125, as cited in Jandot, "La stratégie albanaise dans l'évolution mondiale," pp. 116-17. See also "Albaniens Kritik an Chinas Drei-Welten-Theorie," *Osteuropa* 28, no. 2 (1978): A88-A100; "Albanien verurteilt chinesische Theorie von den drei Welten als antirevolutionär, nicht klassenkämpferisch, den Kapitalismus schützend und die Antagonismen verschleiernd," *Archiv der Gegenwart* 33 (1977): 21273-77; S. Jaschek, "Zwei oder drei Welten? Der ideologische Konflikt Albanien-China," *Osteuropa* 28, no. 2 (1978): 141-49.

[30]See, for example, *Chinese Warmongering Policy and Hua-Kuo-Feng's Visit to the Balkans* (Tirana: Nëntori, 1978); "The Social-Imperialist China on the Road to Further Militarization and Warmongering" [in Albanian], *Ne shërbim të popullit*, no. 7 (1980): 32-33.

[31]Hoxha, *Problèmes de l'évolution*, p. 125.

[32]See, for example, Fatos Nano, "The 'Four Modernizations'--Reforms of State Monopoly Capitalism in China" [in Albanian], *Rruga ë partisë* no. 6 (1979): 76-89.

[33]Patrick F. R. Artisien, "Albania in the Post-Hoxha Era," *The World Today* 41 (June 1985): 107. See also Horst Dieter Topp, *Der Konflikt zwischen Albanien und der VR China und Tiranas aussenpolitische Optionen* (Cologne, 1979) (Berichte des Bundesinstituts für Ostwissenschaftliche und Internationale Studien, No. 37).

[34]Hoxha, *Rapport*, p. 236.

[35]A comprehensive analysis of Albania's isolation policy is found in Tönnes, "Grundlagen der albanischen Isolationspolitik."

[36]A strong nationalist sentiment pervades the works of Hoxha. For example, in his last work, *Salut au peuple à l'occasion du 40e anniversaire de la libération de l'Albanie* (Tirana, 29 November 1984), he uses such terms as "my beloved fatherland," "my Albania," "my people." Quoted in Jandot, "La stratégie albanaise dans l'évolution mondiale," p. 128.

[37]Ramiz Alia, "Address on the Occasion of the 40th Anniversary of the Liberation of Albania and the Triumph of the People's Revolution," quoted in Jandot, "La stratégie albanaise dans l'évolution mondiale," p. 127.

[38]Severe restrictions on access of foreigners to Albania and a ban on foreign travel by Albanians, except on official business, are examples of this moat-building mentality, although in recent years more tourists have

been allowed into the country (between 5,000 and 6,000 in 1984; Lendvai, *Das einsame Albanien*, p. 13). Soviet and U.S. citizens are not allowed, except that Americans of Albanian origin are welcome and many of them have visited their country of origin, another indication of the nationalist attitude of the Alia regime. On tourism in Albania see Derek R. Hall, "Foreign Tourism under Socialism: The Albanian 'Stalinist' Model," *Annals of Tourism Research* 11, no. 4 (1984): 539-55. See also Jandot, "La stratégie albanaise dans l'évolution mondiale," p. 125.

[39]See Catherine Regnault-Roger, "Albanie: Succès d'une politique alimentaire," *Tiers Monde* (October-December 1977): 849-860.

[40]See Berit Backer, "Self-Reliance under Socialism: The Case of Albania," *Journal of Peace Research* 19, no. 4 (1982): 355-67. See also Michael Ellmann, "Albania's Economy Today and Tomorrow," *World Economy* 7, no. 3 (1984): 333-40.

[41]See elaboration of this theme in Tönnes, "Grundlagen der albanischen Isolationspolitik," pp. 444-45.

[42]Bujar Hoxha, "Revisionism and the National Question" [in Albanian] *Rruga ë partisë*, no. 10 (1973): 68, in Tönnes, "Grundlagen der albanischen Isolationspolitik," p. 449.

[43]Ibid.

[44]Constitution of the Socialist People's Republic of Albania, 28 December 1976. For an analysis of this constitution, see Lothar Schultz, "Die neue Verfassung der sozialistischen Volksrepublik Albanien von 28 Dezember 1976," *Jahrbuch des öffentlichen Rechts der Gegenwart* (1980): 325-51.

[45]Article 15.

[46]See a definition of the isolationist foreign policy orientation in K. Holsti, *International Politics: A Framework for Analysis* (Englewood Cliffs, NJ: Prentice-Hall, 1983), p. 99.

[47]Boleslaw A. Boczek, "Global and Regional Approaches to the Protection and Preservation of the Marine Environment," *Case Western Reserve Journal of International Law* 16, no. 1 (1984): 39.

[48]Jandot, "La stratégie albanaise dans l'évolution mondiale," p. 123.

[49]*Britannica Book of the Year 1985* (Chicago: Encyclopaedia Britannica, 1985), p. 821. Membership in the World Bank and International Monetary Fund is out of the question for ideological reasons. See Ilir Boçka, "The 'Assistance' and Credits of the World Bank Are Imperialists' Shackle Round the Neck of the Peoples" [in Albanian], *Zëri i popullit*, 24 October 1981.

[50]"Tired of Being Alone," *The Economist*, 22 March 1986; "Better Connected," *The Economist*, 20 September 1986.

[51]N. Roshi, "The American Imperialism and the Soviet Social-Imperialism Are the Greatest Robbers of Countries and Peoples" [in Albanian], *Rruga ë partisë*, no. 3 (1979): 63-74.

[52]Alia, "Address on the Occasion of the 40th Anniversary," p. 127.

[53]Artisien, "Albania in the Post-Hoxha Era," p. 110. The Chinese message of condolences on the death of Hoxha was recognized by Albania, whereas the messages of the Soviet Union and other Eastern European parties were returned. Veljovic, "Albania after Enver Hoxha," p. 30.

[54]According to Albanian sources, in 1982 the share of these countries in Albania's overall foreign trade amounted to 39.9 percent of its exports and 36.7 percent of its imports. *Statistical Yearbook of the Socialist People's Republic of Albania*, cited in Jandot, "La stratégie albanaise dans l'évolution mondiale," p. 125. The share has since grown further. Veljovic, "Albania after Enver Hoxha," p. 30.

[55]Robert Lindner, "Albanien (August 1983-Juli 1984)," *Osteuropa*, no. 4 (1985): 203.

[56]The Albanian position toward Yugoslavia is explained in Enver Hoxha, *Les Titistes (Notes historiques)* (Tirana: Nëntori, 1982).

[57]On this issue see Patrick F. R. Artisien, "A Note on Kosovo and the Future of Yugoslav-Albanian Relations: A Balkan Perspective," *Soviet Studies* 36 (1984): 267-76; Patrick F. R. Artisien and R. A. Howells, "Yugoslavia, Albania and the Kosovo Riots," *The World Today* 37 (November 1981): 419-27; Elez Biberaj, "Albanian-Yugoslav Relations and the Question of Kosovo," *East European Quarterly* 16, no. 4 (1983): 485-511; Michele Lee, "Kosovo between Yugoslavia and Albania," *New Left Review* (July-August 1983): 62-91; Louise Lief, "Kosovo: Surface Calm Masks Old Troubles," *Christian Science Monitor*, 4 January 1983; Pedro Ramet, "Problems of Albanian Nationalism in Yugoslavia," *Orbis* 25, no. 2 (1981): 369-88. For the Yugoslav position see *Socialist Autonomous Province of Kosovo* (Belgrade: Socialist Thought and Practice, 1981). For the Albanian argument see Hoxha, *Les Titistes*.

[58]See "A Great Historic Victory for the Iranian People," *Zëri i popullit*, 19 January 1979.

[59]Albania is a great power in this regard, occupying the sixth place after the Soviet Union, the United States, China, West Germany, and Great Britain (the BBC). Lendvai, *Das einsame Albanien*, p. 85.

[60]In September 1986 freight trains started to run along a new track between Albania and Yugoslavia. See Eric Bourne, "Isolated Albania Seeks Stronger Economic Ties with Outside World," *Christian Science Monitor*, 25 September 1986. Whereas in the past Albanians went to study in the Soviet Union, and subsequently to China, today some one hundred young Albanians are studying in France, Italy, Austria, and Sweden. Lendvai, *Das einsame Albanien*, p. 80. In August 1985, Alia spoke of "obvious progress" in relations with Italy and Greece. David Binder, "Albania's New Leader Consolidates His Power," *International Herald Tribune*, 22 October

1985.   Diplomatic relations with Italy have existed since 1950.   Despite memories of the occupation, a love-hate feeling seems to prevail among Albanians about relations with Italy.   Trade and cultural relations have been steadily growing, a ferry service has opened between the two countries, and a chair of Italian studies has been established at Tirana University. Lendvai, *Das einsame Albanien*, p. 96.   For economic relations see Tito Favaretto and Angelo Masotti, "Le relazioni economiche tra l'Italia e l'Albania dal secondo dopoguerra a oggi," *Est-Ovest* 15, no. 2 (1984): 7-13.

A snag in Italo-Albanian relations developed in December 1985 when six Albanians got into the Italian embassy in Tirana and asked for political asylum, an unprecedented occurrence.   They were still there by the end of March 1986.   The Italians rejected demands to hand them over to Albanian authorities.   In retaliation Albania cancelled all tourist visits from Italy in March and April 1986. "Tired of Being Alone."   Relations with Greece, strained by Greek territorial claims to part of southern Albania, have entered a stage of rapprochement with renunciation of these claims by Greece, reopening of a border crossing, and expanding cooperation in cultural, economic, and scientific fields.   Artisien, "Albania in the Post-Hoxha Era," p. 109.

[61]Albania is willing to establish diplomatic relations with Great Britain if the British government returns the 2.5 tons of gold once seized by the Germans during World War II, and now held jointly by Great Britain, France, and the United States.   Great Britain is unwilling to do so until Albania pays it the $2.5 million awarded by the International Court of Justice in the Corfu Channel case of 1946.   Direct negotiations between Tirana and London began in 1985, as admitted by Ramiz Alia.   Binder, "Albania's New Leader Consolidates His Power."   On the historical background see Leslie Gardiner, *The Eagle Spreads Its Claws: A History of the Corfu Channel Dispute and of Albania's Relations with the West, 1945-1965* (London: Blackwood, 1966).

[62]Preliminary talks about establishing diplomatic relations with the Federal Republic of Germany started in March 1986. "Tired of Being Alone." They are complicated by the fact that Albania demands $2.5 billion in war reparations from Germany as a condition for normalizing relations.   See Heinz-Günther Boerner, "Enver Hoxha's Milliarden-Poker mit Bonn," *Deutschland-Archiv* (1975): 903-5.   It is possible that Albania may waive its reparations claim if Germany can find a way of giving it economic and technological aid without formal appearances of credit which--as noted--is banned under Albania's constitution. "Tired of Being Alone."

[63]Lendvai, *Das einsame Albanien*, p. 10.   In and around Shkoder alone, Lendvai could count 188 such pillboxes, many overgrown with weeds. Lendvai, "Albania: An Impenetrable Fortress," p. 18.

[64]Lendvai, *Das einsame Albanien*, p. 103.

[65]The standard slogan repeated to foreign visitors is that every would-be attacker "should know that our country is an impenetrable fortress." Lendvai, *Das einsame Albanien*, p. 102. That the Albanian armed forces are on guard against any intruders was demonstrated by the shooting of an innocent French tourist, fishing in a dinghy off the Albanian coast in 1984. See Patrick Forestier, "Bouffonne et sanglante Albanie," *Paris Match*, 12 October 1984. The regime's besieged fortress mentality may, to a certain extent, be explained by foreign intelligence services' attempts from 1948 to 1952 to overthrow Hoxha's Communist regime.

The most notorious instance was the case of a landing organized by the British Intelligence Service, of which the Soviet spy Kim Philby had advance knowledge. As a result, the abortive invasion ended with a slaughter of thousands of anti-Communist Albanians. The story is told in Nicholas Bethell, *Betrayed* (New York: Times Books, 1984). The mysterious affair of the landing in 1983 of what the Albanian government called an "armed gang" of five men, led by the "bandit Xhevdet Mustafa" and liquidated five hours after the landing, can be explained as Hoxha's ploy in his campaign against the followers of Mehmet Shehu. As officially admitted in February 1985, Shehu had been liquidated as an alleged U.S., Soviet, and Yugoslav spy, but the most probable reason was that he was the rival of Alia, whom Hoxha had chosen as his successor. Artisien, "Albania in the Post-Hoxha Era," p. 108; Lendvai, *Das einsame Albanien*, pp. 105-6.

[66]Lendvai, *Das einsame Albanien*, p. 101.

[67]*Military Balance, 1986-1987*, p. 212.

[68]Lendvai, *Das einsame Albanien*, p. 102.

[69]*Britannica Book of the Year 1986*, p. 547; *Military Balance, 1986-1987*, p. 81.

[70]In 1980, 37.3 percent of the population were under the age of 15, and 28.9 percent between ages 15 to 29. Altogether, 82.7 percent of Albanians were under age 45. *Britannica Book of the Year 1986*, p. 619.

[71]Ibid.

[72]Lendvai, *Das einsame Albanien*, p. 102.

[73]*Military Balance, 1986-1987*, p. 81.

[74]Ibid.

[75]Lendvai, *Das einsame Albanien*, p. 69.

[76]*Military Balance, 1986-1987*, p. 81.

[77]Gypsies represent 2.5 percent and Greeks 2.4 percent. *Britannica Book of the Year 1986*, p. 619.

[78]For a discussion of the party-military relationship in Albania see Peter R. Prifti, *Socialist Albania since 1944: Domestic and Foreign Developments* (Cambridge: MIT Press, 1978).

[79]Stephen F. Larrabee, "Whither Albania?" *The World Today* 34 (February 1978): 61-69.

[80]See generally "Die führende Rolle der Partei in der Armee," *Österreichische militärische Zeitschrift* 1 (1975): 61-62. See also Nikolaos A. Stavrou, "The Political Role of the Albanian Military," *Intellect* 104, no. 2367 (July-August 1975): 18-21.

[81]Artisien, "Albania in the Post-Hoxha Era," p. 110.

[82]*Military Balance, 1986-1987*, p. 80.

[83]Ibid., p. 81. For example, it is reported that most aircraft and boats obtained from China are out of action because of spare parts shortages. Lendvai, *Das einsame Albanien*, p. 103, referring to R. Marmullaku, *Albania and the Albanians* (London: C. Hurst, 1975), pp. 173-75; and Eugene K. Keefe, *Area Handbook for Albania* (Washington, DC: Government Printing Office, 1971).

[84]*Military Balance, 1986-1987*, p. 81.

[85]Ibid. On the Sino-Albanian naval contacts see "Pekings Marine in der Adria," *Allgemeine Schweizerische Militärzeitschrift*, no. 7 (1975): 291; "Chinesische Boote an Albanien," ibid. (1976): 300.

[86]*Military Balance, 1986-1987*, p. 81. Lendvai reports that during his stay in Albania he saw only one fighter aircraft; Lendvai, *Das einsame Albanien*, p. 103.

[87]See, for example, Artisien, "Albania in the Post-Hoxha Era," p. 108; Veljovic, "Albania after Enver Hoxha," p. 31.

[88]Binder, "Albania's New Leader Consolidates His Power."

[89]"Albania Opens Party Congress," *New York Times*, 4 November 1986; "They've Heard of Maradona," *The Economist*, 8 November 1986.

[90]A scenario of such a development is outlined by Ducci. In his pessimistic view, the Soviet Union could with impunity put NATO before an accomplished fact by taking control of Albania, with disastrous consequences for the strategic position of the Western Alliance and Yugoslavia. See Roberto Ducci, "Albania: The Spark That May Cause a Fire. Why the Soviets Might Want to Invade Albania: A Scenario," *The Atlantic* 255, no. 2 (February 1985): 16-26.

INDEX